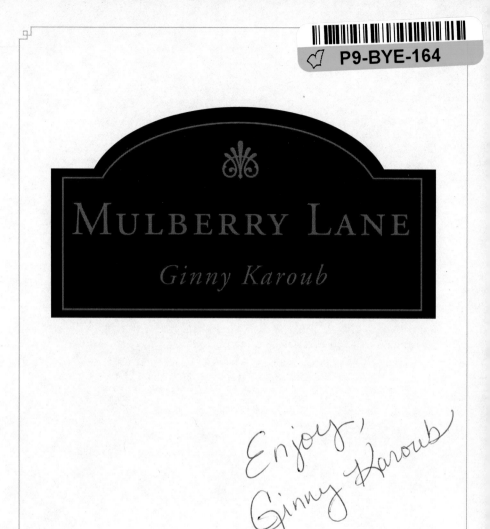

MULBERRY LANE

Ginny Karoub

Enjoy,
Ginny Karoub

TATE PUBLISHING & *Enterprises*

Published by Tate Publishing & Enterprises, LLC
127 E. Trade Center Terrace | Mustang, Oklahoma 73064 USA
1.888.361.9473 | www.tatepublishing.com

Tate Publishing is committed to excellence in the publishing industry. The company reflects the philosophy established by the founders, based on Psalms 68:11,
"The Lord gave the word and great was the company of those who published it."

Book design copyright © 2007 by Tate Publishing, LLC. All rights reserved.
Cover design and Illustration by Janae Glass
Interior design by Luke Southern

Published in the United States of America

ISBN: 978-1-60247-519-9
1. Christmas   2. Gift Book

07.08.27

This ornament is for you, Aunt D

There was a little pine tree at the corner of Mulberry Lane. At Christmas time one year it made a difference in its world. It could be seen from Heaven, so it received its first ornament one day. The lives of every person who placed a ornament on the little pine tree was changed in a very special way. The Spirit of Christmas reached down from Heaven and blessed each of them. From that time on they shared the blessing they received that Christmas.

JOY, PEACE, LOVE, FAITH,
CHARITY, FORGIVENESS, HOPE.

CHRISTMAS.

There was a little pine tree at the corner of Mulberry Lane. At Christmas time one year the little pine tree made a difference in its world. Mulberry Lane was a quaint little street in the village part of town. The neighborhood of Mulberry Lane was very quiet during the day and even more still at night. A Victorian street lamp brightened the area at the corner of Mulberry Lane. Every night the light was shone all around the little pine tree. In the deep of the night, if you listened, you could hear the snowflakes falling down on Mulberry Lane from the sky above. As the snowflakes lightly landed on the little pine tree, it made the corner of Mulberry Lane a beautiful sight. The little pine tree was one of those soft needle pines with lots of branches. The little pine tree was not that tall, only about six and a half feet, if measured. It had a lot of years left to grow.

No one until that Christmas had paid much attention to the little pine tree, it just kept the corner of Mulberry Lane company.

One day in the beginning of December, a little girl, named Melissa, who lived on Mulberry Lane walked down the street with the freshly fallen snow dancing around her fur lined boots. She was all bundled up in her wool coat, striped wool hat and matching mittens. Melissa ducked her head while pushing her way through the snowflakes that were coming down. The snowflakes were as big as cotton balls that day. As Melissa walked, she thought she was inside a snow globe that someone had just shaken up.

She walked up to the little pine tree and placed a Christmas ornament on it. Looking up with hopeful eyes full of the sparkle of tears, Melissa spoke silently to her mother. Melissa had made the ornament for her mother, who was now in Heaven. It said "To Mother" on it, and glued inside the paper ornament was Melissa's school picture, that was taken just that fall. Every year before, Melissa and her mother had made a Christmas ornament with Melissa's new school picture tucked inside. Melissa wanted her mother to know that she did not forget to make their Christmas ornament. Melissa's hope was that from Heaven her mother could see the Christmas ornament she had made on the little pine tree. Somehow this made Melissa feel as though they still had made their ornament together that Christmas.

The neighbors on Mulberry Lane had always stayed to themselves in the past. It wasn't that they weren't friendly people; they were just caught up in their own lives. For most of the neighbors, they were only guilty of being too busy to notice anything else around them, which included their neighbors. There had never been a reason for all the neighbors to notice the little pine tree before, but the little pine tree started to attract some attention with the Christmas ornament on it. The neighbors who saw the Christmas ornament were beginning to wonder to themselves, "Who put that Christmas ornament on the little pine tree and why?" None of the neighbors knew one another so they never thought to ask each other.

Everyday the little pine tree with the Christmas ornament now on it, silently spoke to each neighbor as they drove by. Some of the neighbors pulled back the drapes in their living room window just to look out at the little pine tree. Unspoken questions and curiosity was being stirred among the neighbors.

The Christmas ornament and the little pine tree started a buzz around the homes on Mulberry Lane. The quiet neighborhood was starting to wake up to what was around them.

W hat started as a tug in their hearts that Christmas became something very magical for them all.

A few days later, the little pine tree had three more ornaments on it. At different times three of the neighbors had walked out of their homes in secret hoping they would not be seen by anyone else. They had fought the feeling of embarrassment, but they just could not stop themselves. They had been drawn to the little pine tree. Each one of them had searched through their own ornaments and each of them had found a special ornament to add to the first one. The "To Mother" ornament had deeply touched them. They had heard of the little girl who lived on their street who had lost her mother that year. Each of them were happy in their hearts that they had added a Christmas ornament to the little pine tree. Each of the three neighbors had someone they thought of as they placed their

Christmas ornament on the little pine tree in the still of night.

As the sun set and rose again, each day something new had taken place at the little pine tree on Mulberry Lane. The little pine tree had a star placed at the top now and even some candy canes were hanging from its branches. A wish list that was hand printed on cardboard with most of the words misspelled was also tied to one of the branches with red yarn. The wish list had Christmas stickers placed very carefully all around the edges. The little hands that had made it had taken great care to put it all together.

Mysteriously no one saw anyone else putting the Christmas ornaments on the little pine tree. As each day towards Christmas unfolded, the neighbors on Mulberry Lane could not wait to see the new Christmas ornaments on the little pine tree at the corner. The neighbors slowed their vehicles as they passed the little pine tree so they could get a good look from their car windows. A few waves of hellos and smiles were being made from the automobiles that happened to pass by each other at the corner of Mulberry Lane. Not only were things happening at the corner of Mulberry Lane but things were beginning to happen in each of the homes too. Christmas decorations were being brought out and dusted off that had been seeing the basement walls for so many years. The Christmas cookies that had not been baked in years suddenly were warming the kitchens.

Christmas cards that were shoved in the mail every year before, were being written out with a heart felt note inside. Traditional Christmas's that some of the families did years before were being planned again and even more important, remembered.

In one warm kitchen on Mulberry Lane, Christmas cookies were being baked. The smell of the kitchen was of warm vanilla and freshly baked Christmas cookies. Scattered all over the kitchen table was construction paper of all different colors, glitter and glue. The three children who lived in this home were making their additions to the little pine tree. There they sat at the kitchen table,—Timmy, Todd and Trisha busy making their Christmas ornaments. They were so caught up with making their Christmas ornaments they had completely forgotten the wonderful baking Christmas cookies in the oven.

As their mother was taking out yet another tray of Christmas cookies from the oven, she marveled at how quiet and concentrated they were over their project. Looking at their serious little faces she did not dare interrupt them. This really means a lot to them, she

thought. It was so important to them today to make these Christmas ornaments. For some reason, it warmed her heart and made her feel very proud of her children.

A few days before Christmas Eve, as the sun was coming up you could see that there was a new addition near the little pine tree. A nativity set was placed by the little pine tree. Someone carefully placed some straw on the ground next to the little pine tree. Then placed on top the manger, baby Jesus, Joseph, Mary and the three wise men. That someone must have taken a lot of time and care to set the nativity scene up because it was beautiful! The little pine tree at the corner of Mulberry Lane had come to life!

The little pine tree had come to mean something to this neighborhood. No one could walk or drive past the little pine tree without thinking about what was happening at the corner of Mulberry Lane. Something warm and cozy was taking place in the homes of Mulberry Lane. Christmas was coming alive again in their hearts that year! Where had the Spirit of Christmas gone before? What had made each of them stop feeling the Spirit of Giving? The neighbors wondered to themselves those unspoken questions.

Each ornament placed on the little pine tree had meant something special to the person who placed it there, you just knew it, you could feel it. With the Spirit of Christmas coming alive in the hearts of the neighbors, all the ornaments placed on the little pine tree began to mean something special to each of them. They could not explain it; even if they tried, they each felt the hope of Christmas tugging at their hearts. Every neighbor started to feel for their fellow neighbor.

They were all strangers but somehow they were experiencing the joy of Christmas together.

That night as the neighbors looked out their windows they could not believe their eyes. The little pine tree was all lit up! It just glowed luminous with light. The light from the little pine tree twinkled into the night. The little pine tree was wrapped with Christmas lights; the manger was also trimmed in lights too! With all the strands of Christmas lights in every color, the corner on Mulberry Lane looked as bright as the noon day.

As the snowflakes fell that night, it was a wonderful sight to see what the neighborhood had done together. Without words or a plan, they had brought the Spirit of Christmas back to each of their lives.

As Christmas Eve approached, the feeling in every home on Mulberry Lane was different from the years before. No matter what the situation in each of their lives, they all were experiencing hope again. The simple Spirit of Christmas was being stirred again in their hearts. Stringing popcorn, hand making bows for gifts, and some of the other Christmas activities were also being enjoyed again.

There were children from Mulberry Lane that could not be home with their families that Christmas, some of their pictures were made into Christmas ornaments on the little pine tree with "Wish You Were Here" or "Missing You" written on them. They may not have been able to get home for

Christmas, but with their ornament on the little pine tree, it seemed to all, they were there in spirit. To Robert and Carol Taylor, who lived on Mulberry Lane, placing their Christmas ornament on the little pine tree meant a lot to them. Their son Brian, who was over seas on duty, would not be home that Christmas. Something so simple as his picture made into a Christmas ornament and placed on the little pine tree was so special to them both. That simple act made all the difference to them that Christmas.

The hurts and the walls that were part of the neighbor's lives that had kept them from enjoying that time of year before, were being washed away by what was happening at the corner of Mulberry Lane. What was happening in their hearts wasn't talked about much in the homes of Mulberry Lane; it was just silently taking place.

Hearts that had never meant to harden were being softened as every moment ticked by.

Christmas Eve was finally here! The neighbors on Mulberry Lane were running around their homes with their pajamas and stocking feet, trying to get ready for the day. Cups of half drunken luke-warm coffee, and cut up unused wrapping paper were scattered over most of the neighbor's kitchen tables. Some of the children were still in bed sleeping, buried under mounds of blankets and oblivious to what was happening downstairs in their homes.

It had turned out to be a beautiful day on Mulberry Lane that Christmas Eve. The sun was shining and snowflakes floated down like diamonds. Each snowflake as the sunlight shone on it sparkled with a rainbow of colors. It was cold and crisp outside, but inside the fireplaces were warm and burning; the Christmas trees were lit up and garland decorated several staircases. In some homes, Christmas music was playing from the stereos in the family rooms. The movie *Scrooge* was being watched in one home with everyone bundled up under blankets lying around the family room. Bowls of popcorn with M & M's sprinkled on top were warm and ready to be eaten and the movie, *It's a Wonderful Life* was on television in another home.

Not having anything in common before, the neighbors of Mulberry Lane had something in common that Christmas Eve. That night they each planned to visit the little pine tree. They did not know what they would do, but they knew they were going to pay their respects to the little pine tree that had somehow touched their lives that Christmas.

Most of the neighbors were making plans in hopes that they would not be alone that night at the corner with the little pine tree. Some of the neighbors were packing up Christmas cookies in gift bags to share. One of the neighbors, Paul and his wife Sue, were making a kettle full of hot cocoa;

they had gone out and brought Christmas cups with little trees and bells printed on them. They too, had hopes that they were going to be able to share their hot cocoa with their neighbors.

Another neighbor, Mrs. Smith, who is a retired school teacher, remembering what she used to do for her students at that time of year, wrapped each gift with bright red wrapping paper and tied a candy cane to each gift with a ribbon to make it extra special. Her gifts were all the things children loved, coloring books, crayons, colored pencils and reading books. Her basket was loaded down with some of the things that had put a smile on her student's faces in the past. She hoped that night on Christmas Eve she would see all the children of Mulberry Lane and be able to give each of them a gift from her.

Leah, a single mother that had recently moved to Mulberry Lane with her daughter, Amanda, knew no one in the area. Being new to the neighborhood, Leah wanted to do something special to finally meet their neighbors. Leah and Amanda were making Christmas cards for every home on Mulberry Lane. Leah, being very artistic, was hand painting the front of every card. The hand painted picture on every card was of Mulberry Lane and the little pine tree all decorated at the corner. Amanda following in her artistic mother's foot steps was a great help; she wrote out the message in every card. Leah and Amanda had hoped they could give their cards to each of their new neighbors in person.

With no family near, and living in a new town it was hard for Leah raising Amanda alone. Somehow the little pine tree helped them feel less alone that Christmas. Watching what was taking place at the little pine tree everyday made Leah and Amanda feel part of something special. Leah was beginning to feel hope replacing the fear in her heart. Maybe this new neighborhood was exactly what they needed in their lives.

If you could have seen inside every home on Mulberry Lane that day, you would have liked what you could feel that Christmas Eve.

It was warm and comfortable like a cozy blanket, full of that something special you can remember from your grandmother's house at Christmas time. That wonderful feeling you got every year at Christmas, sitting in the same chair in the living room, near the end table at your grandmother's house where she always placed that special Christmas candy dish filled with that special Christmas candy you can only get at that time of year. The hard candy that is made of  all different flavors and came in all different colors, with a little jelly inside; you remember sneaking a piece when no one is looking, but you're not really sneaking, because your grandmother had put it there every year just for you. That childlike feeling was what you felt on Mulberry Lane that day.

As the day progressed, the neighbors were excited with anticipation at what would take place when they visited the little pine tree that Christmas Eve night. Dinners of light snacks were being prepared and eaten in each home. Most were eating lighter because of the big meals prepared for Christmas day.

As the sun was beginning to set, each home began to get their things ready for their walk down the street to the little pine tree. Everyone young and old could not wait to see up close all the Christmas ornaments that were placed on the little pine tree, and everything that they represented and all that they had come to mean.

As evening came, the Victorian street lamps brighten up the street of Mulberry Lane. Mulberry Lane seemed very still and quiet with anticipation, like a hush had come over the neighborhood. Snowflakes lightly fell without a sound to the neighborhood as if they were blessing what the neighbors were about to do.

The Christmas lights were plugged in now and the little pine tree and manger was lit up in hundreds of lights. It seemed that it was a sign, as if the neighbors had been waiting for the lights to be plugged in on the little pine tree. Some of the neighbors were coming out now. Paul and Sue were setting up their table with hot cocoa and coffee. Trays of baked Christmas goodies and gift bags of cookies were being brought out.

One by one the neighbors came, walking down Mulberry Lane with their gifts and cards. Shy smiles were received with big hellos. Each neighbor helped the other place their gifts on the tables. A few more tables had to be brought out; there was much to be shared!

It took only a few minutes and everyone who lived on Mulberry Lane that Christmas Eve had come out to the little pine tree. Introductions were being made. Shaking of hands and introducing themselves, the neighbors of Mulberry Lane were finally meeting each other. Cups of hot cocoa and coffee were being passed out among the neighbors and the Christmas cookies were being eaten. The handmade cards were given to each family and the gifts were passed out to the children.

The evening surpassed everyone's expectations. Not one neighbor would have ever believed before, that a little pine tree could have been responsible for such a wonderful Christmas Eve! The neighbors wanted to thank Melissa, the little girl, whose ornament "To Mother" had started it all, but Melissa did not want to be thanked. Shyly, holding her dad's hand, Melissa told them that the little pine tree made that Christmas special. She just knew, believed somehow, that her mother could see the little pine tree from Heaven; that was why she put her mother's ornament on it that day. The neighbors on Mulberry Lane believed too, each of them felt, that the little pine tree could be seen from Heaven.

With everyone warm from the hot cocoa

and full from the Christmas cookies, without saying a word they started gathering hands around the manger and the little pine tree. A gloved hand reached for a mitten hand. A grown hand reached out to a little hand. When they had formed a circle around the manger and the little pine tree, someone started singing, *O' Christmas Tree* when that song was done they went on to *Silent Night* and then *Away In The Manger.*

Childhood Christmas's were being remembered. Special times in Christmases past ran through their minds. With tears running down some of the faces of the neighbors, Christmases of long ago were being remembered. They continued singing till they had run out of songs, *O' Come all Ye Faithful* being their last.

With smiles on every face and warmth in their hearts the neighbors refilled their hot cocoa and had a few more cookies. A neighborhood sledding party was being planned for the day after Christmas, the talking and sharing among them went on into the night.

They came that Christmas Eve night as strangers to the little pine tree and went away as friends.

The little pine tree had made a difference in the life of the neighbors on Mulberry Lane that Christmas. It had stood alone at the corner of Mulberry Lane and could be

seen from Heaven, so it received its first Christmas ornament that day. From that day on, Mulberry Lane was never the same. The people who lived on Mulberry Lane were never the same either. They took what they learned that Christmas and shared it with others the rest of their lives. Christmas had meant something! It was about love, sharing, leaving your comfort area and giving to others from what God has given you.

May the Spirit of Christmas live
in your hearts all year long,

—Ginny Karoub
2007

e|LIVE

listen|imagine|view|experience

THE XERONINE-SYSTEM:

*A New Cellular Mechanism That Explains the Health
Promoting Action of Noni and Bromelain*

The Xeronine-System: A New Cellular Mechanism That Explains the Health Promoting Action of Noni and Bromelain
Direct Source Publishing
15 East 400 S.
Orem, Utah 84058

For questions or comments concerning noni use directed to the author, please send correspondence to the above address.

The information in this book is for educational purposed only and should not be used to diagnose and treat diseases. All serious health conditions should be treated by a competent health practitioner. Neither the publisher nor the author of this book in any way dispense medical advice, prescribe remedies, or assume responsibility for those who choose to treat themselves.

Printed in the United States of America

ISBN 1-887938-58-3

To Anne
Understanding, Supportive, Fun to Live With

Table of Contents

Preface

This book contains the first detailed description of a fascinating and important new biological system that occurs in all cells. I call this system the xeronine-system. This system is absolutely necessary for the proper metabolism of cells. I believe that this system works at such a basic level in the cell, that less than optimal functioning of this system in various organs can lead to a variety of health problems, such as some types of arthritis, some types of diabetes, some types of asthma, some types of cancer, many types of memory problems, etc.

That such an important cellular system should have gone undetected for so many years seems unbelievable. There are several reasons for this long delay in discovering this system. One reason is the extraordinary chemical reactivity of free xeronine. Although xeronine is actually present in relatively large amounts in all tissues, it only lasts an extremely short time as free xeronine, or as xeronine unattached to any other substance. As soon as a unique package of all of the ingredients necessary to synthesize xeronine (I am calling these grouping of specific molecules assemblages) releases xeronine, the xeronine immediately reacts with its target molecule.

Another reason for the long delay in discovering the source of the biological activity in certain biological extracts, such as those prepared from noni, pineapple harvested before the 1970s (bromelain), pancreatin, yeast, bacteria and yeast, is that the biologically active compound does not occur in the extract. Only the ingredients and the "recipe" for making xeronine are present in the original extracts. The traditional and logical approach for discovering the source of biological activity in a product is generally a series of purification steps. The traditional purification steps destroy the organized arrangement of the molecules that synthesize xeronine. Therefore the classical isolation techniques failed to discover xeronine.

I had a unique advantage over other groups working on the discovery of the nature of the biological activity in bromelain. For my isolation studies, I had access to the acetone supernatant solutions left over from the commercial processing of bromelain by the former Dole Bromelain

Processing Plant. After the plant operators removed the acetone from the left over supernatant solution, they concentrated the leftover liquid-like substance for my work. Thus, I worked with material collected from twenty-five tons of pineapple stems! Without this unique source of raw material, I would have had difficulty in isolating sufficient xeronine by my empirical methods for isolation work.

The other reason why solving this problem was so difficult was that we had a "Catch 22" situation. I could not identify the nature of the active ingredient until I had devised a proper method for isolating the compound. On the other hand, I could not devise a proper method for isolating xeronine until I knew the nature of the active ingredient and how the cell synthesized this compound. After many empirical experiments and many seemingly dead-ends, in 1977 while I was working at Jintan-Dolph in Japan, I eventually isolated a trace of a volatile, nitrogen containing material I now call xeronine. Pharmacological tests run in the laboratories of Jintan-Dolph in Japan showed that this volatile material was the active ingredient for which I had long been searching.

Expansion of this work in Honolulu suggested that free xeronine existed only temporarily in the body. Either the pertinent organelles had not synthesized the xeronine or when they had synthesized the xeronine, the cell immediately used the synthesized xeronine to modify the functions of specific proteins. This means that at no time is there enough detectable xeronine in the body to isolate and then study. With an abundant supply of raw material from Dole, I had no difficulty in isolating crystalline xeronine. However, its stability was so poor that I had to run all of my experiments within a few hours after I had isolated the crystals.

Although this brief explanation leaves several unanswered questions, namely the nature of "the organelle" that assembles and packages the critical ingredients (including xeronine) to perform critical cell function, it is important to understand before moving forward with the explanation of how xeronine works in the body. In this book, I shall propose that the organelle that assembles the appropriate molecules for packaging is the Golgi complex. The package that the Golgi assembles I am calling an assemblage. I am suggesting this term instead of using the classical term vesicle since the word assemblage implies that the molecules in the package are arranged in a critical manner and in a critical ratio.

This new concept makes much more specific a previous suggestion that I have been making about hormones. For several years, I have been suggesting in talks that many hormones require that both the hormone and xeronine be present on adjacent sites on specific protein receptors. If either component is missing, no hormone action occurs.

The assemblage theory makes certain that both xeronine and the hormone are presented at the same time to an appropriate receptor. Both the hormone and the xeronine-assemblage occur together in unique super-assemblages. Some assemblage contains the address of the appropriate receptor protein. When the assemblage reaches the proper address, it immediately synthesizes xeronine and releases the hormone. This explains why free xeronine does not normally appear in the body.

My empirical success in isolating crystalline xeronine depended on my accidentally having discovered how to allow one reaction, namely the biosynthesis of xeronine, to proceed faster than the normal reactions that practically immediately used the newly synthesized xeronine.

In various talks that I have given since 1996, I described the dramatic effects of crystalline xeronine on certain physiological reactions in animals as well as in people. I also mentioned that I had run laboratory tests with crystalline xeronine and that these tests with crystalline xeronine confirmed the "unusual" properties of commercial bromelain. I did not elaborate on the laboratory tests in my talks for a practical reason. Everyone knows that listening to someone describing laboratory tests is a certain cure for insomnia. Yet, these laboratory tests are important. They provide irrefutable evidence that crystalline xeronine shows properties in the laboratory that no other biochemical compound has ever shown. They also show one well-documented action of what the adsorption of xeronine onto a specific site of a protein does to that protein.

Since these initial talks, I have been re-examining a portion of my old data in preparation for writing this book. This has been a most exciting period for me. I discovered that the literally thousands of disc electrophoretic pictures that my group took during the period from 1956 to 1973 contained a wealth of previously unassimilated information. Putting this information together led me to the concept of assemblages, a new use for an old word. Assemblages led me to the Golgi complexes. These led me to a new concept about how certain hormones function. This also led me to the gene. This is just the beginning.

During the past four years, I have been able to develop an integrated picture of the xeronine-system concept. This is a concept that describes all of my data, explains how xeronine might act at the molecular level and makes some very exciting predictions that scientists can test and evaluate. Since much of my data come from experiments devised for entirely different objectives than studying the properties of the xeronine-system, scientists should repeat some of my early work with experiments designed specifically to study properties of the xeronine-system.

I believe that the xeronine-system hypothesis will mesh well with some of the microbiological and genetic research that is currently exciting the world.

The Book

I have divided the book into four sections: "In the Beginning," "Xeronine in the Laboratory," "What Does it All Mean," and "Xeronine in the Future."

The "In the Beginning" section contains stories of strange medical, agricultural, technological and food observations and practices that classical biochemistry and physiology could not satisfactorily explain. These observations suggested that the cell must contain a biological system that had escaped our notice. It was these observations that stimulate, me in 1956 to search for this "unknown active ingredient" in bromelain.

In the "Xeronine in the Laboratory" section, I cover the work that I and other cooperators did in our attempts to work out the nature of the unknown system. When we started this work, we had few clues to guide us. In this section I cover in an abbreviated and non-technical manner my actual discovery of xeronine and how I crystallized it.

In the "What Does it All Mean" section, I suggest how the xeronine-system works. This is just the beginning of an important branch of biochemistry. I hope that this account will stimulate other laboratories to produce additional data to advance the concept.

In the last section, "Xeronine in the Future," I suggest a few specific problems for study and what we might expect from such work.

The Compact Disc and the Printed Book

My original plan was to present this story at several levels. One level—this book—is a relatively simple description of the xeronine story without extensive documentation. Accompanying this book, I had planned to have a CD that would contain two additional levels of presentations. One level would amplify details of the story that would interest people desiring to have additional, but not too technical information. The third level of presentation would contain the experimental details, the methodology and the literature references.

The CD portion of this project will probably take several years to complete. Transcribing barely legible, fifth carbon-copies of data on aging and fragile paper is a tedious and time-consuming task. Commercial typists, who were not chemists, could not transcribe the barely decipherable data.

The illustrations that I have included in the present book are mostly diagrammatic. I have based them on actual photographs that I shall present on the CD.

The third part of the story is strictly technical. Only scientists who may wish to repeat some of the work that I mention in the second section will use this part. Here I present technical details, such as assay techniques, the type of resins that I used, the concentrations of reagents, pH values, temperatures, etc. In this part, I have also included copies of some of the critical papers that I refer to in the first and second parts of the story.

The CD does have certain distinct advantages over the printed page. On the CD, the distracting but necessary footnotes and qualifying statements are tucked away in an obscure corner of the disc. Yet, a click on the colored hyperlink will immediately bring the footnote to the current window. This facility makes it possible to present the same story at several different levels. Each reader should be able to access just the material that interests him or her.

General Policies

When referring to specific companies who have participated directly or indirectly in the xeronine-system project, I have frequently refrained from naming the companies. Their administrations and their objectives have changed since my contacts with them. Also many of their research workers—all of whom have long since retired—had generously shared some of their confidential data with me. Not all company administrations approve of such a close relationship with an outside research worker.

In some parts of the book, the reader may feel that I seem to be introducing much irrelevant material. Yet, practically everything in the book has a direct or an indirect connection with the xeronine-system. The connection may be obscure at first, but I promise it is there. This is understandable since the xeronine-system is one of the basic units in the metabolism of the cell.

Acknowledgements

Many different people contributed to the development of the xeronine-system concept. Certain people played an especially important role in the development of this project. My early exposure to pharmacology and clinical work came from my association with the late Dr. Robert Hunter, a gynecologist in Hawaii. His work led to the discovery of the unexpected pharmacological action of some unknown material in commercial bromelain. We worked closely together on a range of exciting medical projects. Some of this material we published in a series of papers. Some valuable material, especially the role of the xeronine-system in fertility problems, we were not able to complete before new management at Castle & Cooke eliminated a number of departments in the company; this included Basic Research.

My introduction into formal pharmacology came from two groups of people. The late Dr. Gus Martin, formerly the Director of Research at Rorer Drug Company and a close personal friend, was an iconoclastic research worker. He was willing to challenge conventional ideas. Although today practically no one believes his hypotheses about the inflammatory process and the role of "bromelain" in curing this problem, yet his research group produced excellent data. I still use his data—but not his concepts about the inflammatory process—to explain certain aspects of the xeronine-system. Had he lived longer, we probably would have worked out the nature of the xeronine-system together.

Another important introduction to medical physiology for me was my several years of association with the Research Group of the former Smith Kline and French Drug Company. The late Bill Holmes and Art Heming generously shared their research data and concepts with me. This enabled our two companies to participate jointly in working on certain problems. This company proved conclusively that the purified bromelain that my department prepared for them was a 100% placebo whereas commercial bromelain contained some unknown substances that caused all of the dramatic physiological activity.

After this definitive work, they proposed that our two companies set up a joint research project to discover the nature of the materials that we had removed during the purification process. This would have been an open-ended research project, with regard to both costs and time. Since Dole had already spent large sums of money in start-up costs, Dole management elected to make an arrangement with another drug company that already had a marketable bromelain product. This company had a New Drug Permit from FDA and had an impressive list of both laboratory and clinical studies.

The late Dr. Gerold Klein, a Maine doctor who pioneered the use of bromelain (a potential source of the xeronine-system) as an almost miraculous tool for treating severely burned patients, introduced me to burn research. Together we worked out some of the factors involved in this book and important medical application for "bromelain." During this work, we confirmed that even for an application that theoretically required a protease action, the protease bromelain was a 100% placebo. Some other unidentified "associated material" was the crucial ingredient.

For basic research I am especially indebted to two University of Hawaii professors, Dr. Paul Scheuer, of the Chemistry Department, and Dr. Ernest Ross, of the Animal Science Department. During the years that I worked at Dole, Dr.Scheuer and his graduate students investigated some of the chemical compounds that occurred in commercial bromelain. Later, after Castle & Cooke eliminated my department at Dole, Dr. Scheuer generously invited me to work in his laboratory as an invited guest scientist.

Dr. Ross and I investigated the effect of the "unknown biological factor" in commercial bromelain on various aspects of animal physiology. I know of no other work in medical research in which the investigators used chickens to study pharmacological actions. Actually, chickens proved to be excellent experimental animals to use. They were inexpensive, they had a uniform genetic background and their nutritional requirements had been intensively investigated. After we had finished our tests, a commercial company processed the chickens.

In one study, this led to a completely independent and unplanned confirmation of an anecdotal report that something in pineapple juice (proxeronine) improved the complexion of a woman who was on a special pineapple diet test. The poultry processor, who did not know what treatments the chickens had received, called Dr. Ross and asked what treatment the chickens of code # xx had received. He told Dr. Ross that after the defeathering operation, this group of chickens had skins that were significantly less bruised than that of chickens raised on a conventional diet and handling method. (This meant that he could charge a higher price for these chickens!)

Two commercial companies were critical to the success of this project. The early management of Dole Company gave me generous and excellent support for seventeen years. While I worked for them, as head of the Chemical and Food Research Department, I was able to visit all of the major users of bromelain and all of the research workers who were studying the properties of bromelain. Later Hideto Kono, as President of the East Asia Division of Castle & Cooke (the former parent company of Dole, Inc.), enlarged the scope of the research and the pharmacological applications of bromelain by establishing a joint venture drug company with Morishita Jintan of Osaka Japan. This joint venture drug company not only carried out basic research but established close ties with many of the important pharmacology departments in Japanese Universities. Jintan-Dolph is still very active in this field.

After Castle & Cooke changed management and eliminated the Basic Research Division along with many other departments, Hideto Kono, now the head of Research and Development for the State of Hawaii, persuaded the legislature to fund a research project that might make pineapple a more profitable crop for Hawaii. It was during this period that I patented several aspects of the xeronine-system.

Although my primary interests were in the health aspects of the xeronine-system, I knew that getting the medical profession in the U.S. to use the xeronine-system would be difficult. I also knew that obtaining the necessary FDA approval would require enormous amounts of money. Therefore, I accepted an invitation from a group of Hawaiian friends and entrepreneurs to investigate the nature of a "Magic Elixir" that a Californian entrepreneur had invented.

This "Magic Elixir" did everything. It "magically" cleaned accumulated grease from drainage pipes, it made plants grow better—most of the time-, it killed insects, it cured algae problems at Lake Tahoe, it cured distemper in dogs, it made hair grow better and it caused mares to produce more milk for their foals. No snake-oil salesman had ever made such preposterous claims. Yet, they were true!

I knew of only one substance that could produce these unbelievable and seemingly unrelated results, namely the xeronine-system. For introducing me to this new source of the xeronine-system, I must thank Harry Arakaki, Al Mosher and a former Dole colleague of mine. From the very extensive, well documented and impressive results that we obtained by using this material to treat waste water treatment problems, we obtained data that beautifully support, supplement and extend the data that we have from clinical reports of the effect of the xeronine-system on people.

Although using a source of the xeronine-system is now a well established practice in the waste-water-treatment industry, I felt frustrated that my original interest in the xeronine-system, namely the improving certain aspects of our health, was being neglected. After I moved from Hawaii to Louisville in 1986, I told my brother-in-law that I had information that could benefit our health but that I had no contacts to carry this message to the public. (The old adage that Benjamin Franklin used to inspire young people, namely: Build a better mousetrap and the world will beat a path to your door, does not apply to our modern world.)

For making this pertinent information and a product containing the xeronine-system available to the world, we must thank Kerry and Kim Asay, John Wadsworth, Stephen Story, Kelly Olsen, and all of Morinda Inc. They are the people who deserve the credit for making and distributing a product containing the xeronine-system and for introducing the xeronine-system concept to the public. I feel deeply indebted to them.

SECTION I: IN THE BEGINNING

CHAPTER 1

The Discovery of
the Xeronine-System

The xeronine-system is a completely new biochemical system. To understand the role this system plays in cells, we need to examine some of the observations that led to the conclusion that an undiscovered biochemical system exists in cells. In this chapter I shall describe how I became involved in this subject as well as some of the early reports and observations made by people who used commercial bromelain that was extracted from pineapple plants in the early 1960s and that contained essential components of the xeronine-system.

The xeronine-system plays important roles in many aspects of our lives. In industry it cures certain wastewater treatment problems; in food technology it tenderizes tough steaks and makes quick cooking cereals; in ecology it speeds up the removal of oil spills; in agriculture it affects the flowering and fruiting of plants. Its most exciting effects are in the health field. Here clinical reports with bromelain—at one time an excellent source of components of the xeronine-system—indicate that it favorably affects inflammation, high blood pressure, arthritis, some types of cancer, high cholesterol levels as well as many other ailments. People taking noni juice have reported similar benefits.

In all of these diverse fields, the reactions of people who have seen what this system does are similar—amazement and initial incredulity. I recall the remarks of the world authority on waste water treatment—at least that is what his business card said he was—when he saw what the application of a few quarts of a product containing components of the xeronine-system did in almost miraculously cleaning the clogged pipes of an outdated, overworked sewage system. He said that even if his mother had told him about the action of this product, that he would not have believed her. He had to see the effect with his own eyes to be convinced.

Other highly respected people have been similarly impressed. The head of the research division of one of the largest drug companies in the United States stated in 1957 that in his opinion the discovery of the medical applications of commercial bromelain—at that time an excellent source of the xeronine-system components—would rank as one of the major medical discoveries of the last fifty years. This is an important statement; it comes from the vice president of a company that bases its conclusions on verifiable data. Forty years later practically all of the exciting clinical results that this drug company discovered with bromelain in their laboratory and in their clinical trials are now being repeated with noni juice.

My discovery of the xeronine-system has a long and fascinating history; it has several distinct phases. It began when the Pineapple Research Institute of Hawaii hired me to devise a commercial method for isolating bromelain from the pineapple plant. Although bromelain was described in the seventeen-seventies, no one had previously been able to devise a commercial method for isolating this enzyme. I was able to solve this problem rather quickly and assigned the rights to the patent to the Pineapple Research Institute.

Shortly after we began producing bromelain commercially, our customers began telling us about the unexpected and highly desirable actions that bromelain had. They reported that no other commercial enzyme had ever performed so well in their applications. These reports suggested that some unknown material in commercial bromelain had unusual and very beneficial actions in a wide range of different applications. Discovering the nature of this unknown material was difficult. Eventually I discovered that the active ingredient was a strange volatile, nitrogen-containing molecule; it was a new alkaloid. However, this alkaloid differs in several critical respects from the classical alkaloids that we are all familiar with, such as cocaine, heroin, Novocain® and many others.

Let me start at the very beginning of the story.

Hawaii Beckons

As a graduate student, I had spent four years in Minnesota studying phospholipids, a subject which at that time did not appear to be leading anywhere. About ten years later, phospholipids became the key building block of all cell membranes. As I approached the end of my graduate schoolwork and began looking for a job, I discovered that the world did not exactly need the services of a specialist in phospholipids. Accordingly, I began exploring other job opportunities. Two looked interesting. One was to work on the hoof and mouth disease of cattle at a research station located on a small, desolate, quarantine island off the coast of fog shrouded Denmark. The other was in Hawaii and dealt with some technical problem connected with pineapple. After having spent four long, cold winters and four hot summers in Minnesota, the choice between these two jobs required no great soul searching.

When I arrived in Hawaii, I discovered that the research job for which I had been hired, namely to find a commercial method for isolating the protease bromelain from the pineapple plant, did not look very promising. The more I learned about previous studies, the less promising were the prospects of solving this problem. About eight years earlier, the University of Hawaii had hired the best chemist, A.K. Balls of the U.S. Department of Agriculture, to study the possibility of isolating bromelain commercially from the pineapple plant. His report, which was the definitive paper on the subject at the time, was not encouraging. He said it could be done but not at a profit. Next I learned that my immediate predecessor at the Pineapple Research Institute had spent two years on this problem before he decided that he had better find another job which offered a better chance for success.

I Did It! Commercial Bromelain is Possible

Fortunately, my specialty training in graduate school did not include any specific training in enzymes or pharmacology. Never having isolated an enzyme, I tried methods that properly trained enzymologists would have avoided. Also, since I had been hired specifically to discover a commercial method for isolating bromelain, I decided to restrict my studies to techniques that were commercially feasible. Since this meant that I would work with large quantities of pineapple plants, I asked Dole to set aside a field of pineapple for my use.

A large commercial company, whose business is growing and canning pineapples, cannot casually afford to set aside one of their good fields for basic research at the request of an unknown young chemist. Consequently, they did what was logical and economically feasible. They allowed me to use one of their fields that had been so weakened by worm damage (at least so they believed at that time), that they were going to plow it under and replant it whenever they had a break in their regular planting schedule. Little did anyone know at that time that this particular field contained more bromelain per acre than any field that we would harvest during the next thirty years.

The physiological action of the pilot-plant bromelain that I made from this particular pineapple field has never been equaled by us or anyone else. This was the enzyme that I sent to various potential customers while I was still working at the Pineapple Research Institute. The dramatic action of the bromelain from this initial pilot plant production immediately caught the attention of a wide range of potential customers.

Commercial Bromelain and its Enzymes

Bromelain is one of the earliest enzymes to have been discovered and used as an enzyme. The great Italian scientist, Lazzaro Spallanzani (1729-1799), in his studies on digestion showed that pineapple juice could digest meat. Since his day, many people have attempted to isolate bromelain commercially. They were unsuccessful until 1955.

The commercial bromelain that we produced and sold was not a pure enzyme; it was a mixture of all of the materials in the pineapple stem juice that did not dissolve in acetone solutions. It contained a mixture of different enzymes, proteins, complex carbohydrate polymers and inorganic salts. It also contained appreciable amounts of an unknown organic material that was not a protein, lipid, carbohydrate or plant pigment.

Commercial bromelain contains many other enzymes. We could have standardized and labeled the dried powder as an acid phosphatase, as an oxidase, or as a peroxidase, but we didn't. Because people associate the protein digesting enzyme bromelain with the pineapple and because a commercial market existed for proteases, we labeled our principal product as a protease and called it bromelain.

Although initially customers evaluated bromelain because they believed that they needed a protease for their particular problem, very quickly people began evaluating bromelain because it had other unusual and desirable actions. People in the brewing, tanning and especially in the pharmaceutical industry found that commercial bromelain produced results shown by no other commercial enzyme.

Fortunately, in the very early stages of my attempts to find markets for the tons of bromelain that were beginning to pile up in our warehouse, I met the research director of Princeton Laboratories. He had received a sample of my original batch of enzyme that I had made while I was still working at the Pineapple Research Institute. He told me about the strange, potent pharmacological actions that he found in the sample. He then made a comment that I took seriously. He told me that neither he nor I knew what ingredients in commercial bromelain caused the strong pharmacological activity that he had observed. He advised me that since I had unwittingly done something right, I should never make even minor changes in any part of the enzyme isolation procedure that I had developed. He said that even trivial and theoretically inconsequential changes in the processing method might decrease the amount of this unknown but desirable product.

He was presciently correct! I wish that I could give him the credit that he deserves. Unfortunately his name has been lost during the shredding of the Dole Research files.

Discovering the nature of the pharmacologically active ingredients was to be a long and difficult research project. Several drug companies as well as university research people have worked on this problem without success.

The Search for Sources of the "Unknown Ingredient"

As soon as reports about the strange and desirable properties of commercial bromelain began appearing regularly in the medical literature, research workers and drug companies searched for other natural products that might show similar valuable pharmacological activity. Papain, the only other commercially available plant protease at that time, showed small amounts of these desirable non-protease actions. However, the amount was much less than that found in bromelain and the variation in physiological activity between different batches of papain was so great that customers never knew what to expect from each batch of enzyme.

Eventually one drug company, Toshiba Drug Company of Japan, developed a commercial protease preparation that was as effective as bromelain in treating inflammation. They produced this "protease" preparation from the cells of a specially grown bacterium, Serratia marcescens. Soon they too discovered that an unknown and unstandardized component in their protease preparation was responsible for all of the desirable physiological actions of their product. They made the discovery of the nature of this unknown pharmacological material their primary research goal. Eventually, after three years of expensive and intensive research, they gave up and went on to projects that were easier to solve.

Since Dole was firmly committed to making bromelain and being the market leader, the president of Dole asked me to keep him informed of any potential competitors of bromelain. To fulfill this request, I closely monitored all natural products and all synthetic drugs that might either contain this unknown but valuable ingredient or that might produce by some other physiological method the same beneficial pharmacological actions in people.

The obvious competitors of bromelain were the related plant proteases papain and ficin. The quality of papain with respect to the amount of this unknown material was so much lower than that of bromelain, that even with a lower price per pound, papain would not be a serious competitor for bromelain in the pharmaceutical market. The protease ficin, which was isolated from the latex of the fig tree, was a more serious competitor. Some samples of ficin contained almost as much of this unknown factor as bromelain. However, I did not consider ficin a serious competitor for bromelain because the high cost of harvesting the latex from wild fig trees in the tropics was higher than the cost of our mechanized harvesting of pineapple plants.

The plant that did rival bromelain in potency was noni. Whereas pineapple fruit juice contained two MCU per ml (Milk Clotting Units, a measure of protease activity), noni juice contained between 45-55 MCU per ml. However, pineapple stem juice at that time (1956) contained between 75-125 MCU per ml. Since we had access to thousands of tons of readily harvestable stems a year, I could not envision noni as a serious economic competitor. Therefore at that time (1956) I dismissed noni as an economic competitor of bromelain. That has since changed. As I already mentioned, the pineapple plant changed after the 1960s (mostly because of soil conditions), and noni juice from Tahiti has now been marketed in an economical way.

Two synthetic products did pose a serious threat to one particular market for bromelain in the pharmaceutical industry. These were the industrial solvents DMSO (DiMethylSulfOxide) and Dilantin®. When I compared some of the reported clinical actions of bromelain, DMSO and Dilantin®, many of the actions were identical. This strongly suggests that all three products were affecting the same biological system in the body. Of these three products, explaining the action of DMSO was the most difficult. It took me several years before I finally had a theory that explained the action of DMSO.

The action of Dilantin® is an entirely different story. I shall cover that and DMSO in Chapter 10.

Clues that Protease Was Not the Key

When I transferred to Dole Inc. in 1955, my primary and most immediate job was to find applications for the tons of bromelain that were beginning to accumulate in the Dole warehouse. The obvious, traditional markets for a protease enzyme were meat tenderizers, chill-proofing agents for beer, recovery of by-products from the food processing operations and producing "instant" cooking hot cereals. When I visited various potential customers, I quickly learned two things. One was that the customers knew much more than I did and the other was that much I had learned in the ivory towers of the universities or research laboratories was inapplicable to real world problems.

Bating of Hides

My first contact with a person who knew how to solve real world problems lived in Milwaukee. In an area just south of the center of the city and not too far from one of the several famous breweries was a hide processing plant. The man in charge had rightly been concerned about the odors that his plant was producing. To "bate" the dried, salted hides that came into his plant by train, he soaked the hides for several weeks in large vats of water containing dog dung. In India starving villagers earned a little money collecting sun dried dog dung and sending it to him in large sacks. The dog dung contained bacteria that were particularly effective in making the stiff hides soft, pliable and receptive to dyes. In addition to this desirable action, the bacteria produced odors that the plant manager characterized euphemistically as "strong." To eliminate the use of dog dung to hasten the bating process, he had evaluated in his operation every commercial enzyme that was available.

Of all of these many enzymes that he tested, only bromelain worked. As he proudly showed me his new operation he mentioned that to further reduce odors he added mercury salts to his vats to kill the bacteria. When I heard this I was horrified. I explained to him in a rather know-it-all manner that mercury would completely inactivate bromelain and make it ineffective. He looked at me with patience and said, "Young man, you may know biochemistry but I know how to bate hides. Your product works. Now you go back to the laboratory and find out why your product works."

This was good advice, which I accepted. However, it took me several more years and another contact (Dr. Klein), this time in the medical field, before I had the answer to the hide bating problem. The answer has many important medical as well as technical applications.

The Healing of Burns

About four years later when our primary market for bromelain was the pharmaceutical market, I came across a very critical medical application for bromelain. This was an application that was related, in a way, to the hide bating operation. The difference was that in the medical application, the "hide" was not from an animal but was the burned skin from a living person. (I shall cover this application in the following pages.) Dr. Klein's and our studies in using commercial bromelain to remove damaged skin on burn victims conclusively proved that the protease action of commercial bromelain bore absolutely no relationship to its dramatic action in removing the burned skin of the patient.

This discovery explains why the Milwaukee hide processor could add mercury to his vats of soaking hides and still obtain an action that appeared to be a protease softening action. The action came not from the protease bromelain—mercury would have destroyed the protease—but from an inactive pro-collagenase that occurs in human skin and hides. Some unknown physiologically active "contaminant" produced in commercial bromelain was activating the normally inactive skin collagenase.

The unknown ingredient explains the highly desirable "plumping" action in the hide-bating process that commercial bromelain produced. Theoretically a true, external protease would have produced a slimy film on the surface of the hide with a minimum amount of plumping. To obtain true plumping, the potential protease must be distributed throughout the hide. The only way that can be achieved is by having the enzyme already distributed throughout the hide but in an inactive form. Whereas an enzyme applied externally would diffuse very, very slowly into a hide (many days), free xeronine diffuses rapidly, within a matter of minutes. The free xeronine activates the inactive form of many enzymes.

Exactly the same concept explains the rapid and painless removal of a burn scab in the medical field and the tenderizing of meat and making fast cooking cereals in the food field.

Food Technology Suggested a New System

Four important food applications also indicated that the protease component of commercial bromelain was an irrelevant diluent of some unknown and unstandardized natural, physiologically active ingredient. These are chill proofing beer, the in vivo and the in vitro tenderization of meat, the conversion of wheat grits into an "instant cooking" cereal, and the recovery of useable by-product from the wastes of fish and meat packing companies.

Chill Proofing Beer

From 1950 to 1965, chill proofing beer was a unique part of the American brewing process. When freshly brewed beer is bottled and chilled, frequently a precipitate forms in the beer. This gives the beer a cloudy appearance, as though someone had spilled milk in the beer. Of course, in Germany where beer is traditionally drunk in dark basement taverns that are filled with smoke and dirndiled outfitted waitresses and the beer is drunk from porcelain mugs, a little cloudiness in the beer is no problem. Also in Britain cloudy beer is never a problem. In that country no self respecting pub visitor would ever consider drinking cold beer, a fetish-so they will tell you most vociferously—of uncultured Americans. In America, however, customers demand chilled beer that is sparkling and clear enough to serve in champagne glasses.

Today breweries use physical methods to "chill-proof" beer. Back in the 1950s, however, all major U.S. breweries—with two exceptions— used the Wallerstein enzymatic method to chill-proof beer. The biochemist Wallerstein theorized that the barley proteins extracted during the malting process became insoluble when beer is chilled. (This part is true.) To correct this problem, he theorized that adding a protein-digesting enzyme to the beer would break the large protein molecule into small fragments that would be soluble at any temperature. (This is theory only; it does not work in practice.)

He tried his proposed method. It worked. Therefore he assumed his theory was correct. He patented the process and became a modestly wealthy person.

For many years, all large brewers—with only two exceptions—routinely chill-proofed their beer. The only significant differences between different types of chill proofing agents were in the enzymes used. Most producers of beer chill-proofing products used papain in their product. Papain was the traditional enzyme, it worked and it was relatively inexpensive. A few of the more adventuresome formulators used bromelain. This gave a superior chill-proofing agent that was more expensive than those based on papain.

The chill proofing operation inadvertently provided critical information on the extreme potency of the xeronine-system. I have never released this information previously since the man who supplied this information to me in 1956 had asked me to keep the information confidential. However, he has long since died, the brewing company that he worked for has been taken over by another company, and no brewery uses the chill-proofing process today.

Before his brewing company used the Wallerstein process for chill-proofing beer, as director of research for the brewing company this man tested not only the effectiveness of the process for chill-proofing beer but he also tested the effect of chill-proofed beer on the people who drank such a beer. He reported that the process did not affect the flavor of the beer significantly. However, chill-proofed beer passed through the stomach significantly faster than untreated beer!

If such information had been released, the FDA would probably have asked the company to supply data about the specific component in papain that was causing a more rapid emptying of the stomach. Since no scientist had any information about any material in papain that might have such an action, the officials of the brewing company decided not to make his report public. When I heard this interesting piece of information, I immediately thought of Dr. H. Haggard's work at Yale in 1926. Dr. Haggard studied how different types of breakfast drinks affected the passage of food through the stomach. Of the juices that he investigated, orange juice, prune juice, pineapple juice and cranberry juice, only pineapple juice significantly increased the rate of passage of food through the stomach. Many years later we abundantly confirmed Dr. Haggard's work. Although I had no concept of the xeronine-system at that time, I believed strongly that both bromelain and papain contained the same type of physiologically active agent. However, my laboratory data showed that bromelain was about four times more effective in increasing the rate of stomach emptying than was papain.

From these commercial experiences I estimated just how much proxeronine is required to cause the stomach to empty faster. (Assume 1 lb papain chill-proofing agent/5000 gallons beer; assume 50% of chill-proofing agent is papain; assume 1% of papain is proxeronine.) Each bottle of papain chill-proofed beer would contain approximately 0.03 mg of proxeronine. This is such a minute amount of proxeronine that the ordinary microbalance would not be able to weigh it.

Instant Cooking Cream of Wheat®

To adapt to the changing breakfast habits of customers who felt that they could not wait several minutes for Cream of Wheat® to cook, the Cream of Wheat® Company developed "instant cooking" Cream of Wheat®. All that the time-pressed consumer had to do was to add boiling water to her cereal and to her instant coffee and then read the headlines in the paper before dashing off to work. The Cream of Wheat® Company achieved this "instant cooking" property by treating the wheat niblets with an enzyme solution. Dr. I.W. Sizer of MIT, who was their consultant, advised them that even though a pure protease would be worthless for their application, they should evaluate the action of commercial bromelain. He told them that commercial bromelain contained some unknown ingredient that might activate the enzymes that are present in wheat grains when they germinate.

The Problem with Pineapple Pie Filling

A short time after the Cream of Wheat® project ended, one of Dole's customers reported a strange phenomenon that defied all conventional explanations. This problem also involved starch.

Today not many people are still alive who can remember that at one time in our country's history women stayed at home and baked pies. To help them in this husband-pleasing but onerous task, the food companies prepared various fruit pie fillings. Other companies prepared ready-to-bake piecrusts in disposable pie pans.

One day Dole received a frantic call from one of the large food processing companies. Something in Dole crushed pineapple was causing the starch in their crushed pineapple pie filling to liquefy. They said that since apples, blueberries and strawberries caused no problem, some starch digesting enzyme in Dole crushed pineapple must be responsible for the liquefaction of the starch gel. Since Dole was also making pineapple pie filling and was having no problems with the starch liquefying, the Dole manager suggested that the customer switch to another brand of starch for their pineapple pie fillings. This solved the crisis.

This problem intrigued me. Eventually I found that this company had been using a specially prepared starch for their filling. Since companies manufacturing starch do not earn money selling standard starch preparation, each of the starch producing companies attempts to slightly modify their standard starch preparations so that they can charge a premium price for their improvements. The company that sold the starch to the manufacturer of pineapple pie filling was advertising their starch as one prepared with the minimum use of chemicals.

I later discovered that they did not use sulfur dioxide, the standard bacteriostatic agent commonly used during starch preparation. Sulfur dioxide—as I shall point out in Chapter 9—is a specific inhibitor of one step in the biosynthesis of xeronine. For this reason this particular brand of starch, which had not been exposed to sulfur dioxide, could produce xeronine providing proxeronine were present. The canned pineapple supplied the proxeronine and the released xeronine activated the starch-digesting enzyme in the starch. This action liquefied the starch gel that is so important in a pie filling.

I should point out that this action is precisely what the Cream of Wheat® research workers used in making "instant cooking" cereal even though they were unaware of the mechanism of the action. This is also the action that occurs when a kernel of corn germinates.

In vivo Tenderization of Meat

Another food use of bromelain that indicated that the desirable action of bromelain was not related to its protease action but to something else, was the in vivo as well as the in vitro tenderization of meat. Perhaps a few readers can still remember Swift's ProTen® meat, which Swift marketed during the early 1960s. This was an ingenious meat tenderizing treatment in which the operator injected a "protease" solution into the neck vein of the living animal about two minutes before they slaughtered the animal. The circulation of the blood carried the injected "protease" solution to all of the muscle tissue. Theoretically this would ensure a well-tenderized piece of meat. Whatever the mechanism was, their method was highly effective. For this study they received both a patent and an award for the best food-processing discovery of the year. Swift did their original work with papain.

Yet their method had several critical problems. Their principal operating problem with this method was that no known enzyme test could tell them which batches of papain would be effective in their process. The only effective assay was a full-scale animal test followed by an extensive taste panel evaluation of the cooked meat. Since this process was very expensive, they would not even consider an enzyme supplier unless the supplier could guarantee that he would be able to offer them 500 pounds to a ton of enzyme from the same batch.

Of all the enzymes that they tested, bromelain was by far the most effective. In fact, our problem with bromelain was that it was almost too effective. FDA had allowed Swift to inject the enzyme solution into the neck artery of the living animal providing that this injection did not visibly annoy the animal. Thus, one of our problems in selling bromelain to Swift was to be certain that an effective level of enzyme did not cause the cow to salivate unduly or roll its eyes alarmingly.

Since Swift was one of our most important industrial customers and since I had considerable flexibility in making enzyme for a customer of this size, we did considerable basic research on the action of injected bromelain on animals. For test animals, we used chickens furnished through the cooperation of Dr. Ernie Ross of the University of Hawaii. The three samples which we chose for comparison were a special, highly purified, high protease activity bromelain preparation which had a protease activity of 2300 GDU/gram, our standard commercial bromelain, which had a protease activity of 1350 GDU/gram and a special fraction with high UV absorption at 320 nm which had a protease activity of 750 GDU/gram. (The GDU is a measure of the ability of the enzyme to digest gelatin.) We injected chickens with solutions of the three samples at three dosage levels.

The results were definitive and impressive. The highly purified, high protease bromelain caused no adverse animal reactions at any of the concentrations that we tested. Not only did this treatment not tenderize the meat, but also in large amounts it actually made the meat slightly tougher (statistically significant) than meat from untreated chickens. By contrast, both the commercial bromelain and the special high 320 nm UV samples produced startling animal reactions at the highest concentration of samples. Blood poured out of the eyes and the mouths of the chickens; the animals went into a paroxysm of uncontrolled activity, running and stumbling around the room and attempting to fly. Then within a minute, they died spectacularly. Although this meant that we did not have to kill the chickens ourselves, obviously FDA would not be too happy with this vigorous animal response. However, when we cooked the meat from these chickens, it was delicious and unbelievably tender. One could easily cut the meat with the blunt side of a butter knife. At lower concentrations of these two samples, the animal reactions were mild and the meat was tender and tasty.

These data from our chicken injection experiments suggested that Swift had done the right thing for the wrong reason. They had planned to use the animal's own blood circulatory system to uniformly distribute a solution of commercial proteolytic enzyme throughout the body just prior to the time of slaughtering. However, their studies showed that the protease activity of the injected solution bore absolutely no correlation to meat tenderization by their large-scale animal testing and taste panel evaluation. What Swift had actually done was to inject components of the xeronine-system into the animal. The xeronine produced by this system activated the animal's own abundant supply of inactive cathepsin and inactive collagenase. All of the observed reaction to the injected "enzyme" solution came not from the injected enzyme but from the injected "enzyme" solution activating the abundant supply of the cow's own inactive proteases.

Incidentally, I should mention that exactly the same action is true of the standard in vitro meat tenderizers such as Adolf's Meat Tenderizer®. The protease in papain does not tenderize the meat; it is the xeronine-system in the papain that activates the inactive proteases in the meat tissue.

Fish Leftovers: Another Piece of the Puzzle

Recovering by-products from food processing plants was one of our large industrial markets for commercial bromelain. Since the largest fish processing plant in Honolulu was a part of Castle & Cooke, the company that owned Dole, we had great latitude in running important experiments at this plant.

The tuna packing operation is relatively simple. It has essentially two objectives: 1) placing as much of the tuna fish as possible either into cans for sale to people who like tuna fish or to people who have cats that like tuna fish, and 2) converting the fish heads and intestines into two protein byproducts. One byproduct was a soluble, liquid protein concentrate and the other an insoluble protein solid. Since soluble fish proteins sell for a much higher price than the insoluble protein fraction, a good plant manager attempts to convert as much as possible of the fish solids into soluble fish proteins.

First, I should mention some general properties about the action of proteases on proteins. As a general rule, most proteases act poorly—if at all—on undenatured proteins. Undenatured proteins are proteins in a complex, folded form. When they are in a globular form, most of the bonds that the enzyme could attack are securely tucked inside the structure. For a protease to digest a protein, the protein must first unfold, that is the protein must be denatured. The two most common methods for denaturing proteins are heating the protein or exposing the protein to a low pH. Our stomachs denature the protein that we eat by using a very low pH. When we fry eggs for breakfast, we denature the proteins with heat.

At the tuna plant in Honolulu the fish heads and intestines were run through a chopper and the puree dumped into a 30,000-gallon tank. To promote the autolysis of the puree, the operator held the tank at about 40 degrees C. for two hours. He then ran steam into the tank until the temperature rose to 80 degrees C. Then he centrifuged the contents of the tank, concentrated the liquid portion and dried the insoluble residue.

Theoretically to increase the yield of soluble protein by adding a protease to the mixture, the best place to add the protease would be after the steam heating step. At this point the protein molecules would have been denatured by the heat and would be at their maximum susceptibility to digestion by a protease.

When we did that, we increased the yield of soluble protein by 3%, an insignificant amount. When we added the same amount of enzyme just before the heating step, we increased the yield of soluble protein by 9%.

This better yield is contrary to conventional enzyme theory. The undenatured proteins still had their original three-dimensional structure and should have been more resistant to digestion. When we added the enzyme as soon as the tank was filled, the yield increased to 13%. In our last test we dripped a solution of bromelain onto the fish parts as they entered the grinding machine. This treatment increased the yield 22%.

These results clearly indicated that the factor in commercial bromelain that caused digestion of the fish proteins was not the protease in commercial bromelain but some factor in commercial bromelain that activated the pro-enzymes in the undenatured fish protein.

Other Actions

All of the industrial examples that I mentioned in this chapter involve the activation of hydrolytic enzymes, that is enzymes that break down complex molecules into simpler molecules.

The xeronine-system has other important industrial applications that involve different components or different actions of the xeronine-system. So as not to confuse the picture, I shall cover these reactions in another chapter.

Chapter Summary

• Many plant extracts, such as bromelain, papain, ficin, amylases and kelp and certain tissue extracts, such as rennin and pancreatin, owe their physiological potency not to the reputed enzymes in these products but to some unstandardized material. This we now know is the xeronine-system.

• Most of the "strange" industrial examples that I mentioned in this chapter involve the activation of various pro-enzymes by xeronine. This is a natural metabolic reaction that occurs in various parts of the metabolic cycle of all organisms including humans.

• The xeronine-system has many other important functions. I shall cover these in the succeeding chapters.

CHAPTER 2

Discovery of the Medical Uses
for *Commercial* Bromelain

Many plant extracts, such as noni, pineapple and ginseng, just to mention a few, are parts of the herbal lore treatments for various diseases. Although these plant materials had—and still have—a loyal following among herbalists, pharmaceutical companies showed little interest in these materials. No one knew what ingredients in these extracts constituted the physiologically active component. Furthermore the reports of medical activity in these plants were mostly anecdotal.

All of this changed in the 1950s when commercial bromelain became available in tonnage quantities. Before the start of the Dole commercial bromelain operation, while I was still working at the Pineapple Research Institute, I had prepared and distributed to various industrial and drug companies laboratory samples of bromelain. Since drug companies are generally quite secretive when they are exploring new drugs, I was completely unaware that at least two drug companies were planning to produce drugs based on bromelain. My first exposure to this strange—but exceedingly valuable—pharmaceutical activity of commercial bromelain was accidental.

How the "Accident" Happened

While I was still working at the Pineapple Research Institute, I met Dr. Robert Hunter, a Honolulu gynecologist who had a strong interest in basic medical research. He had read about the success of a gastroenterologist in improving the quality of stomach x-ray pictures by first irrigating the patient's stomach with a dilute papain solution. The papain solution liquefied the gastric mucous that had previously prevented taking sharp x-ray pictures. Since Dr. Hunter, as was true of all of his colleagues, had difficulty in obtaining sharp x-ray pictures of the uterus because of the presence of mucous, he wanted to investigate the possibility of removing the mucous with a preliminary douche of a papain solution.

I prepared fresh papain for him by tapping green papaya fruit growing in my back yard and precipitating the "enzymes." When Dr. Hunter tested a solution made from this papain preparation on one of his patients, he found that the technique worked well. From then on he routinely used a preliminary enzyme douche on his patients before taking x-ray pictures.

Making papain is tedious work and lowers the quality of the fruit. Although I was happy to make the papain for him, I had other work to do, namely produce bromelain, an enzyme related to papain, and to find marketable uses for it. Therefore, I suggested to him that he might be interested in evaluating bromelain in his procedure.

He did. He found that bromelain worked even better than the papain preparations. For about a year he routinely used a bromelain douche on his patients before he took x-ray pictures. His pictures were so striking and showed such exquisite details of the fallopian tubes, that one of the publishing companies used one of his pictures in their textbook. Although I was interested in finding markets for bromelain, I had initially dismissed this niche application. This application required so little bromelain per treatment that even if all of the gynecologists in the country were to use this procedure, the total U.S. market was miniscule. About two hours of bromelain production at the proposed Dole plant would have produced sufficient bromelain to supply this market for a year.

Nevertheless, this purely technical application of bromelain, that is getting clearer x-ray pictures, led to a medical discovery. When a woman who had been suffering from intense menstrual pains each month came into Dr. Hunter's office for a check up, he told her that he wanted to be sure that she did not have a tumor that was blocking her menstrual flow. As was now his routine procedure before taking an x-ray picture, he gave her a douche with a 1% bromelain solution and then began making preparations for injecting a barium solution. But before he was ready, she shouted to Dr. Hunter that he should forget the x-ray picture. Her pains were gone and her monthly flow had started. After Dr. Hunter had tested this procedure on several other patients who had similar problems, we published a paper on his findings. This was the first medical paper on the strange pharmacological action of "bromelain." This is the paper that aroused the interests of several large pharmaceutical companies in the potential application of bromelain for various medical disorders.[1]

Dr. Hunter made still another important medical discovery that involved the xeronine-system. Certain women have great difficulty in caring an embryo to maturity. One particular cause of this problem is the sphincter muscle that closes the opening between the uterus and the vagina. If this muscle is weak, the developing embryo slips out of the uterus. Medically this problem is known as an incompetent os.

Women who have such a problem have several difficult choices to make. Either they can spend most of their pregnancy in bed or they can undergo a technically difficult and dangerous operation in which muscles from another part of the body are grafted onto the weak sphincter muscle. Because of the danger and difficulties of such an operation, a physician will rarely perform the operation until the woman has aborted several pregnancies. Then he can be certain that the weak muscle is the problem. Dr. Hunter's discovery meant that a very simple test unequivocally indicates whether a woman has this problem. (One has to see an x-ray picture of a patient who has this problem to appreciate how dramatic the action of bromelain is.)

In this initial pharmacological work, most research workers assumed that the protease activity contained in commercial bromelain was the source of the physiological activity. In the next section I shall describe the study made by one of the largest U.S. drug companies of that period that proved conclusively that for at least one application, namely the treatment of menstrual cramps, the protease bromelain is a placebo.

The Remedy that Failed

Shortly after Dr. Hunter and I began working together, Dr. Paul

Scheuer, a specialist in the chemistry of natural products at the University of Hawaii, told a visiting drug scout that they ought to investigate bromelain. Dole was producing it in tonnage quantities. Furthermore, he told them that this product had interesting physiological activity. The drug company followed his suggestion. This was the start of four years of close and mutually beneficial cooperation between the Drug Company and the Dole Research Group.

For their initial bromelain-based drug product, the Drug Company chose to follow Dr. Hunter's lead and produce a drug for the treatment of menstrual difficulties. Before they started their drug application investigations, they proved to their satisfaction that the protease activity contained in bromelain was the ingredient that was responsible for curing dysmenorrhea. They did this by heating solutions of bromelain for different lengths of time at moderately high temperatures. They then tested the heated solution for protease activity and for pharmacological activity. They found that heating bromelain solutions for different lengths of time destroyed the protease activity and the pharmacological activity at the same rate. These results were compatible with their belief that the protease bromelain was the source of the pharmaceutical activity of commercial bromelain.

During this period of investigation, which lasted almost four years, I worked closely with members of their research group. They generously allowed me to see their internal research reports. So unexpectedly effective was commercial "bromelain" not only in their initial proposed drug application but also in a wide variety of other potential health applications, that their research director stated publicly that he considered the discovery of the pharmaceutical applications of "bromelain" to be one of the major drug discoveries of the last half-century.

This statement by the research director of one of the largest drug companies in the U.S. has an important bearing on the anecdotal reports about the effectiveness of noni juice in treating certain health problems. People who are skeptical about the dramatic action of noni juice from Tahiti in curing certain health problems always ask, "Where are the data to back up these statements?"

Drug companies do not publish their laboratory and their preliminary clinical data until they are ready to market their products; they do not want to tip off competitors. However, because of my personal connections with the research people of this company, I have seen their data on the action of commercial bromelain in curing or helping with such health problems as high blood pressure, memory problems, emphysema, infection and certain types of cancer. Practically all of the anecdotal reports about the action of noni in improving certain health problems had been documented by this Drug Company in their studies on the action of commercial bromelain. Commercial bromelain produced at this time contained the same physiological components as noni juice from Tahiti does today.

The research director's very favorable comments on the pharmaceutical potential of "bromelain" in medicine even made the financial news. Dole, which at that time needed large amounts of capital for a new pineapple venture in the Philippines, was able to obtain favorable financial rates based on the potential profitability of "bromelain" for Dole. The future looked exciting. Then suddenly this part of the "bromelain" venture collapsed.

For their final double blind test to get FDA approval for their proposed product and application, this drug company asked me to supply them with purified bromelain rather than the commercial bromelain that they had been using in all of their initial studies. (The FDA understandably looks favorably on those drug applications that use purified products in the formulations.) When the results of this very expensive and intensive double blind were in, purified bromelain proved to be no better than the placebo used in the test.

These results provoked a financial and theoretical crisis. To determine whether our bromelain purification process had removed some unknown physiologically active ingredient or whether the drug formulation process had destroyed the activity of the bromelain, the Drug Company sought the assistance of Dr. Hunter. Dr. Hunter persuaded a female patient suffering from incompetent os to cooperate in the definitive test. For this test I prepared two bromelain solutions that I had adjusted to contain exactly the same level of protease activity. One sample was a solution of the highly purified bromelain preparation; the other preparation was a solution of our standard commercial bromelain. Dr. Hunter started the test with the highly purified enzyme.

The results of this test were absolutely definitive. When Dr. Hunter used a solution of the purified bromelain as a douche on his patient, it showed absolutely no physiological action. By contrast when he repeated the test a few minutes later with the solution of commercial bromelain, the sphincter muscle relaxed completely. There was absolutely no question that our purification procedure had removed or destroyed the physiologically active ingredient in commercial bromelain. In other words pure bromelain was completely ineffective in this medical application.

Although this had been a very expensive test, the Drug Company was not discouraged. They knew that commercial bromelain contained a valuable ingredient and that the procedure that we used to purify bromelain had removed it. They proposed that our two companies set up a joint venture to isolate and characterize this unknown material. This was an exciting proposal. We knew what type of molecules our purification technique had removed. Ideally with these clues it should not have taken too long to find the answer. However, no one knew how long the research project would take or how much it would cost. Since Dole had already spent considerable money building the bromelain production plant, they were reluctant to commit themselves to a further indefinite amount of money and research time.

While we were still discussing possible terms for this joint venture, another Drug Company approached us. This was a drug company that had acquired one of my original bromelain preparations that I had made while I was still at the Pineapple Research Institute. They already had FDA approval for a bromelain containing product that would reduce inflammation and they were ready to start marketing their product. Dole elected to switch partners and work with a company that was ready to purchase large amounts of bromelain from us immediately.

Bromelain: A Proven Anti-Inflammatory

The use of enteric-coated bromelain tablets (tablets that have a coating that protects the contents of the tablet from the low pH and the enzymes of the stomach but opens in the intestines) for treating inflammation has had a controversial history. At one time Congress asked NIH to investigate certain dubious health remedies and drugs. The number one drug on the list of remedies that NIH was supposed to study was enteric-coated bromelain. Theoretically, these tablets could not possibly work. After an extensive investigation, the panel concluded that even though the theory made no sense, the clinical data showed that these tablets were effective.

The first and only FDA approved use for bromelain in the United States is as an oral anti-inflammatory agent in an enteric-coated tablet. The research director, Gus Martin, of this second drug company with which we worked, had originally been at Princeton Laboratory. The director of this laboratory was the man who had told me about the unusual pharmacological actions of bromelain and that I should not change any details of the isolation method until I knew what I should be doing.

Gus realized that an excellent pharmaceutical market existed for a truly effective, dependable, oral, non-steroidal anti-inflammatory product. He persuaded a drug company to produce an enteric-coated pill containing bromelain. This pill was for many years the best non-steroidal anti-inflammatory product sold.

Today it is difficult to realize that in the 1950s the nature, cause and cure of inflammation were concepts that scientists debated intensely. The Innerfeld-Martin group proposed that injury to a tissue, whether caused by a sharp blow, an infection or a chemical, denatured some of the tissue proteins. The denatured proteins, which are insoluble, clogged the "microreticular" circulation. This caused a buildup of pressure, heat and pain. If this hypothesis were correct, then the cure was simple. Add a protein-digesting enzyme to the circulatory system and the enzyme would digest the denatured protein and restore the "microreticular" circulation.

Physiological scientists objected to this theory on several grounds. The most important objection concerned the difficulty of getting the enzyme into the circulatory system. All human physiology text books state that intact proteins do not cross the intestinal membrane and enter into the blood stream; enzymes in the intestinal tract must first hydrolyze the proteins into peptides or free amino acids. Furthermore, if a foreign protein should enter into the blood stream, the liver would remove the foreign protein from the blood stream. (This is true for a person with a healthy liver.) However, if the liver did not remove the foreign proteins from the blood stream, then the body would make antibodies against the foreign protein. (This is also true.)

Gus Martin, now the Director of Research at the Drug Company that produced the anti-inflammatory pill, suggested that the classical theory of absorption of proteins was incomplete and inaccurate. His laboratory group took commercial bromelain and tagged it with tritium—a radioactive isotope of hydrogen. He showed conclusively that when the tagged "enzyme" was placed into a ligated section of the intestinal tract, a large radioactive molecule appeared in the circulatory system. Since they had set out to tag bromelain, they assumed that this large molecule had to be bromelain.

Furthermore—and this is what lent credence to Gus Martin's theory—the tagged molecule only leaked out of the capillaries at the site of the inflammation! Gus credited the reduction in the size of the inflamed area as being the result of the bromelain leaking out of the capillaries at the inflamed site and digesting the denatured proteins. (Protein digesting enzymes digest denatured proteins but rarely attack normal proteins.)

The concept that I am trying to show is moderately complicated-intact proteins never enter into the general circulating system of a healthy person. Therefore the large, tritium tagged molecule that Martin's group found in the blood system could not have been a bromelain-protein. Since tritium will replace any active hydrogen in a molecule, I am suggesting that tritium labeled both bromelain-proteins and proxeronine. However, only the proxeronine would pass through the intestinal membranes and through the liver to appear in the circulating blood. The size of proxeronine is just large enough to be retained by the normal capillaries. However if the capillaries become leaky, as they do at an inflamed site, the proxeronine is small enough to leak out. Martin's data supports my xeronine-system hypothesis beautifully.

Japanese scientists, principally Dr. Shigeki Nakagawa, conclusively resolved the debate about whether intact proteins could cross the intestinal membrane and appear in the portal vein. Dr. Nakagawa showed that certain small but stable proteins, such as ribonuclease, rennin and chymotrypsin, could cross the intestinal wall of the rabbit. His identification tests for these proteins in the renal blood stream are exquisite. However, since the renal vein that collects all of the blood from the intestines is a short vein that flows directly into the liver, the liver strips out all foreign proteins. Therefore in the intestinal tract of a normal person with a healthy liver, foreign proteins never enter the circulating blood stream. Thus both Gus Martin and his critics were correct in part of the absorption story but they both lacked other critical details.

Effect of Bromelain on the Brain

In his preliminary investigation, Gus Martin made an astounding discovery that was never further developed. At one of the hospitals where he was running his early clinical tests on the effectiveness of bromelain as an anti-inflammatory drug, one of the patients was a comatose woman who had been in bed for three months. She had no muscular control and the nurses had to turn her several times a day. Even with this treatment she developed severe bedsores and her body was severely inflamed. Dr. Martin recommended giving her two bromelain tablets three times a day. Two hours after the first dose—this is approximately how long it would take the pills to travel through her stomach and to dissolve in her intestines—the woman suddenly sat up in bed and asked what she was doing in the hospital. By the next day she was out of bed and began calling her family on the phone. The third day she volunteered to do work around the hospital to keep busy until her family could pick her up.

After three days the original supply of pills had run out. This did not appear to be a serious problem since by this time the drug company was already producing pills from bromelain that they were buying from Dole. Unfortunately these pills were not as effective as the pills made from my original Pineapple Research Institute bromelain. The woman quickly lost her vigor and stayed in bed. Three days after the switch to the new batch of enzyme, the woman again became comatose.

The first batch of pills had been made with the bromelain that I had produced while I was still at the Pineapple Research Institute. I now know what very subtle changes occurred during the change from a large-scale laboratory type of production to commercial production. It should be possible to produce again a product having these unbelievable properties. This should certainly be a project of high priority.

During the period while Dole was working with the second pharmaceutical company exclusively, another important medical application of commercial bromelain developed.

Healing Third-Degree Burns

News about the use of bromelain to produce miraculous cures on burn-patients reached Dole from an irate stockholder. He wrote a letter to the president of Dole asking him to explain why the company was withholding information about this amazing discovery from the world. Eventually this letter ended on my desk. Being intrigued by this new application, I attempted to track down the name and location of this doctor.

I knew the company that had supplied the bromelain to this doctor. When I asked for the name of this doctor, they told me that it was their company policy not to divulge the name of any of their cooperating doctors. Since this company was our largest customer and since they assumed—very legitimately—that they were the people to carry out clinical research and that I was the person to make certain that they were getting good quality enzyme, I could not press them further. I then tried getting specific information from the man who wrote the original letter to Dole. He did not know either the name of the doctor or where he lived. He did know that it was somewhere in the northeastern part of the country. That did not help me very much.

Then I happened to have a lucky break. On one of my visits to the Dole patent attorney in Washington, I mentioned this new application of bromelain and my difficulty in tracking down the doctor. The patent attorney told me that I must be referring to Dr. Gerald Klein. Dr. Klein had been the doctor who had treated his son when his son and his classmate were badly burned in a boat fire. Two different doctors treated the burned boys. Dr. Klein's patient made a complete recovery whereas the other boy was now permanently crippled. Because of his gratitude to Dr. Klein for taking care of his son, the patent lawyer had maintained contact with him after Dr. Klein had left Washington to set up practice in Maine.

The patent attorney gave me Dr. Klein's address and telephone number. This began a long and a productive research relationship between Dr. Klein and myself.

Dr. Klein had an interesting background for this work. During World War II Dr. Klein was a young medical officer attached to Rommel's African Panzer Corp. The patients whom he saw were generally either patients dying from artillery shell wounds or badly burned patients who, because of their intense pain, wished that they could die. Dr. Klein was so affected by the physical and mental damage that his burn-patients suffered, that he vowed that if he ever survived the war, he would spend the rest of his life attempting to alleviate the physical and mental damage from burns. After the war he became a U.S. citizen and moved to a region of our country that he believed would be safe if WW III started. He had hoped to establish a burn center in this isolated area. But this is getting ahead of the story.

Dr. Klein told me that he had told his supplier of bromelain that some batches of bromelain were terrific whereas others were practically worthless. When he had mentioned this to the drug company, they had assured him that they had tested the enzymes that they supplied him and that all of the batches were all equally effective. (They limited their quality control to the protease content in commercial bromelain.) If there were any variation in results, they told him it was probably attributable to the way that he stored or mixed the bromelain.

Since I had learned to listen seriously to any comments or observations that users of bromelain might make, I told Dr. Klein that I believed him and that probably some critical but unknown and unstandardized ingredient in bromelain was varying between different batches. Cooperative work that we did both in Maine and in Honolulu conclusively proved that pure bromelain was absolutely worthless for the rapid and painless removal of burn scabs. My best laboratory preparation for the removal of burn scabs was a sample that was actually low in proteolytic activity but was high in a material that I was beginning to suspect was either the long sought for active ingredient or else a material closely associated with the active ingredient.

Unless one has actually used Dr. Klein's technique on a badly burned patient, describing the almost miraculous response that Dr. Klein was getting strains one's credulity. In his first major test of this method, the patient was a young woman who had been trapped in the back seat of a Corvette when the car was rear-ended and burst into flames. She was brought to the hospital with three fourths of her body extensively burned. Her mother, who had flown into town from Italy, had wanted to transfer her daughter to the Armed Forces Burn Center in San Antonio. However, after listening to Dr. Klein and seeing photographs of some of the patients whom he had treated with bromelain, she decided to leave her daughter in Dr. Klein's care. The standard hospital prognosis for the future of this patient was one year in the intensive burn ward and then several years of remedial treatment. Even after that she would still be a badly scarred person both physically and mentally.

Dr. Klein started his treatment as soon as he had her mother's permission. Three months later, the daughter was well enough to go dancing! Six months later she was married. For her wedding dress she insisted on short sleeves and a low cut neck to show everyone that she bore no scars!

Certainly Dr. Klein's treatment was providing miraculous results. But how did it work? Dr. Klein had originally started with the conventional belief—which is still prevalent among some burn research workers—that proteolytic enzymes might remove the burn scar more easily than the standard slicing the scab off with sharp knives, a procedure that was tedious for the doctor and painful for the patient. The principal enzyme used for the "enzymatic debriding of burn eschars" was chymotrypsin, a highly purified protease made from the pancreas of cows. Pads soaked in the enzyme solution were placed on the burn scabs and then changed several times a day for three or four days. At the end of that time the eschar was sufficiently softened so that the outer portion could be scraped off of the burn. If eschar still remained, then the treatment was continued.

The research doctors liked the chymotrypsin treatment but the patients hated it. I talked with a marine pilot who had undergone this treatment after his plane caught fire during a hard carrier landing. He told me that the pain of the enzymatic debridement treatment was worse than the pain of the original burn.

From elementary biochemistry this is easy to understand. One group of pain hormones are peptides that latch onto specific protein receptors. When a proteolytic enzyme digests proteins, it releases a variety of different peptides. Certain of these peptides act as pain hormones. Therefore one can anticipate that the enzymatic debridement of burns is a prescription for producing intense pain -not a desirable action. By contrast the xeronine-system treatment is painless. I have carried on a normal conversation with a burn patient while the attending doctor applied the bromelain paste to the burned area. There was not the slightest indication of pain or anxiety on the part of the patient.

Incidentally, I might mention a related example of the complete lack of pain from the accidental application of large amounts of a concentrated solution of proxeronine to the skin. I was preparing a plant sample that was high in proxeronine for a research doctor. Since hand squeezing juice from green pineapple fruit was extremely difficult and since I was running short of time, I finally discarded the slippery rubber gloves that I had been using and worked with my bare hands. As I continued the squeezing process, I noticed that my preparation was getting dirty. I could not imagine where the rust was coming from since I was working with stainless steel. Then I happed to raise my hand and saw that blood was dripping from my finger tips like water from a leaky faucet. The proxeronine had gotten under the cuticle and had activated a pro-collagenase protein in my fingers. If the plant juice had produced this action because it contained an active proteolytic enzyme, I would have been screaming with pain.

This incident had another unexpected side effect. I completely lost all of my fingerprints! I had always wondered what other purpose fingerprints served besides littering the police files with difficult to classify smudge prints. I soon found out. When I attempted to pick up a pin, I had difficulty. I could feel that I had a pin somewhere between my fingers but I could not tell just where the pin was unless I looked at my fingers. The technical term for this ability to detect position by sensory points in the skin is kinesthesia. This incident got me a three-line notice in Playboy Magazine as "The scientist who lost his fingerprints."

Now back to Dr. Klein and his work. The astounding results that Dr.

Klein had discovered required a completely new explanation. No protease enzyme could have acted that rapidly, could have brought about the removal of the scabs without digesting the scabs, or could have left a clean dermal bed that was suitable for immediate skin grafting. One of Dr. Klein's colleagues suggested that something in bromelain was activating a proenzyme in the body. It was the body's enzyme that was making a cleavage plane between the dermal tissues and the overlying scab.

This explanation immediately explains the industrial application of bromelain in plumping and softening cow hides during the bating process. I covered this application in Chapter 1. That commercial bromelain was unaffected by the presence of mercury in the vat shows that the protease bromelain is irrelevant in this hide bating process; the protease is also completely irrelevant in burn eschar debridement.

Bromelain and Fertility

The first well-documented example of the effect of solutions of bromelain on fertility came as an unplanned side effect of the study that our original cooperating Drug Company had made. The first application that this company investigated was the effect of a douche of a solution of bromelain in relieving menstrual cramps. Before the drug company went into large scale clinical testing, they tested the effect of the product on volunteers within the company. When the company summarized the results of their in-house test at the end of the project, they were surprised to find that eight of the volunteers had become pregnant during the course of the study.

Of course, it is not unusual for women to become pregnant. What made these pregnancies so unusual is that they were unexpected. Three of the women said that they had wanted children but had not been able to become pregnant. These couples were very happy. Two women said they had thought that they were past childbearing age; they had not planned to become pregnant. Two of the women said that they had been using contraceptives. They were not happy. Three of the women said that they had thought that they were "safe" based on several years of experience without using any contraceptives. They were very unhappy. After reviewing the data, the company paid for all of the costs of the unplanned pregnancies.

Dr. Abduhl Youseff, a gynecologist in Egypt, reported that using a douche of a bromelain solution before the onset of labor, appreciably shortened the length of the labor period and made both the doctor and the patient happy.

Not too long before a new management of Dole changed the objectives of the company and closed the research department, Dr. Hunter and I were working on an artificial insemination project. Previous to this study I had analyzed the "protease" level of all of the semen samples that the hospital had collected in connection with a fertility study. I used a sensitive milk-clotting test. This, I now know, was also an excellent measure of the level of components of the xeronine-system in the semen. On the basis of my research, Dr. Hunter selected one couple for the artificial insemination test.

This was an ideal couple to take part in this study. The woman had three children by a previous marriage. Obviously nothing was wrong with her fertility. The husband's semen showed a low sperm count but it was still adequate for fertilization to have taken place. However, based on my assays, this man had the lowest semen "protease" activity of all of the samples that I had tested. At the appropriate time in the woman's fertility cycle, Dr. Hunter had the couple come in. He sent me the man's semen. I assayed the sample for milk-clotting potential and then added sufficient bromelain to the semen to bring the "protease" level equal to that of the average semen. Dr. Hunter performed the artificial insemination with the "enzyme" treated semen sample. It was a success. Nine months later the wife gave birth to a healthy child.

This technique could be used in animal breeding. Veterinarians have long known that they can dilute the semen of a bull only a few times before the semen becomes ineffective. Theoretically they should have been able to dilute it a hundred fold and still have plenty of active sperm left. They have explained this "dilution-failure" by assuming that some unrecognized factor was lost during the dilution process. Adding "bromelain" —actually any good source of the xeronine-system—should supply the missing factor. We had planned to publish this information. Unfortunately all the Dole research notebooks got sent to the shredder when the management destroyed all files not related to their new corporate objectives.

Chapter Summary

• The examples that I have listed in this chapter show some actions of xeronine that are similar to those covered in Chapter I and some that are considerably different.

• Certainly burn treatment represents the activation of a proenzyme that is present in the skin. This is an action similar to many of the examples cited in the previous chapter.

• By contrast the temporary alleviation of the problems associated with a malfunctioning brain as well as the problem with non-functioning semen probably involves assemblages containing the xeronine-assemblage plus specific hormones. I shall cover this subject in a later chapter.

ENDNOTE

[1] Robert G. Hunter, M.D., George W, Henry, M.D., R.M.Heinicke, PhD. The Action of Papain and Bromelain on the uterus Part 1, Mucolytic Properties of Papain and Bromelain. Effect on Cervical Mucus. American Journal of Obstetics and Gynecology 869-874 1957. Part 2 875-880, 1957.

CHAPTER 3

The Xeronine-System:
From Grease Traps to Genes

Certain microorganisms respond in an unusual and dramatic way to components of the xeronine-system. Their behavior adds important details to our developing picture about the functioning of the xeronine-system in cells. It emphasizes several aspects of the xeronine-system that were not obvious from the clinical and research work that various drug companies and universities developed from their studies on the action of commercial bromelain on various health problems.

During the last several years I have not stressed an important aspect of the xeronine-system in talks that I have given about the action of noni on health. Noni juice provides our body with a critical part of the xeronine-system that many people frequently lack, namely proxeronine; it does not provide the body with the precursor of the enzyme that converts proxeronine into xeronine, namely lysozyme. (I cover this topic in greater detail in Chapter 7.) Generally our bodies contain an abundant natural supply of lysozymes. There is no need to supply lysozyme in our diet. Furthermore, even if the noni juice contained active lysozyme, the gastrointestinal enzymes would destroy the added lysozyme.

My suggestion that the Golgi complex can take any of a large number of different lysozymes and convert them into the same proxeroninase—the enzyme that converts proxeronine into xeronine—is a new concept. Scientists will want evidence that supports this concept. The examples that I shall describe in this chapter are literally unbelievable. At least the experts in this field refused to believe our reports until they had actually seen with their own eyes our demonstrations. No one can contest the data. The U.S. Patent Office awarded me a patent on this application.

In contrast to the body's abundant supply of lysozymes, certain bacteria in certain environments quite frequently lack bacterial lysozymes. This lack causes the bacteria to exist in a comatose condition or to die. Inserting foreign lysozymes into these bacteria brings about an almost unbelievable burst of metabolic vigor. In the next sections I shall describe such examples.

Putting Glamour into Grease Traps

The average person knows nothing about grease traps and has little interest in acquiring such knowledge. I speak from personal experience. When a former Dole colleague phoned me—this was after Dole had closed my department—and ecstatically described the action of a certain "Magic Elixir" in solving the grease trap problem, I was puzzled. I did not know what a grease trap was or why it was important to solve the "grease-trap problem," whatever that phrase meant. He asked me to work with several of his colleagues, who were interested in selling this "Magic Elixir." He wanted me to provide them with a more scientific explanation of the action of this "Magic Elixir" than the fantastic explanation that the manufacturer of the product supplied. (By this time I had already developed the xeronine theory.)

The manufacturer of this product, an intelligent, observant, practical man had little scientific background. He made his "Magic Elixer" by extracting kelp grown close to the North Pole. He attributed the efficacy of his product to his special ability to concentrate into his product the energy of the magnetic lines of force of the earth. This intense stored magnetic energy could transmute radioactive elements into harmless calcium, could transform grease into harmless carbon dioxide and water. He also claimed it could cure cancer in people and distemper in dogs. Although such an explanation is eminently acceptable to many people living in California, my colleagues lived in Hawaii. In Hawaii an acceptable explanation would have to involve the kahunas (Polynesian healers), Madam Pelee or an acceptable scientific explanation.

Once I became involved in this problem, I found the subject fascinating as well as being important economically and environmentally. Working on this problem also supplied me with additional valuable scientific information about the operation of the xeronine-system.

Although the average homeowner does not have a grease trap, eventually everyone with a kitchen sink knows about plumbing problems. The kitchen-plumbing problem is a miniscule example of the problems that restaurants have with their grease traps and that cities have with their sewage collection systems and municipal wastewater treatment plants (also known less euphemistically as sewage plants) have with their sewage digesters.

The grease from kitchen waste eventually plugs the pipes. For the average homeowner this is an annoying inconvenience; for a city this is a problem that affects not only the wastewater collection system but also disrupts traffic as the emergency crews attempt to ream out a hole through the grease clogged pipes. To postpone the day when it has to carry out this costly and onerous job, cities now require that all restaurants must have grease traps.

A grease trap is a simple device. It is a rectangular tank about five feet deep. At the inlet and outlet of the tank are two "T" pipes set vertically. As the kitchen wastewater flows slowly through the tank, the grease rises to the surface and collects in ever increasing amounts while the grease-free water enters the bottom part of the "T" outlet pipe and flows into the sewage collection lines. When the grease layer, which can be over a foot thick, begins to approach the top of the outlet "T" pipe, the restaurant operator calls a grease-pumper. The grease-pumper pumps out the grease layer.

Our initial studies covered the grease traps at several mess halls at Schofield Barracks on Oahu, Hawaii. Al Mosher, a member of our group, had connections with several of the top military officials. He persuaded the General who controlled the Schofield operation to order that the "Magic Elixir" be tested on the mess hall grease traps. The Colonel, who was in charge of sanitation at Schofield had been a bacteriologist before he joined the army. He knew from his extensive bacteriological experience that the chances of any product promoting the bacterial digestion of grease were negligible. Yet, being a scientist as well as having been ordered to conduct the test, he agreed to allow our company to run a test at no cost to the Army.

We could not have found a better cooperator. Colonel Ringle was skeptical about the chances for success. Yet once he agreed to have us install the test, he made certain that everything possible be done to assure that the product was tested under optimal conditions. As a bacteriologist, he knew that if the product had any chance of working successfully, it had to have healthy bacteria. Therefore, he ordered all of the sergeants in charge of the mess halls to discontinue using Chlorox® or quaternary ammonium detergents (frequently used in automatic dishwashers). He also made certain that meticulous records were kept of all emergency calls to clear grease traps.

After one week on the treatment, the results were so dramatic that they were literally unbelievable. Whereas previously the emergency sewage crew regularly received a call to open up the sewage line on Thursday[1] at 8:30 p.m., the sewage lines now remained open and functioning well on Thursday. When the skeptical crew took the cover off the grease trap, they were amazed to find no odor! The grease layer was small and was obviously being digested as the vigorous evolution of carbon dioxide indicated. Furthermore, there were no cockroaches!

Colonel Ringle immediately recognized that the improbable cure had actually occurred. He immediately extended the system to cover the entire base and then sat down to calculate how much money he was saving in operating costs as well as in improving the local environment. In the meantime, the sewage from Schofield Barracks flowed quietly and smoothly out of his jurisdiction into the Armed Force's sewage plant located on Wheeler Air Force base, which is adjacent to Schofield Barracks.

In the Armed Services each branch is an empire unto itself; each one handles its own problems. However, about once a month the top officials from the various branches get together to discuss overlapping problems. At the next combined meeting, the operator of the Wheeler Sewage Plant gave his report. His plant was over-age, undersized, and underpowered. His motors were overheating and burning out and the quality of the final sewage effluent did not meet government standards. The Armed Force

Services had agreed to replace the plant.

At this meeting he reported that for some inexplicable reason, his motors were running cool, the sewage flow through the plant had increased dramatically and the quality of the final effluent had reached quality levels never previously attained. Not knowing what was happening, he disconnected one of the pipes leading to a pump. To his amazement the pipe contained no grease! Previously a four-inch diameter pipe had an effective diameter of only two inches because of the grease deposit. He stated that if the plant continued to operate at this level, no replacement plant would be required. When Colonel Ringle asked him on what day he had noticed the sudden improvement in the operation of the plant, the operator mentioned a day that was about three days after Colonel Ringle had put all of the Schofield mess halls on the "Magic Elixir" system.

Every once in a great while in science one happens to luck out. The Schofield experience was such a case. All of the various parameters in that test were the best that could have been devised. The man in direct charge of the operation, Colonel Ringle, was a bacteriologist with a better understanding of what was going on than we had. He could spot problems connected with bacteriostatic agents, and he knew exactly what to do and had the authority to demand that the personnel fix the problems. Another advantage that we had was that even though some private homes ran their sewage into the sewage collection lines, the bulk of the wastewater came from the barracks. Here—in contrast to private homes— Colonel Ringle could closely monitor and control the handling of the kitchen waste. Another important break that we had was that the sewage collection lines were unusually short. The average time between the entrance of sewage into the system and the entrance of the sewage into the sewage treatment plant was about thirty minutes. For the average city system the transit time can be up to several days.

Colonel Ringle became such an enthusiastic supporter of this treatment that when another division of the Armed Forces had an intractable hydrogen sulfide emission problem with one of their coastal ships, he not only recommended that they try the "Magic Elixir" but he briefed them on the theory of the action. They were skeptical but desperate. They allowed us to install the system on one of their ships.

Hydrogen Sulfide Stinks!

In the 1980s, the U.S. Government mandated that all ships cease discharging raw sewage into the ocean when they were a certain distance from shore. This forced all ship operators to install temporary holding tanks to collect the sewage that accumulated while they were in this prohibited dumping zone. Once they got to port they discharged the sewage into the port wastewater treatment system.

This new law caused much trouble for the Army. Although the Army is more familiar with trucks and tanks, they also operate a few coastal ships. These coastal vessels travel only in the restricted dumping zone. Therefore their temporary sewage holding tanks were always overloaded and were always a source of intolerable hydrogen sulfide gas. Hydrogen sulfide gas is not only an obnoxious gas, but also it can be deadly.

In this test our only objective was to prevent the production of hydrogen sulfide gas. We ran the system for a month on this ship and completely eliminated the production of hydrogen sulfide gas. At the end of the month the ship sailed to a California shipyard to be refitted with permanent holding tanks. About a month later the Commandant of the Hawaii Armed Force Operation received a call from the shipyard manager. He wanted to know what particular treatment the Hawaii boat had received. He said that the first step in refitting a ship with new holding tanks was to use jackhammers to chip away the hardened grease from the walls of the ship. By contrast the ship from Hawaii was so clean that they merely hosed down the walls with water!

With this background of unprecedented successes, we knew that we could handle any problems connected with wastewater—at least that was our overly optimistic belief. When the home owners of a new subdivision, a subdivision with a beautiful view of Kaneohe Bay and the Pacific Ocean but with a sewage plant in their front yard, threatened to sue the city because of the intolerable hydrogen sulfide odors from the sewage plant, we confidently assured the city that we could handle the problem.

Much to our surprise and chagrin, our initial tests at the wastewater treatment plant were completely unsuccessful. We tried varying the amount of product added and the places where we added the "Magic Elixir." That did not help. Then I realized that the treatment had worked so well at Schofield Barracks for two reasons. One reason was that we added the "Magic Elixir" directly to the wastewater flowing from the kitchen sink. At meal times, the kitchen wastewater invariably contained milk waste. Milk—even pasteurized milk—contains milk lysozyme. The other reason was that Colonel Ringle understood bacteria. He personally checked the mess halls to be certain that no one used any bacterial disinfectants.

Conditions were different in the suburbs. Practically all hand detergents and dishwater detergents that the homeowners used contained chemicals to inhibit or kill bacteria. Although dilution of these chemicals prevented them from actually killing the bacteria, these chemicals decreased the vigor of the bacteria. They also prevented the critical ingredient in the "Magic Elixir"—namely proxeronine—from stimulating the bacteria. When these bacteria reached the wastewater treatment plant they were alive but they could not respond to the proxeronine contained in the added "Magic Elixir." Understandably, not a trace of milk proteins was left in the sewage entering the suburban waste treatment plant.

To remedy this problem, I devised a device that thoroughly mixed milk-lysozyme with the 'Magic Elixir" before we added the combination at various places in the sewage treatment plant. This treatment successfully eliminated the production of hydrogen sulfide gas. For demonstrating that a mixture of lysozyme and a source of proxeronine could successfully eliminate hydrogen sulfide gas production in wastewater treatment and collection systems the Patent Office granted me a patent.

Although eliminating the production of hydrogen sulfide gas was our objective in this wastewater treatment plant test, yet this mixture had another surprising action. One day during the test, the centrifuge that concentrates the grease-laden skimmings from the tops of the sewage settling tanks broke. By the time the operators could shut off the power to all of the various pumps that pumped the tank skimmings to the now broken centrifuge, the tank for the grease-free water from the tank skimmings was covered with a six-inch layer of grease. The manager immediately called a grease pumper to remove the grease.

I asked the manager whether he would mind if I tried our mixture of lysozyme and "Magic Elixir" on the grease layer. He told me that I could do anything I wanted as long as I would be out of the way when the grease pumper arrived at 10 a.m. the next morning. I set up the system at 4 p.m. I was confident that the mixture would stimulate the bacteria sufficiently to digest a significant amount of grease. However, since I had only eighteen hours for the test, there was no way that the bacteria could digest all of the grease—at least so I thought. Therefore I measured the depth and the specific gravity of the grease layer so that I would be able to calculate just how much grease was digested per hour.

The next morning when I met the manager he was smiling. He told me that he had canceled the call for the grease pumper since all of the grease had been digested. Never in all reported figures on bacterial digestion has anyone ever reported such vigorous action of bacteria in digesting grease. This is absolutely without precedent.

Sewage Bacteria Sheds Light

Sewage bacteria and humans have a similar problem: neither like fatty peroxides in their diet. Fatty peroxides form readily whenever fatty foods are exposed to air. A single fatty peroxide molecule can seriously damage a cell. If we knew precisely what cell mechanisms the fatty peroxide damages, we might be able to mitigate the cell damage. Our sewage studies provide new clues to help us understand at least part of the fatty peroxide problem. There is no question about the results of our studies on the effect of using only the "Magic Elixer" for curing the hydrogen sulfide problem at the sewage plant; proxeronine—the critical ingredient in the "Magic Elixer"—by itself does not stimulate the sewage bacteria that digest grease deposits. Both field tests as well as extensive laboratory tests gave the same negative results.

Also there is no question that adding milk lysozyme[2] to the commercial "Magic Elixir" before we added it to various places in a sewage treatment plant stimulated the microorganisms unbelievably.

These results indicate that one or more enzymes are absolutely necessary for the production of xeronine, that the "grease-damaged" bacteria lacked this enzyme and that the "grease-damaged" bacteria could convert milk lysozyme into the required enzyme for synthesizing xeronine.

These results provided me with data that helped me to develop an important part of the xeronine-system concept. I used these results to suggest that most organisms contain a complex enzyme system that converts native and foreign lysozymes into proxeroninase. Proxeroninase is the enzyme that converts proxeronine into xeronine.

Although I had postulated that such a sub-enzyme system must exist in the xeronine-system, until we ran into this particular sewage problem, I did not have any data that supported this hypothesis. In clinical work with material containing the components of the xeronine-system, no doctor has reported any disease that is caused by a lack of lysozyme. Our body generally contains an abundant supply of several lysozymes. Only the grease-digesting bacteria appear to suffer a serious lack of lysozyme.[3]

We can assume that in general the metabolic processes of all cells, whether bacterial, animal, plant or people, are similar. If the Golgi complex in a cell has access to an abundant supply of proxeronine and lysozyme, then the Golgi complex can assemble competent xeronine-system assemblages.

Much work still remains to be done to clarify all of the details of these reactions. It is important that research laboratories study these reactions for several reasons. From the theoretical side studying this system can add greatly to our understanding of some of the reactions that occur both in the Golgi complex and also in the transcription of the gene. At present we have little concrete data connecting the Golgi complex and the gene. I also suspect that certain very important health problems are related to a malfunctioning of certain reactions occurring between the Golgi complex and the gene.[4]

Could a Lack of Lysozyme or Proxeroninase Cause Health Problems?

As far as I know, the lack of active proxeroninase might have caused only one health problem. This is the very rare type of diabetes that I shall cover in greater detail in Chapter 11. I am certain that eventually we will discover other rare diseases that have this lack as the cause of the health problem. Fortunately we will have a readily available cure when such diseases are recognized.

Constipation and Xeronine

Several people who have been taking large amounts of noni juice have reported constipation problems. Initially these reports seemed strange since the general effect of noni juice is to increase the smooth muscle reactions. Thus some people find that taking noni juice initially causes diarrhea.

Our sewage studies with components of the xeronine-system give us some clues regarding constipation caused by drinking large amounts of noni juice. The lower part of our intestinal tract operates similarly to a municipal wastewater treatment plant; only it operates much less efficiently. Some people eventually develop a lower intestinal micro flora that is similar to the bacteria found in sewage plants. These bacteria respond vigorously to proxeronine and begin hydrolyzing normally indigestible food fiber. Since this is an oxidation reaction occurring in an environment that lacks oxygen, the special enzymes in the bacteria use carbon instead of oxygen for the oxidation reaction. The end product of this reaction is methane gas. This inflates the intestine and lessens the effectiveness of normal peristaltic contractions. This may lead to constipation.

This is a problem that can be cured by several approaches. From our sewage work, I know that the most indigestible food items are orange and grapefruit rinds. Although not too many people eat orange rinds, many people eat cumquats during the Holiday Season. I have yet to meet a person who peeled his cumquat before eating it. What would be wrong with eating orange rinds?

Chapter Summary

• The normally inactive bacteria associated with grease in various parts of the wastewater treatment system respond dramatically to an external source of a lysozyme and proxeronine.

• Since proxeronine alone has no effect on the original comatose bacteria, this indicates that in these bacteria the lysozyme is the missing factor in the production of xeronine.

• The long lasting beneficial effect of this treatment and the action at extreme dilutions suggest that the foreign lysozyme —through a number of intermediate steps—promotes the synthesis of normal bacterial lysozyme.

• This action could occur at the polypeptide-folding step or it could occur at the level of the gene.

• At present I know of only one human disease that may have been caused by a lack of lysozyme or proxeroninase. Theoretically more of such diseases will be identified.

ENDNOTES

[1] Every Wednesday night the mess-hall operators would dump thirty gallons of used cooking oil into the kitchen sink. By Thursday night this extra load of grease was sufficient to block the trap and cause the sewage to overflow into the parking lot.

[2] Milk lysozyme is readily distinguished from bacterial lysozyme. That milk lysozyme, a foreign protein as far as the grease digesting bacteria are concerned, should reactivate comatose grease-digesting bacteria suggests that bacterial cells have a mechanism that can snip, cut and paste the foreign lysozyme to produce proxeroninase. The various enzymes that accomplish this transformation probably are contained in the Golgi complex. (See Chapters 11 and 12)

Several problems still remain to be solved. What caused the loss of the original bacterial lysozyme in these grease-digesting bacteria? Since this problem occurs primarily with bacteria growing in grease, we can be fairly confidant that fatty peroxides are the initial source of the problem. Normal air-oxidation will quickly convert unsaturated fatty acids into fatty peroxides.

What is still not known is the mechanism whereby the fatty peroxides interfere in the synthesis of bacterial lysozyme. The damage could occur at the transcription of the gene or it could occur in the folding of the synthesized polypeptide chain into lysozyme. Working out the details of the mechanism of fatty peroxide inhibition of a cell could provide both theoretical and potential health and industrial benefits. At present we lack sufficient data to select from a number of interesting hypotheses.

3 We have additional observations that can furnish more clues about the inhibition mechanism. The fatty acid peroxides probably do not damage the nucleic acids; the rate of recovery of the comatose bacteria is too rapid and too consistent. That the recovery appears to be permanent suggests that the recovery and the inhibition steps occur either in the transcription mechanism or in the folding mechanisms of the newly synthesized polypeptide chains. (See Chapter 12 for details on my proposed mechanism for folding the newly synthesized chain.)

4 An intriguing part of the genetic code copying mechanism is its sensitivity to the needs of a cell and also to what is available in its immediate environment. Since we know more about bacterial adaptation to the environment that we do about our cells, let us examine a few examples from bacteriology. Most bacteria use glucose as a source of energy; others can use either glucose or maltose; still others cannot use maltose as a source of energy unless they are first "trained" to use maltose; still others do not have the ability to be "trained" to use maltose as a source of energy. These differences in the physiology of certain classes of bacteria form the classical basis for classifying bacteria.

This "training technique" has now become the basis for an important niche in commercial bacteriology. Frequently the most effective method for removing certain toxic organic compound from the soil is to discover bacteria that have the potential for being trained to use the toxic organic compound as an energy source. Once isolated, bacteriologists can grow these specially "trained" bacteria in large amounts.

An alternate method that is much less expensive for the person attempting to remove organic compounds from the soil is to allow natural selection to take place in the contaminated soil. Quite frequently the organic soil contaminants damage the xeronine-system. By adding appropriate solutions of proxeronine or lysozyme and proxeronine to the soil, the natural selection of the appropriate organism can occur rapidly.

Essentially "training" a bacterium to use a novel form of organic material to produce cellular energy requires either producing a proper "key" (ligand) to open up a section of the gene so that the cell can produce a new enzyme specific for that purpose or it may require a new template for folding the newly synthesized polypeptide chain to "fit" the new substrate.(See Chapter 11)

This same mechanism, namely the production of a proper template for folding a recently synthesized peptide chain or the synthesis of an appropriate ligand that opens a section of the gene for transcription is absolutely necessary for the routine replacement of worn-out enzymes also has a down side. Either of these mechanisms could produce a protein that requires the foreign alkaloid or drug in order for the protein to function properly. This is probably the biochemical basis for drug addiction.

SECTION II: XERONINE IN THE LABORATORY

CHAPTER 4

Xeronine Clots Milk!

Few people and not too many scientists are going to become excited by my report that xeronine can clot milk. Milk clotting is a phenomenon that interests only one very specialized group of food technologists, the food technologists that make cheese. Only they truly appreciate the complex set of biochemical reactions that occur when adding a small bottle of dilute rennin to several thousand gallons of warm milk to convert the fluid milk into a quivering mass of milk curd. They will be surprised and understandably dubious about my statement that a non-enzymatic method can produce the same type of milk curd.

Another group of scientists are also going to be surprised by this reaction, namely the enzymologists. Until recently one of their firm beliefs—a belief that developed over the last hundred years—was that all enzymes are proteins. They also know that only the enzymes that digest proteins can selectively split certain specific links in a long polypeptide chain. Such specificity is important. Many enzymes and peptide hormones are secreted in an inactive form. To become active, one end of the polypeptide chain must be split off from the molecule by some means.

Biochemists have always had trouble describing this activation process. For all of the gastro-intestinal enzymes, which are secreted into the gastro-intestinal tract in an inactive form, they assume that since the gastro-intestinal tract contains various proteolytic enzymes these enzymes must be the enzymes that chop off the blocking peptide chain from the secreted inactive enzymes. With sufficient assumptions such an explanation is tenable. However, frequently no enzymes are originally present before the ingestion of food. In such cases the activation process cannot start. With some of the peptide hormones, no proteases are present to cleave (split) the blocking end. In such cases the suggestion is that the molecule autocatalytically cleaves off the blocking group. In other words the polypeptide chain breaks itself into smaller pieces.

Little Miss Muffet's "Curds and Whey"

At an earlier period of food technology, everyone knew about clotted or clabbered milk. This formed an important milk dessert, Junket®, which conscientious mothers coaxed their children to eat to increase their consumption of milk. Today food conscious young people buy tofu, an analogous type of clotted protein made from soybeans. In each example, the soft curd that an enzyme—or as I shall suggest, —forms from certain protein solutions contracts with time expressing out a liquid called whey. This is a very old and nutritious dessert as the old nursery rhyme confirms: "Little Miss Muffet, sat on a tuffet, eating her curds and whey."

In the early part of the Twentieth Century, milk scientists discovered that an enzyme named rennin (commercial people call this enzyme rennet), which occurs in the gastric juice of nursing mammals, was a potent proteolytic enzyme. This enzyme was similar in its action to pepsin, the principal protein digesting enzyme of the stomach. Its enzymatic action differs from pepsin in digesting protein better at pH 3 whereas pepsin works best between pH 1-2. With one single and important exception, the splitting of a single peptide bond, rennin shows no proteolytic action at the pH of milk (normally about pH 6.5).

The skim milk that we buy at the grocery store is a homogeneous fluid, containing approximately 3% of three slightly different types of major caseins. One of these caseins, kappa casein, acts as a "wrapper" to enclose all of the other casein molecules. As long as the "wrapper" is intact, the entire package remains soluble. When some agent, such as the enzyme rennin—or xeronine—breaks this unique bond releasing a polypeptide chain, all of the caseins become insoluble and precipitate out of solution as a curd. Other non-enzymatic reactions cause the curd to slowly contract and expel out as much as 50% of the fluid, the whey. What is left is the firm curd that challenges the ingenuity of cheese manufacturers to produce a wide variety of tempting cheeses such as cheddars, Camembert, Limburger, Gruyere and others.

The great importance of rennin in manufacturing cheese (today cheese manufacturers use bacterial substitutes) is that rennin—with the exception of this single breaking of an unusual peptide bond—has no other proteolytic activity at the pH of milk. Many other proteolytic enzymes can break this unique bond and clot milk. However, these enzymes continue to breakdown the formed clot. These further breakdown products produce a bitter flavor and make the cheese soft and eventually slimy. (Of course, there is no accounting for tastes. Some people can develop a preference for such cheeses.)

Enzymologists use the ability of many proteases to clot milk to measure the potency of different enzyme preparations.

People who are interested primarily in the effect of the xeronine-system in producing dramatic health benefits may understandably ask why they should be interested in this seemingly obscure action of xeronine. The xeronine-system is a completely new topic in biochemistry. Most scientists have never heard the details of my work or of my conclusions. They want to know what data I have to support my concepts. The very unexpected action of xeronine on casein not only supports my theories but it suggests many reactions in our bodies where analogous actions may occur. These actions have a direct bearing on our health.

"To Be or Not to Be"

As a research scientist hired by a commercial company to produce and market commercial bromelain, I had several incompatible objectives. As a company man I had to view the bromelain project as a potential source of revenue for the company. As a scientist I had to know what we were actually selling and be certain that we continued to produce a product that was effective. I rather quickly learned from a few of our customers that we were standardizing commercial bromelain as a protease but they were buying commercial bromelain because it contained some unknown ingredient that did what no other product on the market could do.

Our largest customer believed it was buying bromelain because of its proteolytic action; I could not afford to contradict them publicly even though I believed that the protease action was absolutely irrelevant in their applications. The Dole management knew that their profits came from selling protease activity; they understandably wanted me to increase the recovery of protease activity. On the other hand I wanted to discover the nature of the unknown ingredient that was making commercial bromelain so valuable to our customers. If I had succeeded, this would have meant that eventually Dole would have had to restandardize and rename the product. This was a prospect that did not make the Dole management people happy.

We reached a compromise. Officially we produced commercial bromelain and attempted to keep the production method constant. In the meantime, if I wanted to search for the active ingredient, the company would not explicitly object, providing I did not publicize my belief that the protease activity in commercial bromelain was without any physiological value.

I had only a few clues about the nature of the unknown, physiologically active ingredient in commercial bromelain. I investigated all reactions about commercial bromelain that I thought were "strange." One of the "strange reactions" was the milk clotting reaction. I had initially used this reaction to follow the progress of isolating commercial bromelain. During my validation of this test as a measure of the proteolytic activity of commercial bromelain, I had some questions about the method. Other scientists also had some reservations about the method. Yet the method appeared to correlate with other conventional tests for protease activity.

The milk clotting reaction that I shall describe in this chapter is a completely new type of reaction in biochemistry. It is one of three critical pieces of data that supports my concepts about the xeronine-system. That xeronine clots milk is important because this "strange reaction" illustrates in convincing detail one of the biochemical reactions that xeronine performs on certain proteins. This is the first specific, confirmed reaction of xeronine with a specific protein. Xeronine probably reacts similarly with other proteins.

Milk Clotting as a Test for Proteases

In some ways milk clotting is an ideal test for assessing the proteolytic activity of samples. The test is fast—generally less than two minutes per sample, simple, extremely sensitive and requires little technical equipment. The only problem with this test is determining just what this test measures.

A. K. Balls concluded—with a few reservations[1]—that it measured the activity of certain proteases. My predecessor at the Pineapple Research Institute had concluded that this was an appropriate tool to use to follow the course of the isolation of bromelain from the pineapple plant. Before I adopted this method for preliminary survey work, I made an intensive study of this reaction. I found that bromelain clotted milk slightly differently than did rennin, the classical milk clotting enzyme. Nevertheless, since the method appeared to provide results that were similar to the classical protein digestion tests, I decided to use milk clotting for my survey and "in-progress" work and to use both milk clotting and the classical protein digestion tests to test the final commercial bromelain product.

In general, the milk clotting test and the standard protein digestion test of bromelain samples rank different sample of bromelain in the same order. Several years after I had transferred to Dole, I had the company statistician examine the correlation between these two tests. As a standard procedure we always analyzed every production batch of bromelain both by the milk clotting test and by the classical protein digestion test. When he finished his study on about 500 samples, he told me that never in all of his statistical work had he ever seen such perfect correlation between two parameters. He suggested that since both assays were obviously measuring the same factor, that I should choose the simplest test and discontinue running the other.

In spite of his report and recommendation, I knew that the two assays were measuring different substances. In the laboratory I could produce "bromelain" samples with either high or low MCU/GDU ratios. (MCU and GDU are the units that we used for measuring the milk clotting potency and the gelatin-digestion potency of a sample.) Since something strange was occurring during the milk clotting reaction, I wanted to investigate the reaction with a different approach.

Allergies to the Rescue

The Dole Bromelain Production Plant was the first large-scale enzyme operation in the world; no information existed on possible health hazards of such an operation. To be certain that the operators in the plant did not develop allergies to bromelain dust, twice a year we took blood samples from every person connected with the bromelain operation. We checked each blood sample for the presence of antibodies against the proteins in bromelain.

In this test both the blood proteins and the antibody proteins diffuse outward from adjacent wells punched into an agar plate. If the worker has antibodies against the proteins in commercial bromelain, then where the outward diffusing molecules from his blood intersect the outward diffusing antibodies against the proteins in commercial bromelain a white precipitate forms. Since proteins are large molecules and since large molecules diffuse less rapidly than smaller molecules, it takes two to four days for the precipitin patterns to develop. (None developed.)

Believing that with a few modifications, I could use this technique to separate in space and time the various reactions that might be occurring in the milk clotting reaction I set up a test. The results were strange, unexpected and obviously important.

The "Strange Milk Clot"

I know of few other experiments in recent times in which the results were as unexpected and as definitive as this one. In Figure 1, I have diagrammed what should have occurred when a solution containing a protease diffuses out of a well cut into an agar plate that contains milk. In Figure 2 I have diagrammed what actually occurred.

Figure 1.   **Figure 2.**

Agar Diffusion Experiment

Anticipated
Results

Actual
Results

Any person looking at these two pictures can immediately see that commercial bromelain contains—or produces—some unknown substance that does something unexpected. Any enzymologist looking at these two pictures will immediately recognize that whatever caused the milk to clot had properties that no other small biochemical compound has ever exhibited.

When I discovered this strange type of milk clotting reaction in 1956, I knew that the material that produced this unexpected type of clot was important. However, I had no clues regarding the nature of the unknown product or what its importance was in biology. I knew for a number of reasons that the protease bromelain could not possibly be responsible for the strange clot. In our survey for potential antibody production in the workers connected with the bromelain project, we had run hundreds of bromelain and blood protein diffusion tests in agar. Therefore, I knew precisely how rapidly both blood proteins and the various proteins in commercial bromelain would diffuse in six hours. I have shown the maximum distance that the bromelain proteins could have diffused during this time period in Figure 1. Whatever was causing the milk clotting reaction, whether directly or indirectly, had to be a relatively small molecule; it had to be much smaller than any protein molecule.

Another feature of the milk clotting reaction was unique. The clotted area in Figure 2 was absolutely uniform from the center well to the edge of the sharply defined circle. This meant that a reaction entirely different from an enzyme reaction was occurring. It meant that the milk clotting reaction that occurred in this diffusion test was stoichiometric and not enzymatic! In other words, a molecule of a particular casein molecule (kappa-casein) reacted with a specific number of unknown small molecules to produce a clot.

I also quickly learned that the small molecule was not preformed in commercial bromelain. Heating or adding a mercury salt to commercial bromelain solutions before running the diffusion test completely prevented this unusual reaction. This proved that the critical small molecule was not originally present in the bromelain solution; it was produced by unknown enzymatic reactions. This reaction occurred only with commercial bromelain; it did not occur with purified bromelain.[2]

The only products that the protease bromelain produces are peptides and amino acids. The milk specialists whom I visited in connection with this strange milk clotting reaction knew of no peptide that could possibly clot milk. In addition, they insisted that the milk clotting reaction had to be enzymatic and not stoichiometric!

I knew that this strange milk clotting reaction was important, and I believed that someday I would discover the chemical nature of the small molecule that caused milk to clot in a stoichiometrically fashion. Consequently, when I finally isolated crystalline xeronine in the early 1980s, I immediately wondered whether this might be the small molecule that I had been looking for since the mid 1950s.

Crystalline Xeronine Clots Milk!

Once I had developed a method for producing crystalline xeronine, I had to prove by both animal and laboratory tests that xeronine was the substance that made our early production of commercial bromelain so valuable. For twenty years I had been trying to explain the "strange milk clot." Now I suspected that xeronine might furnish the explanation.

I used exactly the same test and the same equipment that I had used in the 1956 experiment that showed the unexpected results depicted in Figure 2. This time I added solutions of crystalline xeronine into the wells cut into milk-agar plates. At room temperature no visible clots appeared. However, when I warmed the plates to 40 degrees C, a clotting pattern identical to that shown in Figure 2 appeared.

This temperature effect did not surprise me since I had discovered while I was still working at the Pineapple Research Institute that commercial bromelain clotted milk in a slightly different manner from rennin, the enzyme that cheese manufacturers use to clot milk, Milk treated with rennin will not clot unless the milk temperature is above 14 degrees C. This is also the reason why the directions on a package of Junket® always warn the user to allow the milk to warm to room temperature before adding the contents of the package. (The package contained rennin and flavoring) By contrast commercial bromelain clotted milk down to the freezing point. From this early work I knew that commercial bromelain contained something that enhanced the so-called non-enzymatic phase of milk clotting. Of course crystalline xeronine would not have this extra factor.

One important characteristic of casein that has been clotted by rennin is that with time the clot retracts and expresses out a whey. This contraction process is a physical process and does not involve enzymes. Milk clotted in a test tube by solutions of crystalline xeronine and held in a water bath at 40 degrees C for several hours shows strong clot retraction with the expression of whey. This indicates that xeronine produces a classical milk clot.

Same Job; Different Mechanism

All of the examples that I have mentioned in the preceding sections show that solutions of crystalline xeronine cause the same reactions with casein as does the enzyme rennin. However, a biochemist hearing this story for the first time would want additional proof. The enzyme rennin produces its action on casein by chopping off a polypeptide chain from the kappa casein molecule that acts as a "wrapper" to keep the other caseins in solution. He would want to know how crystalline xeronine affects casein.

I compared the amount of polypeptides released from a casein solution at 40 degrees C by different concentrations of crystalline xeronine and crystalline rennin. The amount of polypeptides released by similar changes in the concentrations of the two reagents was essentially identical. The difference in action between xeronine and rennin was that xeronine released the polypeptide almost immediately whereas the rennin reaction, being enzymatic, took time. This is the expected difference between a stoichiometric and an enzymatic reaction.

To the non-biochemist, my reporting that xeronine can clot milk might appear to be a relatively routine and innocuous statement. To the biochemists specializing in milk, this statement is literally unbelievable. One of the foremost milk biochemists wrote that never in the hundred years that very capable chemists have studied all phases of the milk clotting reaction has anyone ever reported an action similar to what I was reporting. He attempted to explain my results by suggesting that my crystalline xeronine was contaminated by commercial bromelain!

I can state emphatically and categorically that this was absolutely impossible. My method for producing crystalline xeronine involved several distillation steps. I worked solely with the distillates. Furthermore, bromelain, being a protein, could not possibly have diffused as rapidly as xeronine and it would have—if it should have been able to clot milk— produced a clot that had a diffuse leading edge.[3]

So What?

All of this information may seem rather esoteric and have no application to anything important in the metabolism of a cell. Yet it is very important. This is the first documented example of a small, relatively simple molecule, namely xeronine, reacting with a specific protein of known amino acid sequence, namely kappa casein, to release a specific polypeptide.

Biochemists know of a number of examples in which a protein, for example all of the gastrointestinal enzymes (insulin?), or a polypeptide hormone is inactive until a specific portion of the molecule is chopped off. At present biochemists have only one tool, namely proteases, or one mechanism, namely autocatalysis (a molecule breaking itself into smaller pieces), to chop off hunks of a polypeptide chain.

Both of these solutions for converting inactive proteins or polypeptide chains into active molecules are unsatisfactory. The protease solution has several problems. Most proteases are general protein smashers; they attack a large number of different types of peptide bonds. This is the reason why most proteases cannot be used to make cheese. They form a milk clot and then they breakdown the milk clot. Also the cell generally packages the proteases in special organelles that have one specific job to do, namely to break down foreign or waste proteins into small fragments. The problem with autocatalysis is that no one has determined what causes a protein to suddenly decide to break a chunk of itself off.

My demonstration that xeronine reacts stoichiometrically with casein to split off of a critical polypeptide fragment provides biochemists with a new and better tool to explain the activation of certain enzymes and hormones. Although I have explicit data only for casein, yet I have other experiments and observations that suggest that this is a general reaction in cell metabolism.

Significance of the "Strange Milk Clotting" Reaction

In Chapters 2 and 3, I described reactions of the xeronine-system in pharmaceutical, industrial, agricultural and fermentation industries. In almost all of the examples that I have cited, the initial reaction has been the same: "These results are unbelievable!"

In this chapter I have described laboratory experiments with crystalline xeronine. Again the reaction of the scientists in this field has been the same: "The results are unbelievable."

I ran the two tests described in this chapter with crystalline xeronine. I wanted to complement the animal tests that I had made using crystalline xeronine with laboratory experiments using crystalline xeronine. These animal and the laboratory experiments conclusively prove that xeronine is the active ingredient responsible for most of the amazing results with natural extracts containing the xeronine-system, such as noni and the early batches of commercial bromelain.

The reason why no one has previously found such amazing results is that crystalline xeronine did not exist as an isolatable chemical compound until the latter part of the 1970s. I should point out that several Japanese research workers who were studying the reactions of commercial bromelain had also reported that in the digestion of casein two separate reactions occurred, a stoichiometric reaction and an enzymatic reaction. Their reports are completely concordant with the results that I reported in this chapter.

Having a simple and definitive method such as milk clotting helps in detecting "free xeronine." This is critical for carrying out biochemical studies on xeronine reactions. No other non-enzyme molecule can produce the type of clot produced by xeronine. Therefore, this test is a definitive test for free xeronine.

I would like to suggest that many secreted enzymes that the body secretes in inactive forms, such as the pancreatic and the gastric enzymes and possibly insulin, are secreted in the inactivate form. I would like to suggest that xeronine activates these inactive pro-enzymes by splitting off the blocking peptide chain; this would occur in a manner similar to the action of crystalline xeronine on kappa casein.

Xeronine is a unique building block; it has an absolutely rigid structure that probably is critical for many cellular reactions. My experimental data cover just one of probably a variety of reactions of xeronine with proteins.

Chapter Summary

• Solutions of crystalline xeronine produce classical clotting of milk under the proper conditions.

• Solutions of crystalline xeronine release a large polypeptide molecule from casein.

• Physiologically active commercial bromelain can liberate free xeronine. The free xeronine produces the milk-clot.

• The ability of xeronine to react with certain proteins followed by the release of a peptide may be a fairly common biochemical reaction.

   o Xeronine activates the inactive form of bromelain.

   o Xeronine activates inactive pro-amylases in commercial bromelain and in commercial fungal amylase preparations.

   o Xeronine probably activates all of the gastro-intestinal proenzymes.

• The milk-clotting reaction can provide a sensitive test for free xeronine.

• These laboratory studies of the action of solutions of xeronine on casein are a critical part of the documentation of the xeronine story.

ENDNOTES

[1] When the enzymatic activity is plotted against the concentration of enzyme, the plot of the points should be a straight line passing through 0. A. K. Balls, who worked with solutions of papain, found that the plot of milk clotting activity against the concentration of enzyme gave a straight line over most of the concentration range. This is what should happen. However, at low concentrations of enzyme the clotting rate fell off sharply. When Balls extrapolated the straight portion of the curve, it intercepted the milk-clotting-activity axis at a point considerably above the 0 point! A. K. Balls was unable to explain this anomalous behavior.

[2] Since heat and mercury both inhibit classical, pure bromelain, my initial assumption was that the enzyme that produced this small molecule that clotted milk was bromelain. At that time bromelain was the only protein in commercial bromelain that contained a critical, active sulfhydryl group.

   Later, in 1968, Dr. T. Shigei, formerly of Tokyo University, reported that commercial bromelain contained a second sulfhydryl containing protein. This other sulfhydryl protein was critical in preventing experimentally induced pulmonary edema in rabbits. He also proved that purified bromelain was inactive in preventing this induced type of pulmonary edema.

[3] In the disc electrophoresis pictures shown in Figure 4 in Chapter 5, the protease bromelain digests the inner portion of the milk clot formed by xeronine. Also in this picture the bromelain digestion ring—the clear inner portion—has a diffuse leading edge. This is the normal behavior of a protease.

I would like to point out a striking difference between Figure 2 in this Chapter and Figure 4 in Chapter 5. In Figure 2 the picture shows absolutely no trace of digestion of the xeronine-caused milk-clot after six hours of diffusion. The protease digestion action—which I have not shown—did not appear until the following day. In Figure 4 of Chapter 5, the protease action followed closely the leading edge of the xeronine-milk clot. This picture was made after 24 hours of diffusion.

The commercial bromelain that I used in Figure 2 of this Chapter had excellent physiological activity; this was commercial bromelain made in 1955. By contrast the commercial bromelain sample that I used for the experiment shown in Figure 4 in Chapter 5, which had exactly the same proteolytic activity, had very poor physiological activity. They differed in that the sample used in Chapter 2 had the capacity to produce an abundant supply of free xeronine whereas the sample used in Chapter 5 showed no free xeronine. The xeronine that showed in the picture came from a bromelain assemblage.

CHAPTER 5

Assemblages:
The Body's Mobile Mini-Factories

In the Nineteenth Century and early part of the Twentieth Century, chemists studied the properties of the different molecules that compose a cell. To obtain samples of the individual molecules in a cell, they would take a "hammer," smash the cell and then put the fragments through a sieve. After many separation techniques, they would eventually have a number of pure components. They investigated and characterized these components without being distracted by contaminating molecules. This is important and necessary work. To understand fully how a machine functions, one has to know the properties of the various nuts and bolts that make up the machine.

When I began my work at the Pineapple Research Institute in 1950, we were still studying the components that make up the plant cell. My interpretation of the assignment when I started to work at the Pineapple Research Institute affected the technique that I developed for isolating bromelain. Will Gortner, the head of the Chemistry Department, wanted me to develop a commercial method—as contrasted to a laboratory method—for isolating the enzyme bromelain from the pineapple plant. For this reason, instead of using the traditional laboratory techniques for obtaining extracts from the plant, I used industrial equipment to smash the cells. What I did not initially appreciate was that my industrial equipment for smashing the cells was so gentle that I actually isolated a variety of intact cell "microstructures."

Eventually I learned that these complex cell organelles were much more valuable than was the pure bromelain that I had been hired to isolate. One of these microstructures I isolated contained all of the ingredients necessary to synthesize xeronine. It contained proxeronine, potential proxeroninase, energy sources—such as adenosine triphosphate (ATP)—and other essential molecules. In this chapter I shall introduce the assemblage concept. This concept, which I developed primarily from work that my group did on the pineapple plant, suggests how noni and bromelain produce xeronine. Later work suggests how xeronine can produce such startling health benefits for certain individuals. The assemblage concept should also interest physiologists since many different types of secretions, such as gastric and pancreatic secretions, insulin secretions and probably others, may involve assemblages. This concept should also interest scientists who are studying the signals (ligands) that open certain sections of the gene for transcription into messages that contain the code for synthesizing specific proteins.

After I had developed the assemblage concept and after I began to appreciate how complex some assemblages are (some assemblages contain several smaller assemblages that contain still smaller assemblages), I knew that the cell must have a structure that could assemble such structures. Starting with the end products—the complex assemblages—I began "designing" a cell microstructure that could turn out such assemblages. It would have to have a structure similar to an assembly plant with docking stations for receiving a variety of molecules made somewhere else. I had just begun to design the structure when I suddenly realized that the cell already had such a structure, the Golgi complex.

Quite frequently when scientists with different interests investigate a complex structure, each scientist may give the same structure a different name. This has happened to some extent with the terms assemblage and vesicle. I was concerned primarily with the orderly arrangement of a specific number of molecules that functioned as a unit to perform a specific job. By contrast, the cell anatomists studying the Golgi body discovered structures that budded off from the surface of the plates of the Golgi body. They named these structures "vesicles" and then attempted to find jobs for these structures. The terms assemblage and vesicle emphasize different aspects of the same structure: vesicle emphasizes the container aspect of the structure whereas assemblage emphasizes the orderly arranged contents of the vesicle. Although all assemblages have a covering, that is a vesicle, not all vesicles have assemblages. For example, many nerve transmitters, such as acetyl choline, are stored in vesicles near the end of the nerve. These transmitter molecules are not "assembled;" instead they merely are "dumped" into the vesicle.

Making Sense of the Assemblage Concept

Over a period of about twenty years our group at Dole Inc. routinely ran disc electrophoretic patterns on all of our commercial batches of bromelain, on all of our competitors' products, and on a large variety of related products. Since the technique that we used, namely disc gel electrophoresis separation, is a well-established technique that the scientific community uses constantly, I accepted the method and all of the conventional interpretations of the patterns. These disc gel electrophoretic patterns were almost like "finger prints" that enabled researchers to identify different types of plant extracts. These "finger prints" patterns were so unique that we used them to identify which manufacturer produced a particular batch of bromelain.

When we modified and expanded the gel disc electrophoretic technique to include measurements of a variety of enzymes, I did not feel comfortable with the standard interpretation of these patterns. Instead of each band in the electrophoretic pattern representing one protein, as is the conventional interpretation of the patterns, our results suggested that these bands were more complex. (Please see Figures 2 and 3 in this chapter for an example of an electrophoretic pattern.) Occasionally several bands in a gel pattern of a protein mixture showed the same enzymatic activity. (Biochemists call those enzymes that have the same enzymatic activity but slightly different structures isozymes. This is a common phenomenon that enzymologists expect.) What bothered me was that in many of our electrophoretic separations, a single band might contain three very different enzymes. This should not have occurred.

Then something happened that forced me to reexamine completely my original interpretation of the electrophoretic patterns. This event occurred while I was working in Japan and just two years before a new president of Castle & Cooke, the parent company of Dole, eliminated a number of departments including Basic Research. Before I discuss the event that forced me to reevaluate my interpretation of the electrophoretic patterns of bromelain, I shall describe the unusual electrophoretic patterns of the proteins of the pineapple plant that never did make sense.

Why Two Different Bromelains?

After the pineapple companies in Hawaii became interested in producing commercial bromelain, the Pineapple Research Institute bought me a Perkin-Elmer Moving Boundary Electrophoresis machine.[1]

With this machine, I recorded on film the colloid composition of the various products that I was preparing from the pineapple plant. What surprised me was that using the same recovery techniques on pineapple fruit juice and pineapple stem juice gave me two entirely different products! The electrophoretic patterns of the enzymes prepared from fruit juice and from stem juice contained no common electrophoretic peaks.

Figure 1 shows the moving boundary electrophoretic pattern of colloid mixtures prepared from pineapple stem juice (commercial bromelain) and pineapple fruit juice. Note that at pH 6.5, the pH at which I made the electrophoretic separations, the stem juice enzyme had four basic peaks and three smaller negatively charged peaks. By contrast the fruit enzyme had only a single, broad, negatively charged peak.

Figure 1.

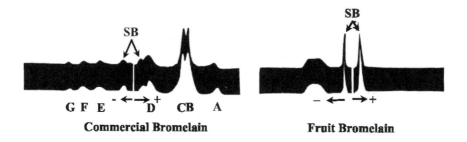

These are strange electrophoretic pictures for two products that theoretically should have been similar. That the pineapple plant should go to the trouble of making two different proteases to do the same job does not make sound biochemical sense. I suspected from the broad shape of the fruit bromelain peak that fruit bromelain was actually a mixture of several different proteins. Yet all of the techniques that I tried at that time failed to resolve the fruit bromelain peak into a pattern of other peaks. This peak was very stable—at that time.

Finally I had to accept the reality of the data. I called the product from the fruit "fruit-bromelain" and the product from the stem "stem-bromelain," or, since this was the only bromelain that the pineapple companies produced commercially, "commercial-bromelain."

It is interesting that even though Hawaiian pineapple fruits of that time had only a single, negatively charged peak, pineapple fruits from Taiwan frequently gave fruit bromelain patterns that contained several other peaks in addition to the major negatively charged peak. Since people in Hawaii believed—and probably correctly so for those days—that Hawaiian pineapple fruit was the best in the world, we dismissed the "abnormal" patterns of Taiwan fruit bromelain as just another indication of the lower quality of Taiwan pineapple fruit. Little did I realize that ten years later Hawaiian pineapple fruit would produce electrophoretic patterns that had even more peaks than did the Taiwan fruit!

Electrophoretic Patterns Change!

I learned about the change in the electrophoretic pattern of fruit bromelain in a strange way. While I was working in Japan at Jintan Dolph, one of the local university professors asked me whether Dole could supply him with the negatively charged proteins from stem juice. I told him that we could either supply him with milligram quantities of fractioned stem proteins or we could supply him with several hundred grams of fruit bromelain. I explained that Hawaiian fruit bromelain contained only a single, negatively charged electrophoretic peak. (Figure 1)

Since he chose the offer of several hundred grams of fruit bromelain, I asked our laboratory in Hawaii to prepare a large batch of fruit enzyme and to send it to me along with disc electrophoretic pictures of the sample. When the sample came, I knew from the electrophoretic pictures that they had sent me the wrong sample; they had sent me stem bromelain instead of fruit bromelain!

I immediately sent a note to our Honolulu laboratory and told them that the sample that we received was stem bromelain and asked them to locate the fruit bromelain sample. When they assured me that the sample that they had sent was indeed fruit bromelain, I realized that a dramatic change had occurred in the colloids of Hawaiian pineapple fruit. This change had occurred within less than a ten-year period. (When we had made our last electrophoretic picture of fruit bromelain ten years previously, the pattern still consisted of a single negatively charged peak.)

This unanticipated finding conclusively showed that the classical fruit and stem bromelain patterns were not distinct entities; they represented different stages in the opening of a large super-assemblage containing different sub-assemblages. Solving my original question of why the pineapple plant would make two different types of bromelain—it does not—immediately raised several new questions. Why were my original preparations of both stem and fruit bromelain so stable and what changes had occurred within a short span of ten years to cause the observed changes?

Why the Change?

As soon as I returned from Japan, I showed electrophoretic pictures of fruit colloids made in 1956 and 1968 to the vice-president of Dole. I told him that the changes in the electrophoretic patterns of the fruit suggested that we probably had a soil micronutrient problem in the Hawaiian pineapple fields.

I am a biochemist, not an agronomist. According to the company policy at that time, any comments about the fertility of the soil should come from the agronomists, not from a laboratory chemist. The vice-president's response to my comment was: "And how many more cases of pineapple can we sell if our advertising people proclaim that only Dole pineapple contains the 1956 electrophoretic pattern of fruit bromelain?"

This was a legitimate question. I took the responsibility of learning what had caused this dramatic change in the electrophoretic pattern of pineapple fruit colloids. When I had the answer to that problem, I knew that I would then have to learn whether these changes affected the nutritional quality of pineapple fruit-it does. After I had developed this information, I knew that Dole would take action—even though the suggestion came from the wrong department.

I had one lead, namely ascorbic acid.[2]

Ascorbic Acid

Getting excited about ascorbic acid seems to be quite a digression from the xeronine-system story. Yet there are a number of reasons why ascorbic acid has a connection the xeronine-system. Studying the effect of added ascorbic acid on the electrophoretic patterns of "bromelain" gave me critical clues about the opening patterns of different assemblages. Furthermore, the effect of ascorbic acid on the stability of assemblages may be a general effect of ascorbic acid in all organisms.

Few vitamins have aroused as much controversy as has ascorbic acid. Everyone knows that we need vitamin C to prevent scurvy. Most people, including government scientists, believe that we need more ascorbic acid than the amount required for controlling scurvy. Just how much more is the issue that divides people into two strongly partisan camps. The government scientists, seeing no data that suggest a role for more ascorbic acid, have increased only moderately the minimum daily-recommended level of ascorbic acid intake. Another group of scientists, which included the late Linus Pauling, believes that we need very large amounts of ascorbic acid. Just why we should need large amounts of ascorbic acid—if we do—remains very much a mystery.

Scientists have identified only a few biochemical reactions that involve ascorbic acid. In preventing scurvy, ascorbic acid is a component of a set of enzymatic reactions that convert the amino acid proline, an amino acid abundant in skin, into hydroxyproline, an amino acid that is necessary for skin to be flexible. This same enzyme system can also add a hydroxyl group to certain steroids. These two critical reactions require miniscule amounts of ascorbic acid. Our present minimal recommended dose of ascorbic acid is more than adequate to cover these requirements.

Most animals synthesize their own ascorbic acid. The goat eats more ascorbic acid per day than the average person consumes. In addition to this dietary supply of ascorbic acid, the goat synthesizes more ascorbic acid than we officially require. Practically all animals synthesize three to four times as much ascorbic acid per body weight as the government recommends that we eat. Obviously this extra amount of ascorbic acid must play some critical metabolic role in the bodies of these animals.

Plants "Know" What to do with Ascorbic Acid

The distribution of ascorbic acid in various parts of the pineapple plant during the growth cycle suggests one function for ascorbic acid in plants. Ascorbic acid is one of the component of the system that controls whether a tissue converts simple building blocks, such as sugar and amino acids into complex storage molecules, such as starch and storage proteins respectively, or whether it breaks down complex molecules into simple building blocks. When the ascorbic acid level is high, the tissue has the ability to build storage molecules. When the ascorbic acid level is low, the tissue has the potential for converting stored food into usable building blocks.

The amount of ascorbic acid in different parts of the mature pineapple plant varies greatly in different tissues. The green leaves may contain up to 10 mg of ascorbic acid per ml of leaf juice! This is such a high level of ascorbic acid, that Dole scientists devised a method for pressing leaves and recovering crystalline ascorbic acid from the juice.[3] Fruit juice has a much lower concentration of ascorbic acid than does leaf-juice. It has about 0.3 mg of ascorbic acid per ml of juice. Compared to orange juice, which has about twice as much, this is only a moderate amount of ascorbic acid. However, what originally (1955 and earlier) distinguished "pineapple juice ascorbic acid" from "orange juice ascorbic acid" was the extraordinary resistance of the ascorbic acid in pineapple juice to oxidation. The stability of "pineapple ascorbic acid" of this period was literally unbelievable.

Trying to Prove the Tour Guide Wrong

When I had a special tour in 1954 of the pineapple company that was to become Dole, I was shocked at their juice processing operation. Being a recent graduate student, I still knew the answers to all problems. I knew that ascorbic acid could not possibly survive their juice clarification process. To remove the fiber from the fruit juice the company sent the pressed juice through a battery of seventeen high-speed centrifuges, The clarified effluent from these centrifuges discharged into an enormous, open rectangular tank. It is hard to imagine a more efficient system for thoroughly aerating pineapple juice.

When I tactfully asked how much ascorbic acid was lost during the clarification process, my guide assured me that the operation did not affect the ascorbic acid level of the juice. Being a guest of the company where I would eventually work, I did not openly express my disbelief in his assurances. However, the next year when I had transferred to Dole, Inc., one of the first projects that I had our people investigate was the fate of ascorbic acid during the juice clarification process. To my amazement, there was no loss of ascorbic acid! What my guide had told me was correct!

This amazing stability of ascorbic acid under conditions that would immediately have destroyed pure ascorbic acid meant that pineapple juice contained one of the most potent antioxidant systems ever discovered. Although this was not my assigned project, I knew that discovering the nature of this antioxidant system was important. Dr. Paul Scheuer at the University of Hawaii had several of his graduate students work on parts of this project. Eventually we identified all of the materials that originally were present in the juice and that provided this amazing antioxidant activity. Unfortunately, by the time that we had identified the several antioxidants and enzymes involved, this highly desirable property of pineapple juice had greatly diminished. In later years the ascorbic acid in pineapple juice showed poor stability to even moderate exposure to oxygen. Furthermore, as I previously explained the electrophoretic pattern of fruit bromelain had also changed during this period!

In contrast to fruit juice, stem juice contains no detectable ascorbic acid. Since the complete absence of ascorbic acid interested me, while I was the Pineapple Research Institute I checked the stem juice for various types of "hidden" ascorbic acid. My measurements detected none. The roots also contain no ascorbic acid.

When the electrophoretic pattern of fruit colloids changed to that of stem colloids, I began to wonder about a possible connection:

Juice	Ascorbic Acid	Electrophoretic Pattern
• Stem juice	No ascorbic acid	Stem electrophoretic patter
• Fruit juice pre-1962	Stable ascorbic acid	Fruit electrophoretic pattern
• Fruit juice post-1962	Unstable ascorbic acid	Stem electrophoretic pattern

Although I knew that the original antioxidant system, which was unbelievably effective, contained at least four discrete components, in my study I choose to work with just a single component, namely ascorbic acid. Working with a single component system is simpler than working with a four-component system.

The hypothesis that I wanted to investigate was that ascorbic acid plus some other molecules was the latch that kept the super-assemblages closed. In work that I did at the Pineapple Research Institute, I showed that ripe, high quality pineapple fruit lasted about eight days. On the fourth day the ascorbic acid dropped to zero. The fifth day the protease level began dropping. By the sixth day all protein and all small nitrogen containing molecules had disappeared from the fruit and appeared in the crown on top of the fruit. A plant physiologist would be pleased. Theoretically this is exactly what should happen in a healthy plant.

I had made fruit bromelain from ripe fruit from the Pineapple Research Institute. (This would have corresponded to fruit from day one to day three in the experiment described above.) The juice had an ascorbic acid level of about 0.35 mg/ml. The electrophoretic pattern of the "bromelain" from such fruit is shown in Figure 1. Obviously the latch on that super-assemblage is closed.

Ascorbic Acid Stabilizes the Super-Assemblages

I did this work in 1971 when I had returned from Japan. This was a time when the stability of ascorbic acid in pineapple juice was poor and the electrophoretic pattern of colloids prepared from the juice by precipitation was that of "stem bromelain." To appreciate the striking changes in the disc gel electrophoretic pattern of pineapple fruit bromelain—and probably in the rest of the plant—during this period, we need to see the electrophoretic pattern of fruit bromelain from the 1950s. Figure 2 is a representative disc electrophoretic picture of the many electrophoretic pictures that we took of fruit bromelain that we produced up to about 1960. This pattern is the "classical" fruit bromelain pattern of a disc electrophoretic separation; it is similar to the moving boundary electrophoretic picture shown in Figure 1. This pattern was so consistent, that after running electrophoretic patterns at monthly intervals for several years, we discontinued running these patterns routinely. Dole had no commercial interest in fruit bromelain, and I had no reason to expect that the patterns would ever change.

Figure 2. Classical Fruit Bromelain (Run at pH 4.5)

Contrast this picture with the lower gel in Figure 3, which contains fruit bromelain precipitated with no additional ascorbic acid. This is the pattern of fruit bromelain made from pineapple juice with unstable ascorbic acid. The latch on the super-assemblage has opened. At lower concentrations of added ascorbic acid, 0.25%, the latch on some sub-assemblages still remain closed. At 1% added ascorbic acid, most of the assemblage remains essentially closed, with only a slight amount of leakage. At 2% added ascorbic acid, which I ran in other experiments, all of the latches remained closed and the electrophoretic pattern was that of Figure 2.

To determine when in the growth cycle of the pineapple fruit this change in the electrophoretic pattern occurred, we harvested pineapple fruits at different times during the growth cycle and then determined the electrophoretic pattern of the colloids in the juice. If we harvested fruit that the plantation people would normally have left on the plant for an additional month, the electrophoretic pattern of the unprocessed fruit juice was similar to the classical fruit bromelain pattern shown in Figure 2. It contained a single slightly negatively charged band. However, when we precipitated the colloids from this juice—a process that inevitably causes some oxidation-we obtained the stem bromelain pattern. We used this juice to test the effect of adding three levels of ascorbic acid to the juice before we precipitated the colloids. Please see Figure 3.

Figure 3.

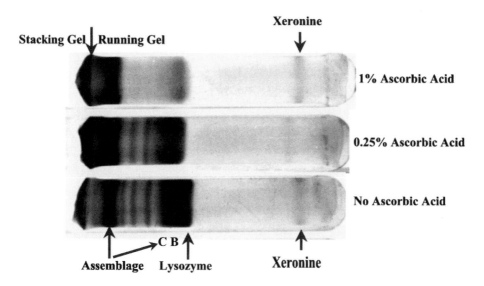

Figure 3. Effect of different amounts of ascorbic acid added to the juice from "green" pineapple fruits on the electrophoretic pattern of the colloids precipitated from the juice by acetone.

We ran the electrophoretic separation at pH 4.5. The narrow bands in the middle patterns in the two lower gels represent discrete enzymes. The broad bands at the leading and the trailing ends of the patterns represent assemblages.

The assemblage band labeled "lysozyme" in the bottom gel is atypical. Normally a clear space separates this band from the BC band. In the bottom gel note the partical clearing of the band at the left end of the pattern.

This particular experiment indicated that high concentrations of ascorbic acid kept the latch closed on the super assemblages until the appropriate time.

By chance I happen to have one experiment that shows the effect of added ascorbic acid on the electrophoretic pattern of stem bromelain. We had run this experiment for another objective, which happened to require the addition of 2% ascorbic acid to the stem juice before we precipitated the stem bromelain. The precipitate from this experiment had very low protease activity and gave an electrophoretic pattern that was similar to fruit bromelain. Since at that period of research (1956) we were committed to producing bromelain with the "stem bromelain" pattern, I did not follow up on this interesting lead.

Based on these results and especially upon a study that I carried out at the Pineapple Research Institute I would like to suggest the following hypothesis about the primary role of ascorbic acid in plants.

• The primary role of ascorbic acid in plants is to stabilize the super-assemblage that contains a variety of sub-assemblages that contain the mechanisms for making five enzymes.

o The function of these enzymes—after they have been activated by xeronine-is to convert reserve foods into small molecules that move to other parts of the plants for storage or new growth.

o Some of these enzymes are proteases, amylases, glycosidases and phosphatases.

o The final assemblages, the ones that actually do the work, have latches that require keys other than ascorbic acid to open.

o The sub-assemblages open in a predetermined sequence.

o The opening and activation of the sub-assemblages can stop at any point in the sequence.

• At a specified time in the metabolic cycle of a plant or in response to a specific signal from the environment, a specific oxidizing molecule lowers the concentration of ascorbic acid sufficiently for the super-assemblage to open and release sub-assemblages.

• Reducing agents protect the ascorbic acid and thus prevent the latch on the super-assemblage from opening. These reducing agents can be a combination of chelating agents, glutathione, excess ascorbic acid or a specific polyphenol.

If we assume that our bodies have analogous assemblages and if we assume that good health is associated with keeping these assemblages intact until the body needs the products produced by the opening of these assemblages, then we have two choices for stabilizing these assemblages. Either we can take massive dosages of ascorbic acid or we can take modest amounts of ascorbic acid accompanied by other appropriate antioxidants. Some fruits contain appreciable amounts of these other factors.

Personally, I favor the latter approach. In pineapple plants grown in Hawaii before 1960, 0.3 mg of ascorbic acid per ml of fruit juice containing a high level of other natural antioxidants, stabilized the assemblages more effectively than did the addition of 20 mg of ascorbic acid per ml of juice containing less than one tenth the level of associated antioxidants!

Receptors: Where the Work Gets Done

Many of the work-assemblages perform their appointed task in the immediate vicinity of various receptor proteins. Scientists know in great detail the structure of receptor proteins. They also know where certain molecules must adsorb onto the receptor proteins to make them active and what the resulting receptor proteins plus adsorbed molecules do. I am suggesting that many receptor proteins require not only the recognized adsorbed molecules—many of these are well studied hormones—but they also must have a molecule of xeronine adsorbed next to the hormone adsorption site. This is a new idea. What information is available to support this concept?

During the 1970s several scientists who were studying the biochemical mechanism of drug addiction, especially A. Goldstein, S. Snyder, E. Simian and Lars Terenius, studied the effect of plant alkaloids on the adsorption of endorphin on the endorphin receptor. These biochemists conclusively proved that the prior adsorption of an alkaloid, such as morphine, on the endorphin-receptor site of the receptor protein blocked the adsorption of endorphin and—visa versa—that the prior adsorption of endorphin on the endorphin receptor site of the receptor protein blocked the adsorption of the alkaloid. From these results as well as from microscopic examination of the interaction of the endorphin receptor protein with tagged molecules, they concluded that both the alkaloid and the endorphin molecules adsorbed onto the same receptor site on the protein. One scientist even demonstrated that he could fold the endorphin molecule so that it had the same three-dimensional shape as the alkaloid.

I am slightly modifying their proposal. I am suggesting that for effective endorphin action two molecules must adsorb onto adjacent sites on the receptor hormone—one molecule is endorphin and the other xeronine. The alkaloids that the University of Chicago biochemists used in their experiments are much more bulky than xeronine. When the alkaloids adsorb onto the xeronine adsorption site-which is what one would expect since both alkaloids and xeronine have a strong positive charge-then the greater bulk of the plant alkaloid would overlap the adjacent endorphin adsorption site, thus blocking the adsorption of endorphin and vice versa.

I have discussed this possibility with a Chicago University Scientist who was familiar with these experiments. He agreed that the optical measurements that the group made and which formed part of the basis for their assertion that both the endorphin and the alkaloid adsorbed onto the same site could not have distinguished between two adjacent sites.

Strictly mechanical considerations suggest that any receptor protein for a peptide hormone, such as the endorphin receptor protein, should have an adsorption site for xeronine. Any small molecule that adsorbs onto a receptor protein and activates the receptor should either modify some property of the receptor protein or should add some property to the protein that the protein did not originally have. A peptide hormone is a chain, a biological rope. Merely hanging a rope on a protein does not provide the protein with any interesting possibilities to do work. However, if a fulcrum is added close to the site where the rope is attached, then the protein has a structure that can perform useful work at the molecular level. Xeronine is an ideal fulcrum.

After I had run a number of animal tests with solutions of crystalline xeronine and observed the dramatic hormone-like actions of xeronine, I proposed that many hormone responses require both the specific hormone and xeronine be present on adjacent sites on the appropriate receptor protein. A receptor protein is a protein that performs its task only after specific molecules, such as various hormones, serotonin, acetylcholine and many specific peptides, such as endorphins and encephalins, adsorb onto certain sites on the protein.

What Assemblages Do

The assemblage concept is partially old and partially new. For many years scientists have known that groups of enzymes work together to perform a complicated task. The ribosomes are an excellent example of such cooperative work. The structures that I am suggesting have a much simpler structure. They contain several enzymes plus an assortment of other molecules assembled together. These move from the site of assemblage—the Golgi complex—to sites where they perform specific tasks. Some are secreted into ducts and move to other organs such as the gastro-intestinal tract. In plants—and probably in our bodies-many of the less complicated assemblages, the assemblages that carry out some biological task, contain a smaller assemblage that synthesizes xeronine.

After I had developed a tentative structure for xeronine (1998), I realized that the extreme reactivity of xeronine would prevent it from wandering around a cell "looking for" a receptor site that needed a dash of xeronine; it would probably latch onto the nearest protein and never reach its intended site.

The solution to that problem was to combine both the xeronine synthesizing system—a xeronine-assemblage-and the hormone in the same assembled package and have the inert package delivered to the adsorption site. Once there, the package would open and the hormone and the newly synthesized xeronine would be delivered to adjacent sites at the same time. This concept can explain many other hormone actions, for example how adrenaline (nor-epinephrine) or certain steroids, can be released into the general blood circulation system but still be targeted to a specific organ under one situation and to another organ under a different situation. I am proposing that the Golgi body assembles the adrenaline into an assemblage containing the xeronine-assemblage. This mechanism gives the cell control over when the tissue should respond to a circulating hormone.

Now let us examine several specific hormone assemblages.

The Endorphin-Assemblage

The endorphin group of physiologically active peptides is essentially a collection of similar peptides affecting the nervous system. Their effects span a most disparate range of actions. They are involved in "good feeling," in the suppression of pain, in promoting sex drive, in suppressing appetite, in curing drug addiction and in increasing endurance. The list goes on and on. What is most amazing is that all of these actions are actions that both the "old fashioned bromelain" and noni also produce. There has to be a connection.

In all of the animal tests that I have run, solutions of crystalline xeronine produced exactly the same actions, good feeling, vastly increased sex drive, suppression of pain and increased activity. I did not have sufficient crystalline xeronine or sufficient time to run a possible test of appetite suppression by crystalline xeronine.[4]

Serotonin Assemblages

The pineapple plant and pineapple fruit contain considerable amounts of serotonin. When pineapple stem juice is passed through a column of resin that separates the different components in the solution by size, serotonin appears in three different places. It appears in a very large colloid, in a medium sized colloid and in the small molecule fraction. The first serotonin-containing colloid probably represents a super assemblage that contains many different assemblages; one of which is the serotonin assemblage. The second colloid probably is the serotonin-assemblage, which is a combination of the xeronine-assemblage plus serotonin. The last fraction is free serotonin. When I originally ran this fractionation and assayed the separated fractions for serotonin, I had no concept about assemblages. I could not satisfactorily explain the reasons for this strange distribution of serotonin.

Prostaglandin-Assemblages

Still another important assemblage may be the prostaglandin assemblage. I am basing this suggestion partially on laboratory data and partially on the similarity of the clinical actions of certain prostaglandins and commercial bromelain. The clinical actions of these two very dissimilar products are so similar, that at one time I believed that the physiological-ly active ingredient in bromelain might be a new type of prostaglandin complex. (I was partially right but not in the way that I had expected.)

After Castle & Cooke had eliminated my department at Dole, Dole gave me a grant to investigate my prostaglandin hypothesis. My laboratory data show that pineapple plants produce prostaglandins; the amount is miniscule. My physiological laboratory data show unequivocally that the material that showed the greatest physiological activity could not possibly be a prostaglandin. (Later—after Dole had terminated my grant—Dole supported other people who continued to pursue my original hypothesis.)

A prostaglandin-assemblage (i.e. an assemblage containing both the xeronine-assemblage plus one of the prostaglandins) could be important in many areas of physiology. Probably the cell synthesizes prostaglandin primarily when some mechanical force, such as a pin prick, a twitch of a muscle, or a sound, momentarily displace the cell membrane. This displacement allows essential fatty acids from the cell membrane to become available for the synthesis of prostaglandins. This is the only mechanism that organisms have for converting a mechanical force into a chemical stimuli that the brain can recognize or that a climbing ivy can use to curl around a stick.

Although I have no direct experimental data showing that a prostaglandin-assemblage exists, yet the clinical reports of the action of both prostaglandin and the xeronine-system strongly support such a suggestion. I remember in particular the fascinating case of a 92-year-old woman who initially had a serious hearing problem. Between two visits to the doctor's office, she began drinking noni juice. During the second visit, the doctor's assistant, who was running the audio test equipment in the adjacent room and recording the data on a computer, accidentally wiped out the previous recordings of her hearing test. He swore softly. The lady, who was in the adjoining room, turned to the doctor and told him to tell his assistant not to worry since the previous hearing tests were no longer valid anyway. She could hear perfectly!

How to Open Assemblages

As long as an assemblage remains unopened, nothing happens; they can remain in a cell for months or even years in this dormant stage. At the appropriate time a specific signal opens and activates an assemblage, releasing xeronine and activating enzymes. Each assemblage requires a unique signal to open it.

As I look back at the various procedures that I investigated during the course of my search for the physiologically active ingredient in the pineapple plant, I now realize that one of the major problems that everyone has in isolating the active ingredient in commercial bromelain is finding a way to open several specific assemblages in the proper sequence. I had empirically discovered a sequence of operations that opened assemblages in the proper order.

When I realized that proxeronine was a critical raw material for the synthesis of xeronine, I thought that I could improve my empirical procedures by concentrating solely on procedures that were based on the properties of proxeronine. When I did that, my "improved" procedure failed completely; I obtained no xeronine. Several of the "unnecessary" steps in my empirical procedure had the specific function of opening certain assemblages in the proper sequence. The final critical step in isolating xeronine was adsorbing the released xeronine-assemblage on a column at one pH and then changing the pH so that the xeronine-assemblage opened and synthesized xeronine.

Obviously the cell does not use the methods that I developed in the laboratory to open assemblages. The cell probably has a variety of very specific signals for opening assemblages. Discovering the chemical nature of these signals could be important in affecting the availability of the xeronine-system. This is an area for much additional research.

Chapter Summary

• The assemblage concept is one of several critical concepts required for the understanding of the xeronine-system.

• An assemblage is a moderately stable structure containing an orderly arrangement of different molecules. At the appropriate time and place the assemblages become activated and the associated molecules work together to perform their specific task.

• The most important assemblage is the assemblage that produces xeronine, namely the xeronine-assemblage.

• The xeronine-assemblage contains proxeronine, inactive proxeroninase, and a source of energy such as ATP or GTP. It may contain still other molecules.

• The xeronine-assemblage is frequently a component of larger assemblages that perform tasks that require xeronine as a necessary component of the final reaction.

• Some of the larger assemblages that probably contain the xeronine-assemblage are:
    o The vesicles of the secreted gastro-intestinal enzymes
    o Assemblages may contain signal molecules such as serotonin, prostaglandin and others.

• This arrangement ensures that free xeronine, which has a very short half-life and is quite reactive, will be synthesized precisely where it will be needed and precisely at the time that it is needed.

• The assemblages of the pineapple plant, papaya latex and fig tree latex are quite complex. The original super-assemblage may contain eight to ten sub-assemblages. The sub-assemblages disassociate from the original assemblage in response to signals from the immediate environment.
    o In normal, healthy pineapple plants most of the assayed protease activity occurs in an inactive form in one special assemblage. This assemblage is packaged with about four other assemblages in a super-assemblage. At the appropriate time each of these sub-assemblages dissociates from the super-assemblage to be converted into active materials that perform a certain operation in the change in the

metabolism of the tissue from a resting stage to a stage of intense metabolic activity.

o Today most producers of commercial bromelain produce a product that does not contain any assemblages that release free xeronine. Either the bromelain protein is preformed or it occurs in bromelain-assemblages. During the activation of the bromelain-assemblage most of the released xeronine is used to activate the pro-bromelain. It is not available for use by a person taking the enzyme.

ENDNOTES

[1] Perkin-Elmer, a company that specializes in making precision lenses—they later built the lens for the Hubble Space Telescope—believed that the medical world was waiting breathlessly for some company to build a desktop Moving Boundary Electrophoresis apparatus that hospitals could use to analyze blood. The original, custom-made Moving Boundary Electrophoresis machines were enormous. They required a dedicated basement room (to minimize vibration), a separate air-conditioning unit and an artist and an engineer to keep the machine running properly.

Unfortunately for Perkin-Elmer, few hospitals had the money, the personnel or the time to buy and operate this convenient tabletop, semi-portable machine. It weighed less than 200 pounds. Four years later another electrophoretic technique, disc electrophoresis, appeared. This technique, which is simple to run, inexpensive and highly sensitive, quickly became the standard research tool for all biochemists. Today variants of this technique are the principal tools that microbiologists initially use to study components of the genes. They are now using even more sophisticated tools. The Moving Boundary Technique is merely a footnote in history books on the development of modern biochemistry. (Few people read endnotes.)

[2] Very early in our research at Dole, a time when the quality of commercial bromelain was still excellent, we attempted to remove all traces of iron from bromelain. This can be done by first reducing the iron with ascorbic acid and then forming a chelate with dipyridyl. The iron complex can be extracted with an organic solvent. When we precipitated "bromelain" from the iron-free stem juice, we obtained a precipitate that had essentially no protease activity and it did not show the classical stem bromelain pattern!. It contained only a single large negatively charged peak! For many years I had been attempting to explain what had happened in this experiment.

I knew of another example where ascorbic acid stabilized an electrophoretic pattern. M. I. Anson, one of the great pioneers of American biochemistry, told me about one of his experiences in the 1920s. He wanted to prepare a very pure preparation of human blood albumin. He attempted to do this by repeated reprecipitations of the albumin with ammonium sulfate. About the time that he felt he was approached the final step, his albumin suddenly disintegrated into free amino acids and small peptides. Believing that oxidation had been the problem, he repeated the isolation but added 2% ascorbic acid at each precipitation step. This time the albumin remained stable. As far as I know no one has ever investigated this important observation.

3 Unfortunately for this project, about the time that the Dole chemists had completed their ascorbic acid recovery scheme, industrial chemists had devised a method for synthesizing ascorbic acid. This was less expensive than isolating ascorbic acid from pineapple leaves. Today, all the ascorbic acid sold commercially is synthetic ascorbic acid.

4 E. Ross of the University of Hawaii and I ran a test on chickens that may be pertinent to the appetite-suppressing action. We fed chickens a diet containing components of commercial bromelain that I now know could lead to the production of xeronine. The chickens initially looked healthy but they soon starved to death. Dr. Ross, who is an eminent authority on the physiology and biochemistry of chickens, examined the organs of the dead chickens. There were absolutely no signs of any organ damage; all of their tissues were perfectly normal. The chickens had literally starved themselves to death! They had no appetite for the abundant food that was available to them. This appetite suppressing action also appears in several anecdotal reports.

In the early 1960s, the Dole sales manager noticed that suddenly the amount of canned pineapple products shipped to the Scandinavian countries increased dramatically. When he investigated the reasons for this sudden interest in eating pineapple, he discovered that someone had published a paper suggesting that eating pineapple caused a decrease in weight. Although I was interested in investigating this phenomenon, the Dole management decided that it was too risky and too expensive a research venture. Their decision was probably a fortunate one. By the time that the research project would have been completed, the compound that might have been responsible for the weight loss, namely proxeronine, was now in short supply in canned pineapple.

CHAPTER 6

Proxeronine and Prostaglandins

The proxeronine story is a story that is still being written. We know that it is the precursor of xeronine; we know many of its physical properties. I have isolated two crystals that are associated with proxeronine. One of the crystals, the golden needles, is crystalline proxeronine. The other—also a relatively large molecule having a structure different from classical biological molecules—may be the residue left from the proxeronine molecule after the xeronine-synthesis process has been completed.

When I sent crystals of these materials to an analytical specialist in 1974, the analytical techniques were inadequate to propose a structure for these two molecules. The chemist who performed the preliminary analysis said that he had never come across a molecule with such a structure.

Proxeronine is an interesting and an important biochemical compound that has escaped detection in our bodies. It has escaped detection not because it is present in exceedingly small amounts but because it does not fall into any of the usual class of biochemical compounds, such as carbohydrates, lipids, proteins, nucleic acids, vitamins or pigments and its action is indirect. It has no direct biochemical action in the body; it is the critical precursor for xeronine. As a result of these properties, scientists had no reason to search for it.

Besides proxeronine, in this chapter I shall also cover a subject that initially appears unrelated to the xeronine-system, namely prostaglandins. However, my prostaglandin investigation played a crucial role in the development of the xeronine-system concept. During this work I obtained the data that led to proxeronine and then to xeronine. This work also led to several new hypotheses about pain and our sense of touch, hearing and space perception.

Early Hints of Proxeronine

After I had developed a pilot plant method for isolating commercial bromelain in 1951, I sent samples of laboratory-produced bromelain to various companies for evaluation. In the preparation of my initial samples of commercial bromelain, I made no attempt to regulate the ash content of the samples; it ranged from 18% to over 30%. Such a range in ash content (the residue that remains after a sample is burned) also occurred in competitive products. However, for the pharmaceutical market, I decided that I should prepare samples that were low in ash. The general method for removing inorganic molecules from a sample is dialysis.

In this method one dissolves the crude protein mixture, places the solution in a cellophane dialyzing sack and then places the dialyzing sack in a large volume of salt-free water that is changed frequently. The salts and small organic molecules diffuse out of the sack but the proteins remain in the sack. Generally this method takes two days for removing most of the salts from a small amount of sample. This is a useful laboratory technique that biochemists still use. Nevertheless, even with commercial dialyzers—which I tested extensively—this method is too slow for commercial work.

To increase the rate at which the salts moved out of the cellophane container while the colloids remained behind, I investigated using an electrical potential to speed the removal of salts. When I used this technique on a five percent solution of commercial bromelain, I was surprised at the rate at which the electrical resistance increased. Normally this would have indicated that the salts were moving rapidly out of the sample chamber. However, the apparent rate was much too fast to be believable. When I disassembled the cell, I found that a brown, gummy precipitate, containing golden needles had completely covered the anode sheet of the electrodialyzer to a depth of about four millimeters. This layer of solid material acted as an effective electrical insulator. This, of course, accounted for the high electrical resistance of the cell.

Since finding new organic crystals is always exciting, I recovered the crystals and attempted to classify them. They gave no test for amino acids, nucleic acids, carbohydrates or fatty acids; they produced no strong absorption peaks in the UV. Since the Hawaiian pineapple companies were interested only in practical research that led either to new products that they could sell or to solutions for some of their specific food processing problems, I knew that spending research time attempting to determine the nature of an unknown crystal that might have no commercial value would be a project that would endanger my financial support. At that time, I could not conceive of any applications for the crystals since I had no idea what the crystals might do that would be commercially interesting. I put the crystal project aside and did not see another yellow crystal until 1973.[1]

The real breakthrough in discovering the nature of the physiologically active ingredient in commercial bromelain came after the new president of Castle & Cooke, the parent company of Dole, had eliminated a number of departments, including Basic Research.

The Prostaglandin Detour

At the time that Castle & Cooke discontinued the Basic Research Department, I believed that I was close to discovering the physiologically active ingredient in bromelain. I decided to continue my research with my own resources and those of people who believed in the project. Fortunately for me, Dr. Mitz Yokoyama, the Research Director at the Kuakini Hospital, allowed me to use his research facilities to continue my work.

In 1973 I developed the hypothesis that the physiologically active ingredient was a prostaglandin-like substance or complex. This was a creditable hypothesis. From the joint work that we did in 1958 with one of the large drug companies, we jointly proved that purified bromelain was a medical placebo. Since our purification process removed lipophilic materials from commercial bromelain during the purification process, I suspected that the physiologically active, unknown associated material in commercial bromelain was lipophilic. Prostaglandins are lipophilic.

Equally convincing was the strong correlation between the clinical action of commercial bromelain and the clinical action of certain prostaglandins. Both commercial bromelain and prostaglandins affect smooth muscle contraction thus relieving the pain of dysmenorrhea; both lower high blood pressure; both are valuable in treating certain birth problems; both relieve the pain of arthritis; both are involved in the immune response; both affect the blood clotting mechanism; both appear to affect the biosynthesis of the important regulatory molecule cAMP. This list could be longer.

I also had laboratory data that were compatible with the hypothesis that bromelain contained prostaglandins. Dialyzing a solution of bromelain at neutrality eliminated the biological activity of the retained colloids. Prostaglandins are soluble at this pH and readily pass through the dialyzing membrane. On the other hand, dialyzing the solution at pH 4.5 did not affect the biological activity of the colloids. At pH 4.5 the prostaglandins are poorly soluble and tend to adsorb onto proteins. Therefore they would not dialyze from the sack. All of these observations are compatible with the prostaglandin hypothesis.

I mentioned my prostaglandin-like hypothesis to George Felton, a vice president of Dole and the man who originally had recommended that Dole become the leading producer of commercial bromelain. George Felton was impressed by the prostaglandin-like hypothesis and obtained a small grant from Castle & Cooke to enable me to continue the investigation of my hypothesis.

The Prostaglandin Project

Initially the new chemical data that I obtained under the Castle & Cooke research grant supported the "prostaglandin-like" hypothesis. In fact, the chemical data were so compatible with my original prostaglandin hypothesis that Castle & Cooke management established a research arrangement with Upjohn Drug Company, the drug company that was at that time the leader in prostaglandin research, and instructed the Castle & Cooke patent lawyer to start drawing up a patent application based on my data. To complete the project, I needed to show that the prostaglandin-like material had the physiological action of commercial bromelain.

For this final phase of the project, I needed large amounts of material. Dole gave me excellent cooperation. In the commercial production of bromelain three volumes of acetone are used to precipitate most of the colloids in pineapple stem juice. Since acetone is expensive, the operators of the bromelain production plant recovery the acetone in a large fractionating tower. They discard the aqueous residue remaining after the acetone stripping operation. For my project the bromelain-production people saved the aqueous residue, concentrated it in a large commercial evaporator and then passed the concentrated residue over a series of commercial ion exchange columns according to the method that I had worked out in the laboratory. The material that I received represented the residue from about twenty-five tons of pineapple stems!

From this concentrated residue I had no difficulty in obtaining sizable amounts of golden needle-like crystals. These crystals were similar to those that I had isolated in 1954 while I was still working for the Pineapple Research Institute. These crystals had biological activity. Although I did not know the chemical structure of these needles, I had enough structural information to know that these crystals could not possibly be related to prostaglandins.

I told Dole management that on the basis of my recent data, I no longer believed that the active ingredient was a prostaglandin-like material; instead I now believed that it was a new material that was unlike any known biological chemical.

When the Dole management people received this information, they were incredulous. My data up to that time had convinced them that the active ingredient was a prostaglandin-like material. Since I was convinced that prostaglandin-like materials could not possibly be the sought for active ingredient, they discontinued my support and supported other people to work on the prostaglandin hypothesis. Although this later work led to some interesting papers that suggested that commercial bromelain showed prostaglandin-like activity, none of this work led to discovery of the active ingredient.

Although prostaglandins are not the material that is responsible for the unusual physiological action of commercial bromelain, there is, indeed, a prostaglandin connection. This connection explains why bromelain could produce prostaglandin-like reactions. Some of these connections have led to certain exciting hypotheses.

Prostaglandins, Cell Membranes and Sensations

While I was investigating the prostaglandin-like hypothesis, I carefully reviewed the prostaglandin literature. At that time (1972) biochemists had worked out the biosynthesis of prostaglandins in great detail. They had also studied the clinical action of administering various prostaglandins at various dosages to various tissues. However, what was missing—and may still be missing as far as I know—was a satisfying reason why the body should produce regulatory molecules that sometimes performed useful functions whereas at other times the same or related prostaglandins caused considerable trouble in the body.

Although the prostaglandins have a hormone-like action, they are not true hormones; true hormones circulate through the blood stream and affect certain tissues far removed from the site of hormone production. By contrast, many cells in our body produce prostaglandins. The cells either use the prostaglandins locally or in the immediate surrounding tissue.

Synthesis of Prostaglandins

Anyone who is interested in the details of the biosynthesis of prostaglandins can find the synthesis listed in any standard textbook on biochemistry. In this book we are interested only in the reasons why the body synthesizes this strange group of molecules, what role the xeronine-system plays in cooperation with the prostaglandins and why the clinical response of commercial bromelain and certain prostaglandins are so similar in many health problems.

The biosynthesis of prostaglandins is relatively simple. Certain enzymes take essential fatty acids and in a few simple steps convert the fatty acid into a prostaglandin. Whereas the normal fatty acids have none or only one unsaturated double bond, the essential fatty acids have two to three double bonds arranged in a special sequence. Our bodies cannot synthesize these essential fatty acids; we obtain them from certain foods, such as sunflower seeds and fish oils. In a cell the essential fatty acids occur in the phospholipids that form cell membranes and the membranes of organelles.

Cell Membranes

A cell membrane is a sandwich of two layers of orderly arranged phospholipid molecules. The hydrophilic (water-loving) ends of the phospholipid molecules are on the outer side of the sandwich and the lipophilic (fat-loving) ends are on the inside. At various parts of this sandwich protein molecules poke through the sandwich; these proteins provide a connection between the extra-cellular environment and the interior of the cell. Some membranes have pores through the membrane that can be opened and closed.

A membrane phospholipid molecule contains two molecules of fatty acids. One molecule is the common type of fatty acid such as occurs in lard, butter, soap and the extra weight that many of us carry around. The other molecule, which is always the middle molecule of a phospholipid molecule, is an essential fatty acid. An essential fatty acid is similar to a vitamin. We must have this essential fatty acid for health but we cannot make this fatty acid; we must get it from our food. Good sources are fish oils and sunflower seeds. We need essential fatty acids to make prostaglandins.

From a casual reading of textbooks on the structure of a cell, we obtain the impression that most of the cell membrane is a relatively static structure that contains certain areas where the cell interacts with compounds in its environment. However, the so-called static portion of the cell membrane is actually very dynamic. Shortly after scientists discovered the phospholipid nature of cell membranes, a Sigma Xi guest lecturer came to Hawaii to tell us about the strange behavior of the cell membrane. (In those days the scientific community believed that Hawaii was a relatively untutored land that needed scientific missionaries to bring us into the scientific fold. In addition Hawaii is a wonderful place to give lectures during the winter season.) About two thousand times a second a particular enzyme releases the essential fatty acid from a membrane phospholipid molecule and then another enzyme puts it back in place.

This seemingly senseless and repetitive operation leaves the cell membrane essentially unchanged. To a cytologist, who studies stained sections of a cell, the cell membrane appears "static." A seemingly useless, repetitive action does not make biological sense; there must be a reason why a cell should spend all of this biological energy removing and replacing a part of its membrane. Apparently people studying the cell membranes felt the same way about this useless action. Since it had no known useful function, they have essentially ignored this action of the cell membrane. Today few textbooks mention this feature of the cell membrane.

I would like to suggest that this "useless" removing and replacing the essential fatty acid portion of a phospholipid molecule is a crucial part of the mechanism for converting motion and pressure into biochemical molecules that become signals. Such an action must occur to provide the chemical signals that our brain interprets as kinesthetic, tactile, auditory and pain sensations.

Normally the essential fatty acids in the cell membrane are unavailable for the prostaglandin-synthesizing enzyme. Even though one enzyme removes the essential fatty acid from the phospholipid that forms part of the cell membrane 2,000 times a second, another enzyme, closely associated with this enzyme, replaces the essential fatty acid onto the phospholipid molecule 2,000 times a second. In the meantime the prostaglandin-synthesizing enzyme waits patiently for something to happen that would interrupt this closely-knit pass and repass team. That something that interrupts this smooth interchange of the essential fatty acid molecule between the hydrolyzing and the synthesizing molecule is a mechanical displacement of the membrane.

Prostaglandin, Pain and the Xeronine-System

Pain is a very complex and intensively studied phenomenon. I do not intend to review the various hypotheses that describe the pain phenomenon. Instead I would like to add still another hypothesis to the list of explanations. This hypothesis will deal primarily with the pain produced by the release of prostaglandins; these are the pains for which people take aspirins and for which doctors prescribe synthetic alkaloids. I shall base this new hypothesis on prostaglandins and xeronine.

Prostaglandins act as agonists (a substance that adsorbs onto a nerve receptor and sends a signal to the brain). For the nerve receptors to function, the agonist must adsorb onto the appropriate receptor site, do its job and then get off the receptor so that the receptor will be ready for another agonist. Probably there are several distinct prostaglandin receptors, one for pain, one for sound perception, one for kinesthetic perception. This is an area that needs much additional work. What I am suggesting is a preliminary scheme. It explains the observations. I know that it must be modified as new experiments provide us with more data.

When a knife blade starts to cut into ones finger, the blade initially indents the skin. This localized pressure displaces the membranes of the affected cells, allowing the prostaglandin-synthesizing enzyme to grab an essential fatty acid and make a prostaglandin molecule. Since only a few prostaglandins are released at this early stage of the cut, the Golgi body has enough proxeronine to assemble a prostaglandin molecule with a xeronine-assemblage. This assemblage exits the Golgi body and locates a prostaglandin receptor protein. Here it delivers both the prostaglandin and xeronine. The brain interprets the signal from this receptor as pressure located at the tip of the left middle finger.

As the knife blade begins to cut the flesh, the prostaglandin enzymes release a flood of prostaglandins. The local supply of proxeronine quickly becomes exhausted and xeronine-assemblages cannot be produced in amounts large enough to satisfy the demand. Consequently some prostaglandin receptors—these could be different receptors—might have adsorbed prostaglandins but no xeronine. To fit the observations, I am suggesting that when a prostaglandin pain receptor having only an adsorbed prostaglandin molecule (no xeronine) sends a signal to the brain, the brain interprets the signal as pain. If the prostaglandin-pain receptor has both an adsorbed prostaglandin and a xeronine molecule, the signal going to the brain would be no pain.

Clinical, laboratory data on both animals and people and anecdotal reports all indicate that xeronine or components of the xeronine reduce pain. Probably the most dramatic demonstrations are my experiments on mice. In this experiment I used solutions of crystalline xeronine, which I injected into the abdominal cavity. The control animals, which received only the same volume of saline solution, were visibly greatly "discomforted" whereas the xeronine treated animals showed absolutely no indications of discomfort; they were lively mice. To appreciate what the control mice must have felt imagine how you would feel if the doctor suddenly injected the contents of a two-liter soda bottle into your abdominal cavity in less than a second.

Feeling no pain and feeling good are two different phenomena. We can either assume that two different receptor proteins are involved or we can assume that the prostaglandin-xeronine pain-receptor can produce both effects. We need more data in this area.

The suggestion that adsorption of prostaglandin only onto the prostaglandin receptor protein produces pain whereas the adsorption of both prostaglandin and xeronine produces no pain gives an explicit explanation for something that we have all experienced. Immediately after we cut ourselves, the pain is intense. Then after a few minutes "we become accustomed" to the pain; it is not as intense as it was originally. Finally— as happens with the tack in the shoe phenomenon—we may forget about the pain completely.

I am suggesting that initially, because of the massive synthesis of prostaglandins, the Golgi body cannot provide enough proxeronine to make assemblages containing both a xeronine-assemblage and prostaglandin. As a result the prostaglandin-pain receptors have only prostaglandin molecules adsorbed. The signal going to the brain is the pain signal. At a slightly later stage in the injury fewer prostaglandin molecules are synthesized and the Golgi body may now be able to make prostaglandin assemblages containing both prostaglandin and a xeronine-assemblage. When the contents of these assemblages adsorb to the prostaglandin-pain receptor no pain signal goes to the brain.

This proposed action makes physiological sense. We need the pain signal to stimulate us to take immediate remedial action. However, once we have done what is possible, further pain signals are redundant and counter productive; ideally the pain signal should stop.

Other Common Pain Relievers

Now let us attempt to explain the action of the alkaloids as pain relievers Compared to xeronine, the alkaloids are bulky molecules. Having a basic charge, they readily adsorb onto the xeronine adsorption site of a pain receptor protein. However, the molecules are so large that they prevent the prostaglandin molecules from adsorbing onto the adjacent prostaglandin adsorption sites. Thus no pain signal goes to the brain. We pay a price for this relief in pain in side effects; we lose our kinesthetic perception. This is why our jaw feels numb.

The action of aspirin and ibuprofen in lessening pain has an entirely different mechanism. Both of these molecules prevent the synthesis of prostaglandins. With a reduced supply of prostaglandins, fewer pain signals reach the brain. Again if these drugs are truly effective in blocking the synthesis of prostaglandins, we pay a price in side effects. This is why some of the more potent drugs warn about operating complex machinery after taking the drug.

The action of the endorphins in relieving pain may operate by still another mechanism. Whereas the first three mechanisms all operate at the site of the injury, the endorphins may act by sending signals to the brain that block the pain messages. I know of no data to support this hypothesis.

With this model, research doctors and medical doctors should be able to devise effective long-term pain relievers. The most important single tool in controlling pain is proxeronine. If we can increase the level of proxeronine in our bodies so that the Golgi complex can produce adequate numbers of prostaglandin-assemblages, then any pain caused by prostaglandins can be blocked. Since this method does not block the synthesis of prostaglandins, there are no side effects. We behave normally.

Proxeronine and Sleep

I believe proxeronine plays in important role in the sleep cycle of animals and humans. Multicellular organisms need to coordinate the operation of all their cells. This is especially true of higher organisms. Mammals do this by secreting various specific hormones that activate specific systems. However, mammals also require a more general type of hormone action that imposes an overall regulation of cellular activity; it needs a general body regulator that switches the organism between wakefulness and sleep.

I suggest that proxeronine is this body regulator. I suggest that the principal warehouses for storing the xeronine contained in the food that we eat are the liver and the skin. At approximately two-hour intervals during the day and night the brain sends a signal to the liver to release a slug of proxeronine from its stores. Normally the amount of proxeronine released in these two-hour intervals is similar. This amount is not quite enough to carry out our normal daytime activities for about two hours. Therefore to continue their daytime activities, the cells of various tissues have to tap into their locally stored supply of proxeronine. Eventually the cell has depleted its local supply of proxeronine and we need to sleep to build up the local store of proxeronine in our tissues.

While we sleep, we require less proxeronine and the slugs of proxeronine released every two hours allows the cells to increase their level of locally stored proxeronine. When the level is finally sufficient we awaken. The REM periods during our sleep probably represent the time when the proxeronine is released into the blood stream.

If each cell produced its own supply of proxeronine—as happens in unicellular organisms and plants—then the brain would not have control over the release of proxeronine. Each cell would make its own decision, a state of cellular activity that would greatly diminish the orderly control over cellular activity that a well functioning brain maintains.

Now let us examine some of the unique properties of proxeronine.

Properties of Proxeronine

Although the biological function of proxeronine is to take part in the synthesis of the alkaloid xeronine, proxeronine has certain physical properties that are important. Every physiologist, every doctor, every research worker and anyone packaging products containing proxeronine should be aware of this property. Proxeronine is an excellent solvent for many lipophilic materials and for certain types of plastic. My first experience with this property of proxeronine came at a time when I knew nothing about proxeronine.

1960 Pineapple Juice and Cholesterol

In the 1960s I knew nothing about proxeronine; I was interested in health problems as affected by the diet. I had come across some interesting suggestions that eating pineapple fruit could lower blood pressure and reduce the blood cholesterol level.

At that time blood cholesterol level was the principal topic in health circles. I personally considered a high cholesterol level not the cause of health problems but as a warning flag that something was seriously wrong with the body's cholesterol regulating system. However, as a commercial scientist, I also knew and appreciated that any product that lowered blood cholesterol level would appeal to doctors and to a large market. Specifically, it could dramatically increase the sales of pineapple products. For this reason I proposed to the President of Dole that we run a controlled test on the effect of eating just a single portion of pineapple a day on the blood cholesterol level.

The president of Dole liked the proposal and sent a memo to all of the executives suggesting that if they desired, they could volunteer for the test. A popular company president's wish is a command. Every executive took part in this experiment. Some executives even volunteered their wives! The results from this test were highly encouraging. Of the thirty-two volunteers, thirty showed statistically significant drops in their blood cholesterol level from consuming just one portion of pineapple product a day!)

I had excellent explanations to explain why the blood cholesterol level rose in the two volunteers who showed an increase in blood cholesterol level during the course of the test. One person did not follow the very specific directions that I had given the volunteers. Since he started his vacation during the pineapple portion of the test, he told me that he could not be bothered about following the very specific directions that I had prescribed. His higher blood cholesterol levels were exactly what I had predicted would happen if he did not follow directions. The other person, whose cholesterol level increased, had just returned from a debilitating foreign trip (Montezuma's Revenge). His initial blood cholesterol level was abnormally low; it was actually in the dangerously low range. His blood cholesterol returned to normal. However, this showed up in the data as an increase.

These results were so promising that the president of Dole contacted Dr. Fred Stare of the Harvard Nutrition Department and suggested that they might be interested in repeating my experiment on hospital patients. The pilot plant test, which a young intern monitored carefully, was even more impressive than my original experiments. All twenty-five of the subjects showed a significant drop in blood cholesterol level. At that point we thought that we had solved the country's cholesterol problem.

Dr. Stare immediately planned a much larger test. This test was so large that Dr. Stare had the hospital food preparation department take charge of administering the test. Of course, the hospital food preparation department had its own work to do, namely to feed patients. They did not have time to explain to each patient how the pineapple juice was to be taken. They merely printed out my instructions and placed the voluminous, finely printed instructions on the morning breakfast tray with a glass of pineapple juice. Supposedly the patients would find their glasses somewhere and would read the instructions. They were supposed to suppress their normal desire to drink the pineapple juice with their breakfast, to remove the juice from the tray and to tell the harassed attendant that they would drink the juice a half an hour before lunch. Understandably, no one read the directions. The result was a failure.

In the review of the results, I pointed out that we had extensive data from experiments on chickens that showed that something in pineapple juice—years later I discovered that it was proxeronine—caused dietary cholesterol to enter rapidly into the body. Dr. E. Ross of the University of Hawaii and I studied the effect of different diets on the cholesterol level in the blood of chickens and on the formation of plaques in the aorta of chickens on these different diet. Dr. Ross prepared iso-caloric chicken feed that contained either no added cholesterol, 5% cholesterol, 5% cholesterol mixed with an equal weight of cooking oil, 5% cholesterol mixed with an equal weight of pineapple juice concentrate and 5% cholesterol mixed with both cooking oil and pineapple juice concentrate.

Chickens fed the check feed and the feed containing 5% cholesterol had exactly the same amount of blood serum cholesterol, namely 90 mg/100 ml of serum. This is the expected result since pure cholesterol does not enter the body. Chickens fed either the cholesterol-cooking oil or the cholesterol-pineapple juice concentrate feed had essentially the same cholesterol level, namely about 450-475 mg/100 ml. The combination of cooking oil and pineapple concentrate with the cholesterol gave the highest blood cholesterol level, about 550 mg/100 ml.

From this experiment I knew that if we included pineapple juice with a breakfast of ham and eggs, that we would certainly cause an analytical increase in the blood cholesterol level. I personally was not worried about the high cholesterol level that might be produced by having pineapple and ham and eggs for breakfast. Our data from the chicken experiment showed that as long as the chickens ate pineapple that even the chickens with 550 mg/100 ml had no plaques in their aortas whereas the chickens with 450-475 mg/100 ml—and no pineapple—did have plaques.

Unfortunately for this very promising alleviation of the country's cholesterol problem, commercial practicality prevented further work on this approach. By chance Dole had just embarked on an expensive advertising campaign in which they suggested "Reach for a glass of pineapple juice for breakfast instead of a glass of orange juice." In contrast to this on-going advertising recommendation, I was recommending that pineapple juice never be taken at breakfast time, when the breakfast might contain ham and eggs, nor should it be taken with meals that might be high in cholesterol. Instead I was recommending that pineapple juice be drunk about 11:30 in the morning or about a half an hour before breakfast.

The advertising people did not like my approach; it was too complicated. They prevailed. Today people once again have the opportunity to control both their cholesterol level as well as their blood pressure by drinking TAHITIAN NONI® Juice. Again—solely for analytical reasons—I would recommend that the user not take the noni juice with meals. Take it either before the meals or several hours after the meals.

Proxeronine Dissolves Plastics

Proxeronine dissolves certain plastics. In a research laboratory, chemists use disposable plastic weighing dishes to obtain the dry weights of fractions that they isolate. The disposable plastic dishes work well for this application. However, if my fractionated samples contained 50% or more proxeronine, the sample would quickly dissolve a hole in the plastic. This was hard on the microbalance.

This solvent action of proxeronine came to light in another way. One time we bought fifty gallons of a special preparation of the plant extract that contained proxeronine. This particular product was unusual in that it contained no additives. Within two months the proxeronine had so soft-ened the thick plastic drum, that the drum split and leaked the entire con-tents of the drum onto the floor. This was an expensive loss of product and a mess to clean up. Since by this time I knew about the properties of proxeronine, we knew what to do to prevent this problem from occurring again.

We alerted the manufacturer of this product about this property of proxeronine. However, he felt that this problem would not bother him. One morning when he came to his plant, he found the floor of his plant flooded with 8,000 gallons of extract. The proxeronine in his product had finally dissolved enough of the thick plastic walls of his tank to produce a leak that completely drained his tank.

The strong solvent action of proxeronine also affected one of our ani-mal experiments. Wanting to have a sterile intestinal tract for certain ani-mal experiments, we used a particular type of a sulfanilamide compound that doctors prescribe to kill microorganisms infecting the intestinal tract. This particular sulfanilamide is very toxic. If it is injected directly into an animal's blood stream, it kills the animal as well as any bacteria that might have been present. If used correctly as an intestinal antibiotic, it is perfectly safe since this particular sulfanilamide does not pass through the intestinal membrane.

In our preliminary experiment we tested four combinations, no addi-tives (the check), the special sulfanilamide alone, a two percent brome-lain solution alone and a combination of sulfanilamide and bromelain. As anticipated, the check, the sulfanilamide and the bromelain treatments caused no change in the condition of the animals. By contrast the combi-nation of the sulfanilamide and bromelain killed every mouse that received this treatment (12 out of 12). We took some of the blood from a killed mouse and tested it for antibiotic activity against bacteria. The blood was loaded with antibiotic. This experiment conclusively proves that proxeronine can affect the absorption of certain lipophilic molecules that, for one reason or another, normally do not pass through the intesti-nal tract and into the blood.

In this connection I should mention that one very successful medical applications of commercial bromelain was a combination of an intestinal antibiotic and bromelain. (The antibiotic was not the sulfanilamide type of antibiotic that we used.) This medicine was for many years the most effective method for treating intestinal infections. It not only rapidly cleared the intestinal tract of bacteria but it also promoted a rapid return of health. This drug produced no side effects.

Proxeronine's ability to enhance the transfer of certain molecules across cell membranes can be of immense value to doctors treating certain medical problems. Several clinical reports from the nineteen-fifties reported that the combination of "bromelain" and an antibiotic controlled meningitis whereas the antibiotic by itself was ineffective. This favorable response was definitely a result of the solvent action of proxeronine. The research doctor took spinal taps of the patient on the antibiotic alone and again after the patient took the same dose of the antibiotic but this time combined with a source of proxeronine. Whereas the control-antibiotic sample showed no antibiotic in the spinal fluid, the bromelain-antibiotic sample showed antibiotic activity. (The bromelain of that period was an excellent source of proxeronine.)

One of the large drug companies had considered combining bromelain with practically all of the drugs that they were selling. This company had originally investigated the application of bromelain solutions to treat dysmenorrhea. Additional research showed that by combining their standard drugs with commercial bromelain they could greatly decrease the amount of drug and still obtain superior results. Reducing the amount of drugs lessened possible side effects of the drug.

The Chemistry of Proxeronine

During the Prostaglandin Research Project that Dole sponsored, I isolated two crystals. Both of these crystals represented large molecules. One, a white crystal, contained no carboxyl groups. Dr. Paul Scheuer ran infrared analyses and NMR studies on this compound. He reported that this material did not belong to any of the usual class of compounds normally found in biological material. An elemental C, H, N analysis of this compound indicated that this was a large molecule with a molecular weight of some multiple of 8,000.

I also isolated the silky, golden needles that I had isolated in 1954.

This molecule was acidic. The UV spectrum was somewhat similar to that of ferulic acid but with a much higher end UV absorption. Since prostaglandins are also acidic, one might wonder whether this molecule might be a special type of prostaglandin molecule as I had originally proposed. After a long series of tests, I reluctantly concluded that this material could not possibly contain the prostaglandin structure.[2]

The beautiful, silky needles are not ordinary crystals. The crystals are lipophilic. Once formed, they are not easy to dissolve. I had to use heat and a neutral pH to dissolve the crystals. If I slowly dropped the pH of a solution of these crystals, the crystals reformed. If I added the acid too rapidly, I obtained a brown gum. These observations exactly match what happened in 1954.

Proxeronine and Xeronine in Smooth Muscles

The first definitive clue that I had that the living cell could convert proxeronine into xeronine came from an interesting experiment that I ran while I was working on the prostaglandin hypothesis. Of course at that time I had not yet developed the xeronine-system hypothesis. I had isolated two different molecules that showed biological activity. One molecule was a solution of the silky needles that I mentioned above (proxeronine) whereas the other molecule (formed after intensive manipulations) was a relatively small molecule (xeronine). Although both fractions affected the aggregation of blood platelets, their actions appeared to be slightly different. I decided to test these samples by an entirely different biological assay, namely the effect of these compounds on the frequency and the intensity of the rhythmic contraction of smooth muscles.

In this test, a strip of stomach tissue freshly obtained from a mouse is stretched in a tensiometer connected to a sensitive, rapid recorder. The mouse tissue is placed in a cell through which a solution of isotonic salts and nutrients passes continuously. Such a strip of mouse stomach contracts rhythmically for several hours after it has been removed from a mouse's stomach. The experimenter can add different chemicals into the stream of nutrient solution that flows constantly through the cell containing the muscle tissue.

The results of this experiment were definitive. As soon as I pumped into the bathing solution the small molecule (xeronine), the stomach strip immediately contracted more frequently and more intensely. When I discontinued adding the solution of the small molecule, the contractions immediately returned to the normal frequency and intensity. Clearly this compound—which I now know was xeronine—increases the intensity and the frequency of contractions of smooth muscles.

When I pumped in a solution of the golden crystalline needles (proxeronine), nothing happened to the stomach muscle tissue. Then a few seconds later the frequency and the intensity of the contractions increased. When I discontinued adding the solution of the golden crystals, nothing happened immediately. Then, a very short time later, the frequency and the intensity of the contractions returned to normal.

The shapes of the curves for the small molecule and the large molecule were identical with one exception. The activity curve for the large molecule was displaced a few seconds on the time axis. My interpretation of the data from this experiment at the time that I ran the experiment was:

1) The small molecule (xeronine) causes an immediate increase in the frequency and in the magnitude of smooth muscle contraction.

2) The solution of the silky, golden crystals (proxeronine) enters the smooth muscles and is converted into a molecule (xeronine) that acted similarly to the small molecule. The diffusion of the large molecule into the smooth muscle cells and the conversion of this molecule into the active molecule (xeronine) required a certain amount of time.

I am assuming that the active molecule formed in the gastric strip was xeronine. All of the clinical work as well as the laboratory work are consistent with this hypothesis.

The Elusive Proxeronine

The difficulty in isolating proxeronine is that proxeronine normally occurs in assemblages. Before proxeronine can be isolated, the assemblage must open under conditions that do not lead to the proxeronine being used immediately to synthesize xeronine. By strictly empirical methods I developed several techniques for opening assemblages.

A further complication in isolating large amounts of proxeronine is that each of the approximately eight assemblages in commercial bromelain requires a different set of conditions for opening. This is a very important and practical area for future research.

Chapter Summary

• Proxeronine is a critical molecule in the synthesis of xeronine•

• Proxeronine is a relatively large molecule that has the shape of a string. The molecular weight is probably above 16,000. It is an acidic, lipophilic molecule that crystallizes readily. The golden needles are difficult to dissolve in water.

• Plants and lower forms of life synthesize their own proxeronine.

• We obtain most—possibly all—of our supply of proxeronine from food.

• Today's food supply of proxeronine is frequently insufficient to supply the increased demands for proxeronine caused by the stresses, strains and pollution of modern life.

• Proxeronine generally occurs in assemblages that must be opened before the proxeronine is available.

ENDNOTES

[1] I would like to make a few comments on this early experiment in light of what I now know about the xeronine-system, assemblages and the Golgi body. What had surprised me originally was the large amount of negatively charged precipitate that formed from a five per cent solution of the commercial bromelain sample. The dry weight of the negatively charged precipitate plus crystals represented an appreciable percentage of the starting material. This is strange and unexpected. The moving boundary electrophoresis separation of pineapple stem colloids predicted that the negatively charged colloids should have comprised no more than 10-15% of the total colloids in bromelain. Instead the negatively charged colloids comprised well over half of the total colloids!

I now believe that electrodialysis removed certain critical cations from the surface of certain assemblages. This removal caused certain assemblages to open and to release free proxeronine. At the low pH at the anode side of the cell, some proxeronine crystallized whereas some became insoluble to form a brown gum. I also believe that some of the strongly negatively charged assemblages did not open. These also moved to the anode and contributed to the large mass of material that became insoluble at the anode.

2 The UV spectrum of this molecule interested me; it explained an empirical observation that I had made many, many years previously. While I was attempting to find some physical method that we could use to identify samples of bromelain that would have good physiological activity (I knew that the protease assay figures were worthless in assessing the utility of a sample.) I found that in general those samples that had high UV absorption around 320 nm tended to be the samples that had the best physiological activity. However, when we searched for the source of the 320 nm absorption, we isolated a ferulic acid containing polycarbohydrate molecule. Isolating pure samples of this polymer was relatively easy.

The pharmaceutical company with which we were then associated tested this fraction extensively. They reported that this product showed no biological activity. At this point I decided that since the ferulic acid carbohydrate polymer was not the "active factor", that possibly it was associated in some way with the active factor. With the re-isolation of the silky crystals, the relationship became clear. Both compounds show absorption at 320 nm in neutral solutions. Distinguishing between these two compounds is simple.

SECTION III: WHAT DOES IT ALL MEAN?

CHAPTER 7

The Enzymes of the Xeronine-System: Proxeroninase and Lysozymes

Proxeroninase is one of the final enzymes involved in making xeronine; it is a new enzyme. By contrast, lysozymes are a group of similar enzymes that biochemists have studied for well over a hundred years. Three groups of research workers have independently isolated from commercial bromelain the protein that I am calling proxeroninase. When these separate groups studied this enzyme, its function was not known. However, each group had its own theory. The Houck-Klein group believed this was the enzyme that worked miracles in treating burns. The Shigei group was the first to document that this protein showed biological activity when injected into animals. My group and the Jintan Dolph Research group believed this protein synthesized some unknown molecule that was responsible for the biological activity.

When these groups carried out their investigations, the xeronine-system hypothesis was still about six years in the future.

Houck-Klein Isolation of "Escharase"

The procedure that Dr. Gerald Klein developed for treating burns was by a considerable margin the most effective treatment that has ever been discovered for painlessly, rapidly and effectively removing burned tissue. The one shortcoming of Dr. Klein's technique was not in his method but in the product that he used; some batches of commercial bromelain were excellent whereas other batches, having exactly the same assayed protease activity and giving the same moving boundary electrophoretic pattern, showed little activity. Before Klein's method could become a standard technique for removing burned tissue, some method had to be developed for producing a dependable product.

Joint work that Klein and I carried out proved conclusively that the protease in commercial bromelain powder had no biological activity. The active ingredient was apparently a small molecule that diffused rapidly across the scabbed burns. Later Jack Houck joined us.

Jack Houck had a well-equipped laboratory and a good research team. He and his group have brought many new biochemical discoveries to the attention of the medical world. Houck was impressed with Dr. Klein's results. He also quickly agreed that the protease activity in commercial bromelain bore no relationship to its pharmacological action. Since his laboratory and the Dole laboratory had different strengths, we worked together on the burn debridement problem for a while and always kept in contact with each other. However, we had different opinions about the nature of the active ingredient; consequently, even though we used some techniques in common, we stopped at different points.

Eventually Houck isolated a protein with a molecular weight of about 45,000 and an isoelectric point slightly on the acid side of neutrality. This enzyme had no proteolytic activity. This protein generally occurred as a dimer (two molecules bound together) and occasionally as a trimer (three molecules bound together). The monomer (one molecule) form showed no physiological action. Since his preparation removed burn eschars, Houck and Klein named their protein preparation Escharase®. In spite of their claim that their protein preparation was the molecular entity that removed burn eschars, they were unable to demonstrate in laboratory tests just what their enzyme did. After considerable delay and questioning, the U.S. Patent Office eventually awarded them a patent for their preparation.[1]

A few years later one of the large drug companies obtained a license from Houck-Klein to produce a debriding agent based on this patent. I knew the research people at this drug company; they were competent and capable of producing protein preparations of exceptional purity. After several years of work on the burn project, they gave up. Their preparations, prepared according to the Houck-Klein method, failed to remove burn eschars.

I believe that the original Houck-Klein Escharase® preparation—which was not purified as extensively as this drug company's product, contained sufficient proxeronine as a contaminant to effectively remove burned tissue. The drug company that licensed the Houck-Klein patent did too good a job in purifying the protein; their preparations contained no proxeronine. (I was all too familiar with the dangers of "over-purifying" a natural product if one did not know the nature of the active ingredient.)

That Jack Houck had isolated and characterized a critical protein from commercial bromelain is a note worthy achievement. I merely am questioning his interpretation of what that protein did in the Klein burn eschar debridement technique. I maintain that the protein that he isolated had no direct action on the burned tissue. The fact that bromelain pastes applied to a burn eschar produced a clean separation of the eschar from the dermal layers within two hours eliminates the possibility that any protein, such as Escharase®, lysozymes or proxeroninase, is directly involved in the debriding action; proteins cannot diffuse that rapidly across a burn eschar.

One of Jerry Klein's colleagues had earlier suggested that some unidentified small molecule in commercial bromelain rapidly diffused across the eschar and activated a skin procollagenase. Since his suggestion agreed with my data, I have accepted his theory. I wish that I could give him credit for his explanation of the burn-debriding action of bromelain. However, I only heard about him from Klein; I never knew his name.[2]

Jintan Dolph Isolation of Proxeroninase

Although Klein, Houck and I cooperated together on certain practical aspects of burn treatment, we each pursued independent courses in isolating the physiologically active ingredient in commercial bromelain. From my early contacts with the Director of Princeton Laboratories, I knew that the physiologically active ingredient in commercial bromelain was not the protease bromelain. From my several years of contact with the drug company that was investigating the pharmacological application of bromelain to treat dysmenorrhea, I learned several critical facts:

1) Purified bromelain produces no pharmacological action.

2) A protein, which was not bromelain, was critical for pharmacological action.

3) The physiologically active factor was a small molecule.

4) The pharmacologically activity components adsorbed onto a polystyrene resin.

For these reasons we searched for a small molecule produced by an enzymatic reaction. During the course of this work, Mr. N. Araki of Jintan Dolph independently isolated the same protein that Jack Houck had isolated. N. Araki isolated this protein not because we thought it was the source of the biological activity but because we believed that it was a key component that produced the physiologically active ingredient.

At the time that N. Araki isolated this protein, I had not yet isolated xeronine. Not too long after this, I isolated my first traces of a volatile compound. N. Araki demonstrated that this volatile alkaloid produced the same physiological actions as commercial bromelain.

Dr. T. Shigei's Experiments

Dr. Shigei and his colleagues, formerly of the Dental College of Tokyo University, ran many experiments on the effect of various materials in preventing pulmonary edema (accumulation of serum in the lung) in rats and rabbits. Their work is outstanding in all respects. Not only did they consider and measure all of the parameters that might have affected the outcome of their experiments, but they also used large enough numbers of animals so that statistical analysis of the results leaves no question about the validity of their data.

They proved three critical points:

1. Commercial bromelain was effective in preventing laboratory induced pulmonary edema in rats and rabbits.

2. The protease bromelain was completely ineffective.

3. This previously unidentified sulfhydryl-containing protein was directly or indirectly active in preventing pulmonary edema.

Since the work of Dr. Shigei and his colleagues is so definitive, I shall describe their experiments briefly.

The Test

Pharmacologists produce a laboratory edema in test animals by injecting intravenously a critical amount of adrenaline. This amount of adrenaline has two effects: it makes capillaries leaky and it increases blood pressure. Under these conditions blood serum exudes from the capillaries, especially the lung capillaries. This causes the animal to literally drown in its own blood serum. Dr. Shigei and his colleagues adjusted the concentration of adrenaline so that a rabbit receiving only adrenaline would die within two hours. As a further test of the effectiveness of various materials in preventing or lessening this action of adrenaline, they removed and weighed the lungs of all of the animals in the experiment. The ratio of lung weight to body weight gave a quantitative measurement of the amount of serum that leaked from the lung capillaries.

The Active Ingredient is a Sulfhydryl Protein

After they had proved that something in commercial bromelain was effective in preventing pulmonary edema, they looked for the compound in commercial bromelain that was responsible for the action. Since heating commercial bromelain destroyed both the protease activity and the anti-edema action in the same ratio, they were certain that the active ingredient was a protein.

If they treated commercial bromelain with chemicals that permanently blocked any free sulfhydryl groups in the commercial bromelain, they again found that the protease activity and the physiological activity changed at the same rate. This indicated that the physiologically active protein—whatever it might be—contained a sulfhydryl group. Up to this point in their work, their results could not tell whether the active ingredient was the protease bromelain, which contains a sulfhydryl group, or another protein that also contained a free sulfhydryl group.

Dr. Shigei and his colleagues then ran an experiment that resolved this question for all times. They treated commercial bromelain to selectively destroy the catalytic site on the bromelain molecule without destroying the sulfhydryl group on bromelain or any other protein. This product, which contained no protease activity, protected the rabbits against adrenaline-induced pulmonary edema just as effectively as did the untreated sample. These data prove that commercial bromelain contains two distinctly different types of sulfhydryl-containing proteins, bromelain and some other protein molecule.

Anyone examining these well-controlled and convincing experiments cannot disagree with their conclusions; commercial bromelain contains a non-proteolytic, sulfhydryl protein that plays a critical role in curing adrenaline-induced pulmonary edema. Dr. Shigei and his colleagues deserve great credit for so meticulously carrying out these experiments. These experiments are definitive.[3]

Clinical Edema and Dr. Shigei's Work

When Tahitian noni, an excellent source of certain components of the xeronine-system, became widely available in 1995, several people with severe edema were in the hospital living in oxygen tents. One person, who was in the process of getting her affairs in order for the inevitable outcome of her health problem, began taking noni. Soon she was out of the oxygen tent and then out of the hospital. A few weeks later she returned to work and is now living a vigorous life. However, not everyone having edema has responded as dramatically.

Skeptics have pointed out that these are strictly anecdotal reports. Such "spontaneous" cures occur occasionally. They ask the very legitimate question, "Where are the hard data?"

Two excellent scientific studies prove that the xeronine-system can cure certain types of edema. Dr. Shigei's work is published.[4] Although he did his work on experimentally induced edema in rats and rabbits, his data are pertinent to human edema; they complement the anecdotal reports.

The other study was done by the first drug company that Dole cooperated with for three years. In addition to their investigation of commercial bromelain to cure dysmenorrhea, this company had planned to produce a bromelain-based product to treat edema. I have seen their data and talked with their research people. Their animal and their preliminary clinical data were impressive and exciting. They had completed an extensive toxicity test on dogs. Since they have never published the data that they developed between 1957-1961-generally drug companies do not publish their work on products that they do not bring to the market-the scientific world is unaware of these studies.

There are many other excellent research papers from Japanese universities on the effect of commercial bromelain on the treatment of experimentally induced pulmonary edema. Of these numerous papers the five or six papers published by Dr. Shigei and his talented colleagues are outstanding. Their conclusions are practically unassailable.

The Lysozymes

Lysozymes were among the first proteins to be crystallized. Scientists have studied these proteins intensively for many years. They are abundant; they occur in many unlikely places and they have no reasonable physiological function. In this section I shall suggest a new function for lysozymes. However, before I do that, let us examine a short history of lysozymes.

The "Unemployed" Enzyme

Sir Alexander Fleming (1881-1955), the bacteriologist who shared the 1945 Nobel prize with E. Chain and H. W. Florey for their work in discovering and commercializing the production of penicillin, spent much of his life searching for materials that had antibiotic action. In 1921 he discovered that tears contained a protein that caused the thick, mucous-like coating of certain bacteria to dissolve. Since the enzyme dissolved or lysed mucous, he named his enzyme lysozyme. Soon biochemists began discovering lysozymes in many tissues in our bodies, in egg whites and in plants. In the body it occurs in tears, the gastro-intestinal tract and the secretions of the cervical cells.

Many plants contain lysozymes. For example, the fig tree and papaya latex have large amounts of lysozymes in their latex tubules. The pineapple plant has a protein that corresponds to lysozymes in many of its chemical properties. In the work that I did in the 1950s I was unable to detect any lysozyme activity in this protein. Since this protein shares all of the properties of the lysozyme proteins, I am considering this protein to be a pineapple lysozyme protein in spite of my inability to demonstrate that this enzyme lyses the mucous-like coating surrounding the cells of certain bacteria. (Commercial bromelain does liquefy mucous as Dr. R. Hunter so ably demonstrated.)

The role that lysozymes play in the metabolism of an organism remains a mystery. Most scientists who have studied lysozymes assume that the role of lysozymes is to kill bacteria. The presence of a lysozyme in tears supports this suggestion; this is the function that A. Fleming suggested. I would like to suggest a new role for the lysozymes; they are the molecules that certain organelles in a cell convert into proxeroninase.

Obviously to convert a wide range of different lysozymes into the same proxeroninase molecule requires modification of the lysozyme; the lysozymes are basic proteins whereas the proxeroninase-dimer is slightly acidic. Very likely a group of enzymes in the Golgi complex accomplish this conversion.

Since my suggestion that a wide variety of different lysozymes are precursors for proxeroninase is new, scientists will want to examine the reasons for my making this suggestion. I shall start with the current belief that function of lysozymes is to kill bacteria.

Lysozymes are Not Effective Antibiotics

I am well aware that the position that I am taking goes counter to the material published in encyclopedias, general magazines and textbooks. In our body lysozymes frequently occur in secretions from various glands, such as the tear glands, the salivary glands, certain intestinal cells and cervical mucous. Generally the statement is made that the function of lysozymes is to inhibit certain bacteria. Yet lysozymes are not very effective antibiotic proteins. One of the richest sources of lysozyme is egg white. Normally an egg does not need an antibiotic since the entire formation of the egg is in a sterile environment. If the oviduct channel should become infected—as happens quite frequently these days—the egg white lysozyme does not inhibit the development of bacteria inside the egg.

Lysozymes act only on the mucous-like envelope that certain bacteria secrete around themselves. Since most bacteria do not have this mucous envelope, the lysozymes have no action against most microorganisms. The bacterium that is especially adept at secreting this mucous coating. Micrococcus leisodeikticus, would not thrive in the fluid in our eyes; this bacterium requires a sugar-rich solution. As far as I know, no one has suggested a specific bacterium that might damage the eye that is inhibited by tear-lysozyme.

Lysozymes also occur in the gastro-intestinal tract. Most bacteria cannot survive in the acid environment of the stomach. (The one egregious exception to this statement is Helicobacter pylori, the cause of most stomach ulcers; in the stomach this bacterium lives in a world of its own making.) It is highly unlikely that the body would synthesize large amounts of a protein that it does not need. Surely this protein must have some other function!

My discovery that the fasting stomach juices contain xeronine indicates that proxeroninase must have been present. On one of the following pages I shall present one of many pictures that we made on the gastric contents of volunteers.

Properties of Lysozymes

All lysozymes have four unique characteristics: 1) they are very basic proteins, 2) they all have excellent heat stability (they easily tolerate the temperatures used to pasteurize milk), 3) they all are lipophilic, and 4) most—but not all-hydrolyze the mucous-like capsule that surrounds certain bacteria.

These proteins have still another feature in common-they all crystallize readily. The most widely available crystalline protein sold today is egg-white lysozyme. Commercial companies recover crystalline egg-white lysozyme in high yields in just a few simple steps. Pineapple lysozyme also crystallizes readily. In the early days of my research, this property of pineapple lysozyme was a definite handicap. When running moving boundary electrophoretic separation of commercial bromelain at pH values above neutrality, the lysozyme crystals that formed during the separation drifted downwards like a miniature snowfall. This was fascinating to watch, but it spoiled my photographs of the moving boundaries. Later while I was fractionating commercial bromelain on gel-filtration columns, the crystals of pineapple lysozyme so completely plugged my gel filtration columns that I would have to disassemble the columns, remove (and discard) the crystals and then rerun the solution over a fresh column.

The Conversion of Lysozyme into Proxeroninase

The evidence for the conversion of different types of lysozymes into proxeroninase is indirect but still convincing. Part of the evidence is based on the changes in the concentration of pineapple lysozyme that occur as the pineapple plant develops; part is based on the ability of milk lysozyme to activate comatose grease digesting bacteria; another part is based upon an analogous protein produced by certain primitive bacteria that can produce a toxin that can kill us.

Lysozyme During Pineapple Growth

Lysozymes show an interesting change in concentration as the pineapple plant shifts from a dormant stage into an actively growing vegetative stage. The stem of the pineapple plant is where the plant stores its food reserves for future vegetative growth. When the plant is in the dormant stage, the most abundant protein in the stem is pineapple lysozyme. When the roots send a signal to the stem that sufficient moisture is available for growth, the concentration of pineapple lysozyme decreases. This decrease is probably caused by the formation of more assemblages.

Since the fruit is not a storage organ for food for current plant vegetative growth, good quality fruit do not have even a trace of free lysozyme. The fruits have super-assemblages, which form as the fruit develops; it has no need to make additional assemblages in response to changes in the moisture level.

It is interesting that two food storage systems for future cell growth, egg whites and the pineapple stem, both contain large amounts of lysozyme.

Lysozyme Peps-Up Sick Bacteria

The most convincing indication that organisms have the tools to convert lysozymes into proxeroninase comes from the examples that I mentioned in Chapter 3. Apparently fatty peroxides prevent bacteria (and us as well?) from forming proxeroninase. However, after I introduced milk lysozyme—a foreign protein as far as bacteria are concerned—into the bacterial cells, the metabolism of the previously comatose bacterial cells increased enormously.

The Hypothesis: Lysozymes and Proxeroninase

The experiments that we reported in a book published by Technicon Autoanalyzer®,Inc.[5] contains data that we developed while we were evaluating the value of the Technicon Autoanalyzer® as a tool to aid in standardizing the proteolytic activity of commercial bromelain and to study the properties of protease enzymes.

Our data contained some unexpected results that I was unable to explain at that time. To understand the significance of the results, we have to understand something about the proteins that we used to test the potency of commercial bromelain. Even before Dole began producing commercial bromelain in 1955 potential customers for bromelain advised me about the difficulty of properly standardizing enzymes. They mentioned that different batches of protein from the same supplier frequently varied greatly in digestibility. To reduce this variability they suggested that I find a batch of protein that commercial bromelain digested particularly well and buy enough protein from that same batch top last for several decades of test work.

The two proteins that we used at Dole for all of our assay work over a period of thirty years were a high-grade gelatin and a special grade of casein, Hammerstan casein. The difference in the digestibility of different batches of Hammerstan casein was one of the topics covered in our research paper. Before we bought the particular batch of casein that we would use over the next several decades, we asked the biochemical processing companies to send us a small sample of the purified casein that they could supply in 20-pound lots. From the seven samples that producers of Hammerstan casein sent to us for evaluation, we selected the casein that commercial bromelain digested most completely.

Although the primary market for The Technicon Autolyzer® were hospital laboratories, we modified this machine so that we could study any parameter involved in enzyme studies. Testing the proteolytic activity of any enzyme was our primary purpose for buying this machine. The assay that I developed was simple, fast and highly reproducible. Once we had prepared solutions of the seven samples of casein, determining how other enzymes would digest these different batches of casein took very little extra time.

We compared the digestibility of seven brands of casein by three enzymes, bromelain, papain and ficin. The results surprised us. With papain and ficin it made no difference which brand of casein we used; all seven brands of casein showed the same degree of digestibility. In contrast to these results, bromelain digested each of the seven brands of casein to different degrees. These values varied by as much as 15%.

The casein digestion test did not rank samples of commercial bromelain samples in the same order as did our gelatin digestion test. Obviously some unknown and variable component of "highly purified casein" was reacting with some unknown and variable material in commercial bromelain.

These data led to several important conclusions:

1. Although both the gelatin digestion test (GDU) and the casein digestion test (CDU) both measure the ability of an enzyme to digest proteins, the casein digestion test also measures some other factor. (Much later I realized that this other factor was milk lysozyme.)

2. Different batches of "purified and standardized" caseins contained various amounts of an associated material that reacted with some unknown material that occurred in commercial bromelain. (Much later I realized that the unknown material in the casein was milk lysozyme and the unknown material in commercial bromelain that reacted with the proxeroninase made from milk lysozyme was proxeronine.)

3. This unknown material in commercial bromelain did not occur in detectable amounts in the commercial samples of papain or ficin that we tested.

Additional work showed that the associated material in casein was a protein with excellent heat stability and a high isoelectric point. Boiling the casein or exposing the casein to a high pH completely destroyed the activity of this protein. These properties match those of milk lysozyme.

Our previous work at Jintan Dolph had shown that the critical enzyme in the biosynthesis of xeronine was a protein dimer that had an isoelectric point slightly on the acid side of neutrality. Therefore something in commercial bromelain must have converted milk-lysozyme, which has a basic isoelectric point, into proxeroninase, which has an isoelectric point slightly on the acid side of neutrality.

I am suggesting that my original process for isolating commercial bromelain isolated both assemblages and some intact Golgi complexes. If we assume that the early batches of commercial bromelain contained Golgi complexes, then the Golgi complexes could have converted the milk lysozyme contained in the Hammerstan casein into proxeroninase. The Golgi complex could then package this with proxeronine from commercial bromelain to produce a xeronine-assemblage that would liberate free xeronine. Free xeronine can release stoichiometrically a peptide from kappa casein. (Chapter 4) This would show up in our automatic analytical technique as increased digestion of the casein. We would calculate this as enzymatic activity, even though a portion of the peptides were produced by a stoichiometric reaction.[6]

Shortage of Lysozymes?

As far as I know, no research worker or doctor has recognized a health problem that might be attributable to a lack of lysozyme. Lysozymes occur in many organs and tissues in the body. What the body generally lacks is a supply of proxeronine.

In contrast to people, certain grease-digesting bacteria frequently lack lysozymes. They lack lysozymes not because they do not synthesize lysozymes but because the fatty peroxides in grease destroy the lysozyme. Everyone knows that fatty peroxides rank as probably the most potent of natural toxins. Yet research workers have not identified the precise place in the metabolic cycle where this inhibition occurs. I am suggesting that fatty peroxide block one of the components of the xeronine-system. Our work with grease bacteria indicates that the molecule affected is lysozyme. However, our work does not indicate the precise method of inhibition.

Our data, which we obtained from both laboratory tests as well as on commercial sewage plants, show that no amount of added proxeronine will activate comatose grease digesting bacteria. The bacteria have no functioning lysozyme. Hence they are unable to form proxeroninase and then xeronine.

When we did this work in the early 1980s, what surprised me was the very small amount of active ingredients that we had to add to the system to produce an unbelievable amount of bacterial activation. I made some rough calculations about the number of bacteria that were present in the entire sewage system that we were treating effectively. I then calculated how many molecules of potential xeronine we were adding to the system. If I assumed that a single molecule of xeronine could convert a comatose grease digesting bacterium into an actively metabolizing bacterium—this is the most conservative suggestion possible—then we were adding much less than one hundredth to one thousandth the amount of material that would have been necessary to activate all of the bacteria. No wonder the experts in the wastewater treatment system were skeptical about our reports!

We need a plausible hypothesis to explain how small amounts of active material can treat so many bacteria. Several very different hypotheses based on the most recent concepts in gene transcription and polypeptide folding might explain the results. However, we have two problems. We have no experimental data in this area and the new theories are still in the process of being developed. Perhaps our experience with comatose grease digesting bacteria can provide the microbiologists with new tools and concepts.

The comatose grease bacteria problem may provide an ideal subject to study to expand our basic ideas about the metabolism of the cell. We know that these bacteria have a lysozyme problem. We know that adding a combination of milk lysozyme—a foreign protein as far as the bacterial cells are concerned—and a source of proxeronine solves this problem. It solves this problem permanently as far as these bacteria are concerned. I believe that solving this problem will have implications for human health.

Chapter Summary

• All of the molecules that are required to synthesize xeronine are packaged by the Golgi complex into a package that I am calling the xeronine-assemblage.

o One critical enzyme in this assemblage is inactive proxeroninase.

o The monomer form of proxeroninase is probably the form that is packaged in the xeronine-assemblage. Activation of this enzyme requires a critical amount of a divalent cation, such as calcium.

o The precursor protein that becomes the proxeroninase monomer is probably lysozyme.

o Enzymes in the Golgi complex apparently have the ability to convert different types of lysozymes into the monomer form of proxeroninase

• Proxeronine, the molecule that the enzyme proxeroninase converts into xeronine, is probably synthesized by enzymes—which have yet to be isolated and studied—in the smooth endoplasmic reticulum in plants.

o People probably depend upon an external source of proxeronine.

• Evidence for the conversion of lysozymes into proxeroninase is indirect but convincing.

o Our report on the anomalous action of commercial bromelain in digesting casein indicates that:

* In protease digestion studies, which measure the production of peptides from proteins, part of the production of peptides is stoichiometric rather than enzymatic.

* Only xeronine produces a stoichiometric liberation of a peptide from casein.

o My U.S. Patent on the activation of comatose grease bacteria.

• In comatose grease digesting bacteria, proxeronine by itself fails to stimulate the bacteria. For stimulation lysozyme must be added to the system. The milk lysozyme that we used is a foreign protein as far as bacteria are concerned. Yet they can use it.

ENDNOTES

[1] U.S.Patent 4,226,854

[2] Active proxeroninase consists of two monomers, in other words a "dimer." Both Jack Houck and N. Araki of Jintan Dolph demonstrated that the dimer form was active whereas the monomer form was inactive. Quite frequently when proteins dimerize and become bound together, they do so by forming "salt" bridges between acid groups (in this particular case between carboxyl groups). The bridging atom is generally calcium or magnesium atoms.

I demonstrated (U.S. Patent 1987) that the amount of calcium was very critical. Either too much or too little calcium inhibited the action of proxeroninase. Inhibition-activation curves, such as those I found by varying the concentration of calcium from zero to high levels, are typical of calcium bridging actions. With too much or too little calcium no bridging can occur.

The discovery of the importance of the calcium concentration explains many of the empirical procedures that we developed for recovering commercial bromelain from pineapple stem juice. During the storage stage of metabolism in the pineapple plant, a high available level of calcium ions prevents the formation of active proxeroninase.

[3] Understandably with this unexpected discovery Dr. Shigei was intensely interested in learning just what role a foreign protein containing a critical SH group could possibly have in producing such dramatic reactions in the body; nothing like this had ever been reported before. We discussed this problem. I mentioned that I had also discovered a sulfhydryl reaction in commercial bromelain that was completely unrelated to the sulfhydryl containing protease bromelain. However, at that time I too had no clue about the function of this sulfhydryl protein.

While I was writing this chapter, I initially relied on my memory of the conversations that we had. As I was writing about the technique that Dr. Shigei used, something that I wrote did not make sound physiological sense. If Dr. Shigei had injected a bromelain solution into the vein of a rabbit, the liver would have cleared all of the bromelain proteins in the first passage of the blood through the liver. Therefore, there should have been no sulfhydryl-protein effect; yet the effect was dramatic and incontrovertible. I wondered whether I had remembered correctly and that the injection was intra-peritoneal or intra-muscular. I checked the original article in a Japanese journal. The injection was indeed intravenous, as I had remembered.

I also found that Dr. Shigei had anticipated the problem that had bothered me and that he had arranged his experimental procedure to circumvent it. If he gave the intravenous bromelain injection five minutes before the adrenaline injection-a time sufficient for the blood to circulate through the liver several times-commercial bromelain provided absolutely no protection against pulmonary edema. By the time that he injected the adrenaline, the liver had stripped out the foreign proteins. Thus these rabbits had no available pineapple colloids to protect them. To circumvent this problem he gave the adrenaline injection first. Then one minute after the adrenaline injection, he gave the bromelain injection.

[4] Shigei, T., Sakuma, A., Nishiwaki, T. A study on thee Protective Effect Bromelain, Crude Pineapple Proteases Against Plimonary Edema. Jap. Heart J. 8: 718-720,(1967)

Mineshitam S, and Shigei, T. Prevention of Adrenaline-Induced Pulmonary Edema by Stemn Bromelain and Analysis of the Hemdynamic Changes, Jap. Y. Pharmacol. 20: 373-381 (1970).

Katori, R.; Mineshita, S., Shigei, T. Depletion of Kinogen I by Stem Bromelain and its Significances in Preventing of Adrenaline Induced Pulmonary Edema in Rats, Adv. Exp> Med. Biol.8: 273-282)1970)

[5] Ralph M. Heinicke, Charles Larson, Oscar Levand and Mildred McCarter The Study of the Use of the AutoAnalyzer on Proteases. In Automation in Anal. Chem., Mediad Inc. 1968, 207-212

[6] The assemblage picture in the pineapple plant is quite complicated. In commercial bromelain there are about five assemblages in the running gel of a disk electrophoretic separation and at least two large assemblages in the stacking gel. These are too large to enter the running gel. However, with time and the proper stimulus they too open and eventually disappear completely. Since this is a subject that is of interest only to specialists working in this field, let us consider just one band, the lysozyme band.

Not a trace of a lysozyme band appears until the third group of assemblages in the running gel opens. The difference between two preparations can be very striking. The two preparations may appear identical except for one striking difference, the presence or absence of the lysozyme band. This is not a gradual appearance of the lysozyme band. The band is either there or it is not. At a still later stage in the opening of the assemblages, the lysozyme band disappears. At this time about three discrete protein bands appear.

Several features about the lysozyme band are interesting.

1) It is the first pure protein band to appear during a sequence of electrophoretic runs made of the acetone precipitates formed from pineapple stems harvested at different stages in the change from the storage stage to the active vegetative stage.

2) It is present in much larger amounts than the other pure protein bands that appear later3)

4) It decreases in amounts as more of the assemblages continue to open, that is as the change progresses from storage stage to active vegetative stage. This decrease suggests that it is either being used in another reaction—namely in the formation of additional assemblages—or that it is being hydrolyzed to produce free amino acids for growth.

CHAPTER 8

Xeronine, the Japanese Puffer Fish, and More

Tetrodotoxin is the most poisonous natural product known. It is an alkaloid found in the puffer fish, the blue octopus and a few salamanders. That tetrodotoxin is so unbelievably toxic indicates that this material blocks a most important regulator molecule in the body. Until my discovery of xeronine, no one knew what regulatory molecule tetrodotoxin was blocking or what this regulatory molecule did in the body. However, before I discuss tetrodotoxin and xeronine, I would like to review the confusion that surrounds the chemical term alkaloid.

Alkaloids

In the early days of organic chemistry everyone knew what an alkaloid was; there was no ambiguity. An alkaloid was a basic, complex nitrogen-containing compound that only some plants produced. This definition was amplified by mentioning that most alkaloids tasted bitter and altered the mental state of people who used the alkaloid internally.

When R. B. Woodward worked out the structure of tetrodotoxin, which occurs in certain tissues of the puffer fish, he classified it as an alkaloid. Because of his prestige, no one questioned his right to call a basic, nitrogen-containing compound an alkaloid. Unfortunately, classifying tetrodotoxin as an alkaloid forced scientists to redefine alkaloids since obviously a puffer fish is not a plant. The modern chemical definition of an alkaloid leaves out the restriction that only certain plants can produce alkaloids. As a result of this change, the definition of an alkaloid is so broad that a large number of compounds that we know are not alkaloids would be included in the alkaloid group. For example, serotonin and the purines and pyrimidines, which are the building blocks of nucleic acids, fit the modern definition of an alkaloid. However, by tacit agreement chemists and physiologists do not classify these important biochemical compounds as alkaloids.

A chemist who is interested only in the chemistry of xeronine would definitely classify xeronine as an alkaloid. However, physiologists, who are interested in what various biochemical compounds do in the body, would demur at this classification; they would point out that since scientists have agreed not to call serotonin an alkaloid, scientists should exclude xeronine from the alkaloid class for exactly the same reason. No basic, nitrogen-containing biochemical that is absolutely essential for the functioning of organisms should be classified as an alkaloid.

Since many years will pass before scientists once again revise their definition of alkaloids, anyone interested in xeronine should clearly know the difference in structure and function between alkaloids and xeronine. The best way to appreciate this difference is to understand why only certain plants make alkaloids.

Plants Have an Excretory Problem

All tissues depend upon a group of signals to coordinate the various activities in a cell or a tissue. Once the signal (agonist) has performed its task, the cell destroys the agonist. It does this either by breaking down the agonist or adding extraneous groups to inactivate it.

Our bodies dispose of the molecular trash from the inactivated agonists by excreting the residue in urine, sweat, or feces. For example one of the breakdown products of serotonin in our bodies is beta indole acetic acid. Most people know this formidable sounding compound as "a gardener's green thumb." It appears in the sweat of hard working gardeners and promotes the rooting of plant cuttings. It also appears in the urine. Too much of this breakdown product can cause problems for plants. This is why gardeners try to prevent the neighborhood dogs from sniffing and adding their own scents to their rose bushes.

Plants do not have the luxury of excretory systems. Since their metabolism is similar to ours, they too must get rid of the inactivated agonists. They have several options. They can break down the inactivated signal molecule and recycle the components parts; many plant use this disposal method. However, this disposal method requires energy. If the regulator molecule does not contain any valuable elements, such as nitrogen, then the "cheapest way" for a plant to dispose of these regulators is to insolubilize them and dump them outside of the cell wall. If the tissue happens to be a leaf, then when the trash load becomes too burdensome, the tree sheds its leaves and starts over again with fresh leaves. If the tissue happens to be a stem, such as a tree trunk, it dumps the polymerized regulator (lignin) into the heartwood on the inner side of the actively growing tissue and into the bark on the outer side.[1] Of course the barks falls off eventually just as the leaves do. On the other hand, the lignin in the heart wood remains there forever. This part of the tree is not very active metabolically.

If the regulator contains nitrogen, a very precious element as far the plant is concerned, the plant always recycles the nitrogen-containing molecule. Most plants use the "expensive method" of first inactivating the regulator and then breaking down the trashed regulator and storing the nitrogen in some form for future use.

A few group of plants have devised a different method for inactivating their nitrogen containing regulators and then recycling the nitrogen. They add a few blocking agents to the molecule and store the inactivated regulator in special cells. We call such "inactivated-regulators" alkaloids; the plants consider them a valuable source of nitrogen. Frequently the plant stores these inactive regulators in a latex or resin in special cells or ducts. The purpose of this latex is to furnish the developing seeds with the extra nitrogen they require to build proteins. The seeds never contain even traces of alkaloid.

I would like to suggest that we define an alkaloid in terms of its function. For example: an alkaloid is a nitrogen containing plant regulator that the plant has inactivated by attaching a variety of substituents. This definition could be expanded by mentioning that although these materials have no regulatory effect in plants, they frequently cause strong physiological actions in people. Also they generally have a bitter flavor.

According to this definition, xeronine definitely would not be an alkaloid (although if the plant converted it into an inactive form and stored this inactive form, then the inactive form would be an alkaloid). From this definition I also do not believe that tetrodotoxin should be considered an alkaloid. However, by most scientists' definition, tetrodotoxin is viewed as an alkaloid, and therefore I will refer to it as such for the remainder of the chapter. Now let us learn more about the Japanese Puffer Fish.

Tetrodotoxin and the Puffer Fish

In Japan, before 1976, one of the great and unique culinary adventures for the Japanese as well as for a few adventuresome foreign tourists was a visit to a fugu restaurant. Even today any visitor to Japan who roams the side streets of one of the large cities at night will be struck by the colorful neon signs of restaurants specializing in dishes made from the fugu fish. In the U.S. we call the fugu fish the puffer fish. We desecrate the glories of that fish by converting it into trashy tourist lanterns.

In the good old days a fugu restaurant served primarily just two dishes, sashimi made from thin slices of the muscle of the fish and a soup. The sashimi is good but relatively mild; it is still available today; it served primarily as a contrast to the soup. The soup or broth was the primary reason for visiting a fugu restaurant. It had bite, character and just a dash of danger.

Only carefully trained and licensed cooks were allowed to make the broth. As a base they would toss in fugu heads and bits of fugu meat; this served as the foundation for the real treat. What made the dish particularly exciting were carefully washed, examined and weighed bits of the ovaries and intestinal linings of the fish. These tissues contain tetrodotoxin, the most poisonous substance known to man. The proper amount of this poison added to the soup produces a pleasant numbness in the lips, then in the tongue and occasionally in the throat. The numbness should never go beyond the throat. More than that can lead to permanent numbness.

During one of my stays in Japan, the inevitable disaster happened. In 1976 the National Living Treasure of the Japanese stage, Mitsui-san, gave a particularly brilliant kabuki performance. Sitting through a kabuki performance, like going to a fugu restaurant, is an acquired taste; a good kabuki performance lasts from four to seven hours and is enlivened by much shouted encouragements and encomiums from the audience. After the performance, as a reward for sitting so long, everyone must go to a sake bar or a fugu restaurant. This is especially true of the performer.

After one particularly brilliant performance, Mitsui-san stopped by his favorite fugu restaurant. He asked the cook to prepare his usual fugu soup and sashimi. Believing that his excellent performance that night deserved something special, Mitsui-san asked the cook to put in an extra bit of the ovaries of the fish into his soup. The poor cook demurred, pointing out that he was already adding the maximum amount allowed. However, when a National Living Treasure, who is still reveling in his performance of Chisangura, roles his eyes inward and thunders out his request, a mere cook can only obey.

A few hours later the career of Mitsui-san came to a crashing end. Since the Japanese government was upset about losing one of their National Living Treasures, they banned forever the serving of fugu soup containing traces of tetrodotoxin. Thus, one of the exciting gustatory treats of Japan is no more.

Although as a lover of fugu soup I regret this decision, as a bio-chemist I believe that this was the correct action. Tetrodotoxin is not a substance made by the puffer fish; it is a substance produced by certain microorganisms that works its way up through the food chain and finally accumulates in certain tissues of the puffer fish. As a result some fugu fish contain moderate amounts of tetrodotoxin whereas other fugu fish contain more than the average. Thus each dish is a bit of a gamble. This increases the pleasure of eating the soup. On the whole, since most cooks wish to have a clientele of living customers, the risks were miniscule.

The fugu fish is the most widely known source of tetrodotoxin. Some other animals that also accumulate this poison are a salamander in California, the blue octopus and the beaver. In the 1970s a group of young men were playing around the barrier reef in Australia. As a joke one of the men picked up a blue octopus, a delightful, timid and pretty creature, and threw it at his friend. Normally being hit by a thrown octo-pus is an interesting experience, which is neither dangerous nor particularly frightening. Unfortunately, this particular octopus must have been feeding on something that contained tetrodotoxin. The poor youth died within a few minutes.

Another well-documented death from tetrodotoxin is that of James Bond. In the last chapter of one of the James Bond novels, Bond, is being shadowed by a foreign agent carrying an umbrella. (In Britain whether it is raining or not, all well-appointed gentlemen carry umbrellas.) This particular umbrella contained at its tip a pin that had been dipped in a concentrated solution of tetrodotoxin. The agent gently stuck Bond with the tip of his umbrella and then disappeared.

By the time that Bond realized that he had been stuck with something, the poison had already begun to act. Bond went into a violent convulsion and collapsed on the street. If the coroner had performed an autopsy on Bond, he would have found nothing in Bond's body that might have caused his death. Thus ended the book.

Fortunately for the loyal followers of Bond, in the opening chapter of the next book a biochemist happens to be in the crowd that had gathered around the convulsing, dying Bond. (Occasionally biochemists do have literary value.) This biochemist immediately recognizes that nothing except tetrodotoxin could cause such a violent death. He also knows that if he keeps James Bond's blood aerated and circulating, that possibly Bond might survive. Which he does and Bond lives to figure in many more tales.

If I had happened to be carrying my trusty syringe and a sample of xeronine, I could have resuscitated James Bond more quickly and with less effort. Besides, James Bond would have felt better. But that is getting ahead of the story.

The Tetrodotoxin-Xeronine Connection

I became interested in a possible connection between tetrodotoxin and the xeronine-system in a strange way. While I was working as a guest research worker in Dr. Paul Scheuer's laboratory in Hawaii, I attended a series of lectures that he was giving on marine toxins. What particularly intrigued me was that many of the techniques that his group used to isolate their marine toxins were similar to the techniques that I had been using to isolate the pharmacologically active ingredients from pineapple plants.

The parallels between the physical and biochemical properties of tetrodotoxin and xeronine are too close to be fortuitous. Tetrodotoxin, the most poisonous substance known, is toxic at such low levels that no chemical tests can detect it in the body; xeronine exerts its physiological effect at very low levels. Both tetrodotoxin and xeronine lack an interesting UV spectrum. From these parallelisms, I reasoned that tetrodotoxin must block the protein receptors for xeronine. I reached this conclusion from an old pharmacological rule. This rule states that if a molecule acts as a super-toxin, then this chemical must have a structure that is similar to a molecule in the body that is necessary for certain critical metabolic reactions.

There can be no question about the toxicity of tetrodotoxin; tetrodotoxin is the ultimate super-toxin. One mg of tetrodotoxin—an insignificant amount of material—can kill over a million mice! It does not just kill the mice; it kills them spectacularly. Shortly after being injected with a small amount of a very, very dilute solution of tetrodotoxin, the mouse becomes excited and then loses control of its muscles. It runs, it stumbles and it jumps around the cage. Finally in one last desperate leap, it jumps into the air and lands on its back as a dead mouse.

Since not too many of us have worked with tetrodotoxin, we may not really appreciate its extreme toxicity. We all know about the toxicity of cyanide. We consider this to be quite a powerful poison. Yet tetrodotoxin is more than a thousand times more toxic! When I first started working with tetrodotoxin, no chemical company in the U.S. sold tetrodotoxin. Therefore, I wrote to the chemist in Japan who had originally crystallized tetrodotoxin. Although he was willing to sell me five mg of tetrodotoxin, we did not know how we could ship the sample from Japan to Honolulu. Neither the mail services nor the package express companies would agree to handle the material. Finally this professor persuaded a friend of his, who was a pilot for Japan Air Lines, to assume responsibility for the package. The pilot agreed providing the material was securely packaged.

The package was a true marvel to see. Five mg of tetrodotoxin is not much material. You can see it and you can weigh it on a sensitive microbalance. But you can easily lose 5 mg of material during ordinary packaging procedures. This miniscule amount of material was placed in a two-inch long heavy walled glass tubing that was fused at both ends. This tubing was then placed in the center of heavy pint sized metal can that was filled with bentonite. This can was then placed inside a four-inch diameter cast iron pipe that was filled with more bentonite and was then capped at both ends. The iron pipe was then encased in a custom-built, heavy wooden crate that had a large base that enabled the pilot to bolt the package onto the floor of the cabin between the pilot and the co-pilot. The packaging weighed 45 pounds! Today any eye surgeon can buy dilute solutions of tetrodotoxin from his local hospital supply source.

Xeronine, the Perfect Antidote for Tetrodotoxin

After I had worked out a method for isolating and crystallizing xeronine, I knew that I would have to prove that this material, which I named xeronine, was the active ingredient that was ultimately responsible for the many truly unbelievable actions of commercial bromelain. From the wide variety of health problems that commercial bromelain had cured, I knew that the active ingredient formed from commercial bromelain must be acting at a very basic level in a cell. Also since tetrodotoxin was the most toxic substance known, I reasoned that this also must act at a very basic cell level.

If xeronine could block the extraordinary toxicity of tetrodotoxin, then this would be very strong evidence of two things. One, that xeronine could block tetrodotoxin from adsorbing onto certain critical receptor proteins and two, that certain of the receptor proteins for xeronine were absolutely critical for the survival of the organism.

Crystalline xeronine has a half-life of no more than a day; therefore, I could not prepare a large batch of crystalline xeronine and then run all of my experiments on this batch of crystals over a period of a week. I could prepare crystalline xeronine in about five hours. Therefore, to run animal tests with solutions of crystalline xeronine I would prepare the xeronine crystals in the morning and run the tests in the afternoon. Any solutions left over from the experiments, I discarded since they would quickly become worthless.

The Crucial Tetrodotoxin Test

For my first crucial test I started the isolation of crystalline xeronine in the morning and had it ready for testing by three o'clock in the afternoon. I divided twenty-four mice into four matched groups. One group was my control. They received only an intra-peritoneal injection of saline solution. Another group was my tetrodotoxin control group. They received a dose of tetrodotoxin that would kill them within less than a minute. Another group was my xeronine control group. They received an amount of xeronine that I estimated would be sufficient to protect them from tetrodotoxin poisoning. The last group received a mixture of xeronine and the toxic dose of tetrodotoxin.

This was my first test of a combination of xeronine and tetrodotoxin. It was successful beyond belief. All of the tetrodotoxin treated mice died a violent death within less than a minute. This, of course, was the expected result. All of the saline control mice survived, as they should have. When I returned them to their cages, they all dug into the wood shavings where they waited in misery for a half an hour until the discomfort from the saline injection wore off. This is the normal behavior for a laboratory mouse that has received a half-millimeter intra-peritoneal injection of saline. As I had hoped, all of the mice that received the combination of xeronine and tetrodotoxin survived. This experiment was the first time that anyone had demonstrated an effective antidote for tetrodotoxin poisoning.

Besides this most satisfying outcome from this experiment, something else happened that was completely unexpected. Both the xeronine-control mice and the xeronine-tetrodotoxin mice behaved similarly. Their behavior was most unusual. When I returned them to the cage, none of these mice buried themselves in the wood shavings. They were comfortable, curious, very active mice. In fact their behavior was so striking, that one of my colleagues, who was unaware of the experiment that I had just performed, asked me where I had bought such active and intelligent mice!

After I finished this experiment, I still had several ml of the xeronine solution left over. I knew that no matter what I did with it, the next day the xeronine solution would be black and would be worthless. Rather than throwing it away, I drank it. Nothing amazing seemed to happen. Since this was at the end of the working day, I went home, had dinner and did some work around the yard. Then I came in and started my long postponed intellectual chore, reading Chemical Abstracts.

Only a chemist can appreciate the necessity of reading page after page of Chemical Abstracts and the boredom of reading page after page of articles that may or may not contain something that might be pertinent. Normally I can only read several pages before I find my attention wandering. That night I eventually thought that I had done enough reading in Chemical Abstracts. When I looked at my watch, I was surprised to find that it was well past three in the morning. I had been reading Chemical Abstracts for over four hours. This is something that I had never done before or since!

During the next several days I continued to study the interactions of tetrodotoxin and xeronine on mice. During this time I found several additional interesting and unexpected findings. Normally when running mouse experiments, one uses mice of the same age, weight and sex. Since I was going through my supply of mice at a rapid rate, I used leftover mice from the experiments that other members of the department were running. This meant that I occasionally used male and female mice in the same experiment.

Anyone who has worked with laboratory mice knows that the male mouse is a considerate creature. If a male mouse suggests a little sexual activity to a female mouse, she may either agree or she may tell the male mouse that this is not the appropriate time. In that case he accepts her decision and finds something else to do.

In one of my experiments I happened by chance to have some female mice as the saline control mice and male mice as the xeronine treated mice. When I returned the mice to the common cage, the saline treated female mice dug into the wood shavings to wait until the effects of the injection wore off. By contrast, the xeronine treated males needed no recuperation period. They were not only interested in exploring the cage, but they were also particularly interested in locating the female mice and suggesting a little sex. When the female mice suggested that this was not the proper time, the males did not take no for an answer. They vigorously forced their attention on the females to such an extent that the female mice would squeal loudly in protest.

This was an interesting result. I decided to reverse the treatments. In the next test I made the male mice my saline controls and gave the female mice the xeronine treatment. When I returned the mice to the cage, the male mice dug into the wood shavings for the required rest period. However, the xeronine treated female mice needed no rest period. They dug into the wood shaving and uncovered the male mice. Then they began sniffing all around the male. I know that a scientist should not anthropomorphize his experiments. Yet I do feel strongly that these female mice were intensely interested in something that the poor male mice were not in a condition to deliver.

I ran still other experiments. I found that the maximum time that pretreatment of a mouse with xeronine would protect the mouse from tetrodotoxin poisoning was approximately ten minutes. This indicates that xeronine must adsorb onto a site and then sometime later desorb from the site. This also suggests that the half-life of xeronine in the body is short. Although these are very preliminary results, they suggest important future experiments that someone should run.

I also found that if I gave the tetrodotoxin first and then gave the xeronine about twenty seconds later, the mice died but it took them about three times as long to die. This indicates that tetrodotoxin and xeronine must have almost identical shapes. Once either xeronine or tetrodotoxin adsorbs onto the critical receptors, the adsorption is so firm, that the other molecule does not displace it readily.

Building a Living Cell

If a team consisting of a structural engineer, a chemist and a microbiologist were given an assortment of all the amino acids, all the complex carbohydrate compounds, all of the nucleic acids, all of the lipids, all of the vitamins, etc., that the biochemists know constitute the constituents of a cell and were then told to build a cell, they could build a structure that looked like a cell. They could—and in fact do so frequently—make cell membranes, make an assortment of organelles and stuff them with enzymes purchased from biochemical supply companies and they could build a nucleus. The problem with this beautifully constructed cell is that it would not work. The structural engineer would point out that although he had enough building blocks for a structure, he could not give the cell movement. A cell that cannot perform work is a comatose or a dead cell.

From strictly mechanical considerations, the engineer would point out that he needed to supplement his supply of building blocks with a short, rigid girder. This would have to be a structure that cannot be stretched, compressed or twisted. Such a structure does not exist among the classical components of a cell. Fortunately for his dilemma, my proposed structure for xeronine is exactly the type of structure that he would need to put movement into a cell. Much of the movement that he would be interested in occurs at the molecular level. For example all enzymes produce movement at the molecular level. This movement, which involves great forces applied to limited areas, is so slight that we would not detect any visible movement even with our newer types of microscopes.[2]

Deducing the Structure of Xeronine

At the present time no one has made a complete chemical and physical analysis of xeronine. Nevertheless, I have sufficient data to enable me to suggest a structure for xeronine. Later research work can confirm or correct these initial suggestions.

My four primary clues for deducing the structure of xeronine are:

1) The xeronine-tetrodotoxin connection.

That these two molecules must have similar shapes enabled me to use Woodwards's structural formula for tetrodotoxin as a starting point for working out the structure of xeronine.

2) The volatility of xeronine.

That xeronine is volatile places strong constraints on possible molecular configurations for xeronine.

3) The UV spectrum of solutions of crystalline xeronine.

That xeronine, similar to tetrodotoxin, has only end absorption in the UV spectrum further confirms the basic similarity in structure between the two molecules.

4) The extreme lability (or instability) of xeronine.

That xeronine is very labile indicates that one of the atoms in the molecule can become a free radical. (Tetrodotoxin is quite stable.)

Of these four clues the xeronine-tetrodotoxin connection is the most important. Although tetrodotoxin and xeronine must have essentially the same three-dimensional shape, these structures must differ in several critical respects. The physical and the chemical properties of tetrodotoxin and xeronine are distinct; no one could possibly confuse tetrodotoxin and xeronine.

From these clues I have deduced a structure for xeronine that meets all of the present observations about this molecule. Although future work might suggest some changes in the structure that I proposed, I feel confident my proposed structure for xeronine is essentially correct. For anyone interested in my proposed structure and for more details about how I arrived at the structure please see the Appendix.

Chapter Summary

• Studies with tetrodotoxin played a key role in working out the physiological properties of xeronine
    o Tetrodotoxin, an alkaloid accumulated by certain creatures from the food chain is the most toxic substance for mammals ever discovered.

• Tetrodotoxin kills by blocking the normal transmission of certain nerve signals to the muscles. (It blocks other reactions as well.)

• Xeronine completely blocks a toxic dose of tetrodotoxin in mice. mice. This indicates that xeronine and tetrodotoxin adsorb onto the same adsorption site on certain receptor proteins. It also indicates that xeronine, being the normal body alkaloid, absorbs more readily and more strongly than the slightly differently shaped tetrodotoxin.

• Physiological Action of Xeronine
    o Stimulates the metabolism of mice (and people)

• Some of the likely receptors for xeronine are:
> * The "good feeling" receptor protein for endorphin.
> * The receptor protein for the sex hormones.
> * Probably other still to be identified protein receptor sites.
> * Chemistry of xeronine
>> o The structure is based on Woodward's structure for tetrodotoxin
>> o Xeronine structure differs from tetrodotoxin

• Has a trivalent-nitrogen whereas tetrodotoxin has a quaternary-nitrogen.

• Has one or two additional three-dimensional "cages."

• Xeronine is very labile or unstable whereas tetrodotoxin is very stable.The reactive atom is probably an oxygen atom that readily forms a free radical.

ENDNOTES

[1] Plants have an analog, dihydroxy-cinnamic acid, of adrenaline that does not contain nitrogen. The plant cell inactivates this hormone by adding a methyl group onto one of the OH groups forming ferulic acid. This polymerizes to form lignin in a series of steps.

[2] Understanding how an enzyme works is simple. In essence the enzyme clamps the molecule that it is going to modify into a vice. It then grabs hold of two parts of the fixed molecule and starts pulling it apart. During the stretching operation at a certain point the bonds holding the molecule together become so weak, that either the enzyme itself or the enzyme with the help of a cooperating enzyme can slip different types of atoms into the weakened bond. This forms a new molecule; this is an enzymatic reaction. All enzymatic reactions are simply mechanical or elementary electrical reactions.

The energy to perform this work comes from the tremendous amount of random energy in water. To direct and control the enormous amount of random energy contained in water, the enzyme uses the leverage principle with the xeronine molecule acting as a sturdy fulcrum. Since so many reactions in a cell require molecular motion, many reactions require that xeronine be part of the system.

The mechanism whereby the enzyme obtains energy from water is important and exciting. This is a new subject and will require several books to fully develop the theory. For the present book, all that we need to know is that a protein—properly fitted with an assortment of accoutrements such as hormones and "active sites"—is a device for focusing the random energy in water to do useful work.

CHAPTER 9

Poisons and Preservatives Supply Clues About the Xeronine-System

Poisons fascinate people for many reasons. Some of these are practical, such as killing worms chewing holes in your favorite apples; some are political, such as the Borgias's subtle way of reducing the effectiveness of their competitors by serving foods containing arsenic or poisonous mushrooms, some are literary, such as the black humor play Arsenic and Old Lace and some are scientific, such as using poisons to provide clues about the nature of complex biochemical reactions.

The xeronine-system is a complex system. It contains a number of different enzymes and molecules that the enzymes work on. These enzymatic reactions occur in a definite sequence. When a biochemist adds a chemical to the system and it inhibits the enzyme, the molecule is called an inhibitor. Ordinary people call it a poison. If the biochemist knows from other experiments the molecules that the inhibitor reacts with, then he or she knows that this molecule is an essential part of the site on the enzyme where the catalytic action takes place. This is basic information to a biochemist, but a little more obscure to a non-chemist; however, it is important to review in order to understand how I began to better understand the xeronine-system

In this book, I have attempted to integrate many of the disparate bits of information about the xeronine-system. Some parts of the story still remained to be worked out in detail; other parts definitely will be modified as we obtain more data. Nevertheless the outline of the entire story is now sufficiently clear to enable scientists to focus on the parts that need additional work.

Since certain poisons (enzyme inhibitors) played critical roles in working out this problem, I shall recount some of the experiences I had with several of these poisons. Some of these poisons operated at the beginning of the sequence of reactions and some at the later stages of the reaction. Some of the poisons are common food preservatives that we use daily but do not know precisely how they work.

Poisons that Affect the Xeronine-System Development

When I transferred from the Pineapple Research Institute to the company that would become known as Dole Inc., I had our research group study the action of certain chemicals on the proteolytic activity of commercial bromelain. At that time we did not suspect that previously unknown critical health promoting components existed in commercial bromelain. In these studies we used a number of classical poisons.

Our initial results with two of these enzyme inhibitors (poisons) were truly amazing. No one had ever reported such results before. No one could repeat our initial work because the unique structure that these inhibitors affected does not exist in purified bromelain.

DFP, a Nerve Toxin, and Mercury

Many enzymologists in the 1950s studied the effects of the extremely toxic nerve gas DFP (diisopropylfluorophosphate) on enzymatic activity. Scientists of both the Allied and the Axis Countries had developed this nerve gas during World War II just in case the other side started using war gases. The biochemists of both sides knew precisely how the DFP molecule reacted with a certain critical nerve enzyme. From these studies, biochemists knew that if DFP inhibited an enzyme, that the enzyme must contain a specific type of active site—that is the part of the enzyme where the catalytic action occurs.

Since no one had ever investigated the action of DFP on bromelain, we started with this inhibitor. To our surprise, DFP completely inhibited the protease activity of the commercial bromelain produced at that time. These results suggested that bromelain had a catalytic area on the protein that was similar to that found in one of the critical enzymes involved in nerve transmission.[1] If this interpretation had been correct—which it was not, this would have been a significant discovery.

We discovered an even stranger result. If we added mercury to a solution of commercial bromelain, we, of course, reversibly inhibited the protease activity. This was not surprising; all enzymologists know that mercury reversibly inhibits any protein requiring a critical sulfhydryl group and all enzymologists know that the protease bromelain has a critical sulfhydryl group. However, if we added mercury to a solution of commercial bromelain and then added the same amount of DFP that had completely inhibited the proteolytic activity of commercial bromelain, we discovered a strange effect of mercury. When we removed the mercury from the doubly treated preparation, we found that we recovered all of the original protease activity! Mercury had prevented the DFP from inhibiting the proteolytic activity in commercial bromelain.[2] This was a significant discovery. The editors of Science readily accepted our paper. Our work represented a completely new discovery, one that could open new approaches in this sector of biochemistry.

There was just one problem. When numerous scientists attempted to repeat and extend our work, no one—including us—could repeat our original work![3] Eventually the scientific community accepted the suggestion of Irvin Liener of the University of Minnesota. He had also worked with this nerve poison. He had found that certain batches of DFP were contaminated with a chemical that reacted with sulfhydryl groups. He suggested this contaminant in DFP explained our data.

However, I knew unequivocally from subsequent experiments that our DFP was not contaminated; there had to be some other explanation for our results. Although I quickly solved the technical reasons why no one could reproduce our original work, I realized that my original interpretation of the data had been incorrect. This published paper presented the first laboratory data that proved conclusively that commercial bromelain contained a previously unknown biological system. However, discovering the nature of this new biochemical system required many years of research work.

Another interesting inhibitor of protease activity, and also one that only inhibited our early commercial bromelain samples, was sulfite.

Sulfite Does Many Strange Things

The two most widely used food preservatives are bisulfite and benzoic acid. When food processors dry light colored fruit, such as peaches or apricots, they generally treat the fresh fruit with sulfur dioxide, a source of bisulfite, to preserve the color and flavor of the fruit and to lessen microbial growth. Most light colored wines contain small amounts of sulfite to preserve the color and flavor. Until a few years ago, operators of fresh salad bars in restaurants kept their leafy vegetables looking fresh by misting them with water containing small amounts of bisulfite; it works. Food technologists have long regarded bisulfite as an effective and safe food preservative.

The French vintners inadvertently made superior wines in certain valleys because of bisulfite. After World War II, a serious crisis developed in France when some of the prime valleys for producing expensive wines suddenly began having a series of "bad" years. This problem became so serious financially, that the French government assigned some of their best food scientists to determine why the quality of French wines had declined. Their study showed that the decline in quality had occurred when the railroads replaced their picturesque, smoke belching locomotives that crawled along the shores of the river valleys with more efficient diesel engines. The sulfur dioxide in the smoke from the coal burning locomotives was sufficient to inhibit the growth of wild yeast on the surface of the grapes. If harvested grapes contain wild yeast, the wild yeast overgrows the special strains of yeast that are so important in producing superior wines.

Starting in the 1990s, the FDA attempted to reduce the amount of bisulfite in foods. Although sulfite consumed in small amounts is not toxic to people, in our fast-food biased culture some people are able, through an unusual choice of diets and restaurants, to ingest sufficient sulfite to cause serious health problems. In spite of the long period of use of bisulfite as a food preservative and color stabilizer, no one knows precisely what bisulfite does. The usual, facile and logical explanation is to suggest that bisulfite is effective because it acts as an antioxidant. This answer has satisfied most people. Nevertheless, the answer may be considerably more complex.

Bisulfite Destroys Protease

My interest in bisulfite started in the mid 1950s. Certain of our customers used bromelain as the critical ingredient in beer chill-proofing agents. In addition to bromelain or papain, chill-proofing formulators frequently added large amounts of bisulfite salts. Other practitioners of this art claimed that adding bisulfite salts was counterproductive. I felt that we should develop data that could resolve this debate.

What we discovered was surprising in several respects. Of all of the enzyme inhibitors (enzyme poisons) that I had tested up to that time, bisulfite was the most toxic! It inhibited the protease activity of 1955 commercial bromelain more than mercury did!

Our work showed that in the chain of reactions that eventually leads to the synthesis of xeronine—and thus to the activation of bromelain—one of the reactants is a critical aldehyde group.[4] Other research workers have also suggested that an aldehyde might be important in the production of certain plant proteases.[5]

Our research work dealt primarily with the storage tissues of plants. Our data show that both DFP and bisulfite inhibit the initial step in the activation of the enzymes that convert stored food into building blocks for new growth. Our bodies probably have analogous systems. When we suffer an injury, we need a sudden supply of building blocks to repair the damage.

Another Food Preservative

At one time sodium benzoate was the most widely used food preservative; it still is used extensively. Benzoate, which is toxic to both bacterial and animal cells, does not harm us because our liver converts all of the benzoate that we eat into a harmless compound called hippuric acid. As the name suggests this acid is related to horses (hippos is the Greek word for horse). This is the compound that gives horse urine its distinctive odor.

In spite of its long-term use as a bacteriostatic agent, no one knows precisely what benzoate does in a cell. Some work that I did in the early 1960s may furnish a clue to how benzoate inhibits cells. As soon as Dole began manufacturing commercial bromelain, one of my assignments was to set up standards for the finished product. In addition to the obvious need to have every shipment of bromelain have exactly the same amount of protease activity and a maximum amount of inorganic material, I also added several additional standards for our internal use.

One of these dealt with the color stability of a dilute solution of enzyme held at neutrality for twenty-four hours. I had discovered that certain batches of enzyme could be dissolved in water and held for twenty-four hours without turning black whereas other batches of enzyme, supposedly manufactured in exactly the same way and having exactly the same protease activity, turned black. The solutions that turned black quickly lost all of their protease activity.

All food technologists know that when food products turn dark, generally oxidation is the problem. However, none of the antioxidants that I tested had any effect in preventing the development of the black color in solutions of bromelain. Therefore the problem was not the usual type of oxidation. During the course of testing a wide variety of additives to prevent the darkening, I discovered that benzoate and several related molecules completely prevented the appearance of the dark color and the subsequent loss of protease activity. Since this was such an unexpected action for the benzoate ion and since this was a discovery that had utility, the U.S. Patent Office awarded me a patent on this action. Nevertheless, I was bothered by my not being able to explain how the benzoate ion prevented the darkening.

Many years later I isolated pure crystalline xeronine. One of the problems that I had with xeronine was that it had a very short half-life. A perfectly colorless solution of xeronine crystals would start turning pink within a few hours. The color quickly deepened, becoming red and then black by the next day. Again I thought that if I prevented oxidation by working under an inert gas or by adding antioxidants, that I could prevent the appearance of the black color. Nothing that I tried—including benzoate—prevented the xeronine solution from darkening; the darkening was not caused by oxidation but by a free radical reaction.

Therefore, if the "color stability" test of commercial bromelain measures the decomposition of xeronine, the benzoate must act to prevent the formation of free xeronine. To explain all of the data and observations, I am suggesting that benzoate blocks the biosynthesis of xeronine at one of the latter steps of a chain of reactions. Possibly benzoate blocks the enzyme that converts an alcohol into an aldehyde. The aldehyde, which no one has identified, may be one of the molecules that becomes part of the xeronine molecule

If this hypothesis is correct, then this explains why benzoate can kill bacteria and not harm us—providing that we are in good health. However, if a person has a damaged liver, this hypothesis suggests that the person should not eat foods containing benzoate.

Chapter Summary

• Commercial bromelain occurs in several forms.

1. The original product (1952-1956) contained no preformed proteases or amylases. All of the potential enzymes occurred in assemblages. This product also differed from later commercial bromelain products in having a unique type of xeronine-assemblage. This assemblage functions as a "master-switch;" it initiates the series of reactions necessary for converting stored food into building blocks.

2. The currently produced bromelain contains mostly preformed enzymes. It contains no trace of the unique xeronine-assemblage (the "master-switch" assemblage) that characterized the initial bromelain production.

• The nerve poison DFP (diisopropylfluorophosphate) and dilute concentrations of bisulfite inhibit only the xeronine-producing reactions in the "master-switch" assemblage.

o This assemblage is the master switch for controlling all of the reactions involved in getting ready for growth or repair reactions in plants.

o Neither of these two potent poisons affects the activity of formed bromelain.

o DFP does not affect the formation of bromelain in the bromelain-assemblage. This sub-assemblage also requires free xeronine.

• The inhibition studies suggest the following conclusions.

o The DFP inhibition data suggest that the master-switch assemblage contains an enzyme having a serine-histidine active site.

o The bisulfite inhibition data suggest that a molecule containing an aldehyde group is critical in the synthesis of xeronine.

o The benzoate results suggest that an oxidase reaction converts a molecule containing a hydroxyl group into a molecule containing an aldehyde group. This aldehyde may become part of the xeronine molecule.

ENDNOTES

1 Acetyl choline esterase

2 In our Science paper, we had suggested that the DFP inhibition of the protease activity of bromelain indicated that bromelain had an active site that contained serine and histidine. We also suggested that since reacting the enzyme with mercuribenzoate, a moderately large molecule, before we added the DFP prevented the DFP inhibition, the SH group must be adjacent to the active site of bromelain.

3 One common feature in all of the responses to our paper was that no one could repeat our experiments! Dr. Murachi, then at Nagoya University, Japan, found that DFP did not inhibit the protease activity of bromelain. However, by running the experiment at a much higher pH and using higher concentrations of reagent than we did, he found that DFP reacted with certain tyrosine groups. Dr. I. Liener of the University of Minnesota gave a plausible explanation that appeared to explain our data. He reported that in his early studies with DFP he found that certain batches of DFP contained a contaminant that reacted with sulfhydryl groups. He suggested that we had obtained a contaminated batch of DFP. Dr. Paul Boyer in his review of our work accepted Liener's explanation.

If Liener's explanation had applied to our experiment, then this would explain why blocking the sulfhydryl group in bromelain with a reversible mercury inhibitor gave complete protection against the SH-reacting contaminant in our DFP product. The DFP would have had no effect on the enzyme bromelain. Dr. Liener's explanation is still currently accepted by all of the authors of review articles, including the Annual Review of Biochemistry, to explain our data.

Obviously, as soon as we learned that other people could not confirm our results, we reran our original experiments. In our original experiments DFP produced 100% inhibition of commercial bromelain; now (1959) it produced 30-40% inhibition with commercial bromelain and 0% with purified bromelain. The latter result is what other people had already reported. We took stem juice from the bromelain processing plant and prepared "commercial bromelain" in the laboratory. DFP inhibited our laboratory bromelain sample about 60%. This suggested that minor "improvements" to our bromelain precipitation procedures had adversely affected certain unknown properties of commercial bromelain.

We next investigated possible changes in the pineapple stem harvesting and stem pressing technique. We hand-harvested pineapple stems and pressed the stems in laboratory presses and precipitated the colloids with acetone. With this technique we found that DFP inhibited the protease activity by 70-80%. This was getting closer to our original results. However, we still had not accounted for the 25% discrepancy between our 1955 results and our later results.

I am certain that changes in the quality of the pineapple plant during this short span of time accounted for the other 25% discrepancy. In 1955 all Hawaiian pineapple fruits were 100% golden colored at maturity; there was no suggestion of a green colored border around the eyes of a pineapple as there is in "ripe" pineapple today. By 1964 almost all the pineapple plants in Hawaii were "green-shell" ripe at maturity. Physiologically "green-shell" ripe pineapples are permanently immature pineapple fruit. "Green-shell" ripe fruits never senesce properly.

When I told one of my Dole colleagues about this decline in bromelain quality and my hypothesis that the pineapple plants had changed, he was incredulous. He said that as an agronomist, he could not imagine the soil deteriorating that rapidly. Yet when we look at the history of growing pineapple in Hawaii we see that on the average a crisis in growing pineapple occurred every ten years. That our DFP sample did not inhibit purified bromelain proves conclusively that our DFP sample had never been contaminated. Our original published data are still valid but I must provide a new explanation for our results.

4 In addition to forming complexes with aldehydes, sulfite forms a complex with nitric oxide forming the salt dinitric oxide sulfite. ($Na_2(NO)_2SO_3$). Since this complex forms only on the alkaline side of neutrality, this reaction could not have been a factor in the bisulfite inhibition of bromelain. It could be a factor in a different type of inhibition that we have observed with some samples of bromelain.

5 Commercial papain is a proteolytic mixture obtained from the latex of green papaya fruit. As is true of commercial bromelain, it contains a variety of materials in addition to proteins. Purified papain, as is true of purified bromelain, also contains a sulfhydryl group that must remain free for proteolytic action to occur. All research enzymologists studying papain generally purify the papain before they start their investigations. A few research workers have purposefully worked with commercial papain. The literature at the time that I became interested in the properties of commercial papain (1950-1960) contained poorly documented reports that papain might contain an aldehyde group.

While I was working in Japan at our joint drug venture company, Jintan Dolph, I met a research worker at the University of Osaka who had carried out interesting research on papain. He had published a paper on papain that was now causing him considerable embarrassment. He had reported that papain contained an aldehyde group. Since this was a piece of datum that none of his colleagues had ever reported and since he was a respected scientist, his paper immediately stimulated other research workers to repeat his work. They all reported that papain contained no aldehyde group. When the Osaka University research worker repeated his original work but this time with purified papain, he also found that papain contained no aldehyde group. He was in the process of writing a paper apologizing for his previous report.

I visited his laboratory and examined the tests that he had used to determine the presence of an aldehyde group. He was an excellent analytical chemist. I am convinced that in his original work—with commercial papain—that he did discover an aldehyde group. However, the manipulations that any enzymologist uses to purify a plant protein would have caused papain assemblages to open and to release recently activated papain. Any structure containing the aldehyde group would have been discarded during the purification process.

CHAPTER 10

Confronting the Claims of "Snake Oil"

Anyone following the health literature is probably amazed at the similarity in health claims that specialists make for the particular product or process that they are promoting. The purveyors of noni, aloes, kelp extracts, bromelain and other enzyme preparations, yeast extracts, mushroom powders, colostrum milk, etc. all make almost identical health claims. Because of these similar health claims, some people oppose natural health products claiming they are only a modern form of the traveling salesman's "snake oil" made famous around the turn of the century. I know, however, from my laboratory investigations that the active ingredients in many of these products are components of the xeronine-system; I believe that many of the others, which I have not had time to investigate, probably also contain modest amounts of the xeronine-system, or they have an indirect ability to release xeronine by opening pre-packaged assemblages containing xeronine (see Chapter 5). However, only noni and properly prepared bromelain have a sufficiently large amount of these components so that crystalline xeronine can be isolated from them. In this chapter, I shall not spend time covering the differences between different sources of the same product; there is no mental challenge in describing these differences.

What is intriguing is to discover why certain drugs, certain inorganic molecules, certain industrial chemicals and certain physical and mental activities, such as exercise, meditation, chiropractic and the placebo effect-produce reactions in the body that are similar to the actions of xeronine. I shall suggest hypotheses that might explain these actions. I hope that these hypotheses will stimulate other research workers to corroborate or to disprove these hypotheses.

Let us start this chapter with an examination of certain relatively simple non-biological organic and inorganic materials that produce physiological and biochemical actions that are similar to those produced by xeronine.

Chemicals that Copy Cat Xeronine

DMSO

DMSO (dimethyl sulfoxide) is a by-product produced during the manufacture of Kraft® paper. It is a most unusual industrial solvent, dissolving both lipophilic and hydrophilic compounds. Gasoline service stations use preparations containing DMSO to dissolve oil stains on their concrete floors and then flush the dissolved oil into the sewer with water. Manufacturers of synthetic fibers use DMSO to dissolve the polymers that they spin into fibers. By-product processors in the citrus industry use DMSO to extract the orange flavor from waste orange rinds.

In the 1960s someone discovered that DMSO relieved the pain of inflamed joints. Very quickly magazines sold at the grocery store checkout counters that had cover pages touting DMSO as the Miracle Drug of the Century. Not only did it relieve the pain of sore joints but it also promoted the healing of wounds, cured certain skin problems and helped to heal burned skin tissue.

There was no question about its efficacy; there were many questions about its mode of action. Understandably, the FDA became interested and concerned when they learned that people were promoting an industrial chemical that anyone could buy in fifty-five gallon drum lots. This industrial chemical appeared to be just as effective as many of the more expensive drugs. The FDA asked the producers of DMSO to explain how their product relieved the pain of arthritis. Of course the manufacturers of DMSO were not in the pharmaceutical business; their customers were the large chemical companies. They had no interest in spending large amounts of money to develop an annual market that they could supply with a few hours of one day's production of DMSO.

The government then funded research on the effect of DMSO on animals. In general, research workers found that DMSO was relatively non-toxic. Finally one group reported that if DMSO were instilled into the eye of a rabbit, cataracts developed. This was the data the FDA wanted. They instituted an immediate ban on the use of DMSO for the treatment of inflammation and other health problems. The FDA ban on the use of DMSO to treat inflammation had one exception. Veterinarians could use—and still do use—DMSO as a liniment to treat the legs of racehorses. (Someone on the FDA Review Board must have loved the Kentucky Derby!)

The government enforced the ban on the use of DMSO vigorously. At the time of the ban, my colleagues and I had been investigating the use of DMSO to introduce certain radioactive amino acids into pineapple fruit. Within a few weeks after the ban had been instituted, a Federal Inspector visited our laboratories to determine whether our use of DMSO was legitimate—it was.

DMSO was potentially a strong competitor for bromelain in several pharmaceutical markets. Hence, I followed the medical implications of this product closely. When FDA banned the use of DMSO in medicine, I was relieved. Quite a few years later, after I had developed the xeronine-system theory, I could suggest several reasons why DMSO was so effective.

One reason involved its solvent action. DMSO is an excellent solvent for proxeronine. One of the "warehouses" for proxeronine in our bodies is the skin. If a sharp blow to the arm produces a swollen, inflamed area, the body immediately uses the local supply of proxeronine in the dermal layer to begin the healing process. When that supply is exhausted, the movement of additional proxeronine into the area is slow. However, if one rubs DMSO in the general area of the swelling, the DMSO dissolves proxeronine from the outer edges of the swelling and moves it into the swollen area. This provides immediate relief. This theory explained why the first application of DMSO frequently gave dramatic relief from pain whereas subsequent applications of DMSO gave less and less relief.

DMSO might have still another effect. Being an excellent solvent for both lipophilic and hydrophilic substances, it might open the wrapping around certain assemblages. (See Chapter 5 for information on assemblages.) I no longer have the disc electrophoretic pictures that might have the data bearing on this possibility. (In 1971 a new president of the parent company of Dole shredded all "unnecessary" files. These included all of the research files.)

Although as a chemist, I personally felt that the FDA banned DMSO on insufficient evidence (after all, who would put DMSO in their eyes!), I now believe that the ban is definitely justified. The proper way to treat an injury or an inflamed area is to supply additional proxeronine to the site. Applying a salve containing proxeronine and at the same time drinking Tahitian noni is a more effective treatment than temporarily "robbing" one part of the body of its stored proxeronine to help another part.

Still another explanation for the effectiveness of DMSO in relieving the pain of inflammation might be the conversion of DMSO in the body into MSM.

MSM (Methylsulfenylmethane)

Similar to DMSO and closely related to it in structure and in its commercial production is another sulfur derivative, namely methylsulfonyl-methane. This is also known chemically as sulfonylbismethane.[1] MSM is an excellent high temperature industrial solvent for a variety of chemical compounds.

Whereas DSMO does not occur naturally in plants or animals as far as I know, MSM is found in primitive plants such as the horsetail (Equisetum) and in the adrenal cortex of cattle. In Japan, one of the more or less mandatory spring rituals is to collect fresh stalks of the horsetail plant for the preparation of a spring tonic broth.

The claims for the health benefits of MSM are identical to those reported for DMSO and the components of the xeronine-system. Since the recommended dosage amounts of MSM are large, about one gram at a time, I believe that the effectiveness of MSM is indirect. It probably acts as a solvent for proxeronine thus making it more available.

Dilantin®

Dilantin® (diphenylhydantoin Na), patented by Parke Davis in 1946, is a drug that doctors use to control convulsions. It works by decreasing the sensitivity of the diencephalon region of the brain. This drug is moderately effective for this application. However, it does have a number of serious side effects. Another action of this drug is to displace certain hormones, such as the thyroid hormones, from the blood globulins that serve as carriers for the thyroid hormones.

I became interested in this drug when reports appeared in the medical literature that indicated that Dilantin® could be a competitor of commercial bromelain in certain of the pharmaceutical markets for bromelain. Most of the detailed reports came, not from a drug research laboratory, but from a private medical laboratory that the financier, Jack Dreyfus, the founder and head of the Dreyfus Fund®, had established.

Jack Dreyfus spent his early career carefully examining the assets, the personnel and the future of companies before he would decide whether to buy, hold or sell shares in the company. He was eminently successful. Then suddenly he found that his brain was not working properly. As he described his problem, his brain seemed to have developed a short-circuit. He kept going over the same material, again and again but he was unable to make a decision. This problem also extended to other parts of his life. Even selecting which tie to wear to work became a critical problem. As a result of all of these stressful decisions, his normally outgoing and congenial personality changed. Fortunately, he realized that he had a serious problem and needed help. Unfortunately, none of the doctors or psychiatrists could help him.

Finally he decided to solve his own problem. He read all of the pertinent medical articles that described how the normal and abnormal brain operates. From this material he developed a theory that he believed explained why his brain had the tendency to dwell on a problem without moving on to a solution or to a decision. He then read books on pharmacology and selected a drug that he believed would correct the problem. His doctor did not subscribe to his theories—nor do I—but since the doctor could not help Dreyfus, he agreed to write a prescription for low dosages of Dilantin®.

The drug worked. Soon Dreyfus was able to return to work. Once again he had no difficulty in making crucial decisions. Also his personality returned to his previous congenial state. Having gone through this problem, he was able to detect various stages of this problem among some of his friends. All of them experienced the same rapid return to a normal life after taking the low dosages of Dilantin®. (Just recently, a writer who has written about President Nixon mentioned that Jack Dreyfus persuaded the president to try Dilantin®. Perhaps this is not a good example of its effectiveness.) Since this problem seemed widespread but not well recognized by the medical community and since the treatment was simple, rapid and relatively inexpensive, Jack Dreyfus attempted to get Parke Davis Co., the owner of the patent, interested in publicizing this application of their product.

They were not interested in doing the basic work to support his observations. Jack Dreyfus then funded his own private research laboratory to develop more data. What surprised me was that the pharmacological actions of Dilantin® were identical to the pharmacological actions of xeronine. In addition, there were even similarities to a few laboratory reactions of xeronine. If a drug, such as Dilantin®, operates at low levels to produce dramatic responses that are similar to those produced by xeronine, one possibility is that the drug acts as a "key" to open the xeronine-assemblage and to start the synthesis of xeronine.

The xeronine-assemblage hypothesis is new. My data from the storage tissues of plants strongly support this concept. My data for the body is limited to the gastrointestinal tract; our data from these studies also supports the xeronine-assemblage concept. I have no data from body organs or blood since our laboratory objectives did not include work in this area. Although basically plant cells and animal cells have similar metabolisms, yet there are certain peculiarities that are unique to each group. Certainly each group has unique types of assemblages. If my hypothesis that low doses of Dilantin® unlock xeronine-assemblages, then we should be able to discover other "keys" (ligands), produced by the body, plants, micro organisms or synthesized, that will open assemblages.

One excellent candidate for being one of the natural keys that cells—both animal and plant cells—use to open and start the reactions in certain assemblages is nitric oxide. In addition, nitric oxide could have even another role that I shall discuss.

Nitric Oxide

Nitric oxide is a most unlikely substance to show desirable biological activity. Under ordinary conditions it is a gas. The gas itself is toxic, irritating the eyes, nose and throat and causing delayed pulmonary edema. Its oxidation product, which forms readily when the gas is exposed to air, is highly toxic nitrogen dioxide. Chemically it acts both as a reducing and as an oxidizing agent. In the body it is generally present as a free radical. As a free radical, nitric oxide can cause cell damage. Certain research workers believe that nitric oxide may be a key factor in causing Alzheimer's disease.

That such a poisonous substance should be an important cell signal or messenger seemed highly unlikely to most biochemists; most biochemists initially did not believe that nitric oxide played a critical role in the cell. This attitude changed quickly.

Nitric Oxide: Friend or Foe?

Robert F. Furchgott had been studying the dilation of blood vessels in the 1970s. He discovered that the endothelial cells of blood vessels released a substance that caused the smooth muscles of the arteries to relax, thus increasing the blood flow. (Xeronine also affects smooth muscles.) By 1986 he reported that this endothelial-produced substance was nitric oxide. At the same meeting at which he made this announcement, Louis Ignarro, who had been stimulated by Furchgott's work on the blood vessel relaxing factor, independently suggested that nitric oxide acted as a local hormone. He also demonstrated that nitric oxide regulated the diameter of blood vessels. A pharmacologist, Ferid Murad, enlarged the role of nitric oxide to that of a critical regulator of many cell activities. All three of these men shared the Nobel Prize in Medical Physiology in 1998. Since their discoveries, many research workers and drug companies have investigated many aspects of the action of nitric oxide.

Do Plants Use Nitric Oxide?

Between 1953 and 1958 the pineapple company that later became known as Dole Inc. used a unique pineapple juice processing system.

Their objective was to produce an exceptionally high quality frozen juice concentrate. When the consumer reconstituted the juice by adding three volumes of water, the consumer would have a juice that was almost identical to freshly pressed pineapple juice; it contained the same enzyme concentration and the same volatile flavors as the original juice. To recover the volatile pineapple esters from the water removed during the vacuum concentration process, Dole ran the removed-water through a 3-foot diameter 25-foot high fractionating tower. The volatile components came off the top of the tower and went to a very low temperature condensing system and the stripped water went to the sewer.

This fractionating tower was very efficient. It could produce large amounts of volatile materials that only appeared in the juice in trace amounts. For example, pineapple juice contains negligible amounts of alcohol. Yet this tower produced so much pure alcohol that the government insisted that Dole operate the fractionating tower as a Government Regulated Alcohol Facility. This meant installing high security chain fences around the tower, restricting access to the still to just a few key people and maintaining voluminous records of the daily production of alcohol.

The materials that condensed on the cold condensing coils could be fractionated. One of the fractions was a blue liquid. Since no one at that time knew what this fraction was, since it had no aroma and since it had this strange color, Dole discarded this fraction. Today with modern mass spectrometers being readily available, obtaining the identity of this compound would be simple. In 1953 this piece of equipment was not available in Hawaii.

Most volatile organic compounds are either colorless, yellow, red or some combination of these two colors. I know of no volatile organic material that has a blue color. At that time we did not consider the possibility that the blue color might be an inorganic compound!

I am now suggesting the following reactions to explain how this strange and unstable blue color arose in the volatile fraction obtained by stripping the volatile materials from the removed water. Trace amounts of nitric oxide in the pineapple juice volatilized during the vacuum concentration process. In the presence of oxygen—which was present in the pineapple juice—some of the nitric oxide oxidized to nitrogen dioxide. (This is a very rapid reaction.) At the low temperatures of the condensing coils the nitric oxide and nitrogen dioxide reacted to form the blue liquid dinitrogen trioxide. These are all well documented inorganic chemical reactions that can occur under the operating conditions that Dole used. In fact this is the method that a chemist would use to synthesize dinitrogen trioxide.

This is the only series of reactions that I can suggest that explains this strange phenomenon. Because of the small amount of nitric oxide that can be present in pineapple juice, this is a reaction that can only be observed in pineapple-processing plants that process around 100,000 gallons of pineapple juice per hour! Personally I believe that this is impressive evidence for the presence of nitric oxide in pineapple juice.

A Cure For Hiccups

The presence of traces of nitric oxide in canned pineapple juice explains a strange medical phenomenon that has baffled everyone. In 1954 a short report appeared in the New England Journal of Medicine about a simple cure for hiccups. Hiccupping can be annoying but it is rarely life threatening. This doctor had a patient who had been hiccupping violently for three days; this had become a serious medical problem. None of the standard treatments were effective. Then the doctor remembered an old folklore tale about pineapple juice curing hiccups. He opened a can of pineapple juice and had his patient drink a glass of freshly poured pineapple juice. Relief occurred immediately.

Shortly after this article appeared H. Y. Young of the Pineapple Research Institute investigated this phenomenon. Having a moderate attack of hiccups, he cut open a fresh pineapple and squeezed out enough juice to fill a glass. When he drank the juice, nothing happened. Then he remembered that the doctor did not have access to fresh pineapple fruit and had used canned juice. H. Y. then opened a can of pineapple juice, poured out a glass and immediately drank it. His hiccups disappeared immediately. He suggested that the heat used in canning pineapple juice had released some volatile material that collected in the top space of the can. When he drank the juice he obtained sufficient amounts of this volatile material to cure his hiccups. At that time none of us could suggest what this volatile material might be.

In the laboratory we empirically discovered several techniques for opening the assemblages. One involved the sequential treatment of a solution with a reducing agent and a mild oxidizing agent. Nitric oxide is both a reducing agent and an oxidizing agent. Thus it might have functioned as a key to open the xeronine-assemblage.

Similarity between Nitric Oxide and Xeronine

Because my supply of raw material for the production of crystalline xeronine was suddenly discontinued, I have been able to run only a few animal tests with solutions of crystalline xeronine. In every test that I have run, the actions of solutions of crystalline xeronine were identical to that reported for nitric oxide. In general, the tests with solutions of crystalline xeronine solutions performed more dramatically than those reported for nitric oxide.

Anti-inflammatory Action: Nitric oxide has an anti-inflammatory action. In the test that N. Araki of Jintan Dolph ran on my first sample of xeronine, the method of preparation precluded the presence of any nitric oxide. This sample had a powerful anti-inflammatory action.

Good-Feeling Action: Nitric oxide promotes good feeling. My tests with solutions of crystalline xeronine produced probably the most dramatic examples of good feeling and alertness of any product ever tested. Nitric oxide could not have been present in this sample.

Elimination of Pain: Nitric oxide lessens pain. My tests with solutions of crystalline xeronine eliminated completely the normal pain caused by injecting a peritoneal solution into mice. There is absolutely no possibility of nitric oxide being present in my solutions.

Increased Sexual Activity: Nitric oxide increases sexual activity. My tests with solutions of crystalline xeronine produced very strong stimulation of both male and female sexual activity.

All of the above examples represent actions of solutions of crystalline xeronine. There is absolutely no possibility that nitric oxide could have contaminated these samples.

Commercial bromelain—the type that Dole produced in the 1950s—

has produced every biological action that has ever been reported for nitric oxide. Of course, since commercial bromelain—the type that Dole produced in the 1950s—also produces nitric oxide, this comparison is not definitive. Nevertheless, I know that these samples all had the ability to produce xeronine.

Nitric Oxide May Be a "Key"

Nitric oxide is not produced in assemblages. Dr. Furchgott in his initial experiments showed that something produced in the epithelial cells of blood vessels moved into the smooth muscles of the blood vessel and caused the muscle to relax. Later he showed that this substance was nitric oxide. Just how one of the simplest of inorganic gases can initiate a physiological reaction requires some explaining.

I am making two suggestions to explain how nitric oxide might operate to release xeronine from a xeronine-assemblage. One proposal is physical; the other is chemical.

In the physical proposal I am suggesting that nitric oxide acts as a "key" or ligand to open the xeronine-assemblage so that the assemblage starts its synthesis of xeronine. The details about how various keys or ligands stimulate the components in various assemblages to commence their work still remain to be worked out. The chemical proposal also involves the synthesis of xeronine. In this proposal nitric oxide would be a reactant in the formation of a critical aldehyde. (I have covered the presence of a critical aldehyde in good quality commercial bromelain and papain in Chapter 9.) Our studies with bisulfite indicated conclusively that an aldehyde is one of the reactants in the biosynthesis of xeronine. I am suggesting as one of several possibilities that an enzyme in the xeronine-assemblage used nitric oxide to convert an alcohol into an aldehyde.

This is a suggestion only; no one to my knowledge has ever looked for an enzyme that could use nitrogen oxide to oxidize and alcohol to an aldehyde. Yet it is a suggestion that has considerable appeal. If further work substantiates this hypothesis, then this would explain how nitric oxide might activate one particular assemblage, namely the xeronine-assemblage.

Hormones that Mimic Xeronine

In all except one of the examples that I shall cover in this section I am making the same suggestion; namely, that the receptor for the specific hormone being studied has two adjacent adsorption sites, one for the particular hormone and one for xeronine. For the hormone to act I am proposing that both sites must be occupied. If the xeronine adsorption site is not occupied, then the normal hormone reaction does not occur.

For the prostaglandin receptor protein I am suggesting a slight modification of the action of the receptor protein. To accommodate the data and observations I am suggesting that the adsorption of the prostaglandin alone will produce a signal at the other end of the nerve. The brain interprets this signal as pain. However, if both xeronine and the prostaglandin occupy their appropriate sites, then the signal going to the brain is a "good feeling signal."

Endorphins

Recently the endorphins have become popular with the general public and with scientists. The general public recognizes endorphins as "the good feeling hormones" and a factor in a "runner's high." The scientists are interested in the endorphin protein receptor as the receptor for either endorphin or alkaloids. Since endorphin is a peptide string whereas alkaloids are odd shaped blocks having these two very differently shaped molecules occupy the same adsorption site to the exclusion of the other molecule does not make good mechanical sense. I am suggesting that there are two adjacent adsorption sites, one for endorphin and the adjacent one for xeronine. For the endorphin reaction to occur both sites must be occupied by the appropriate molecule. I am suggesting that the cell accomplishes this dual adsorption by packaging endorphin and a xeronine-assemblage into a larger assemblage, the endorphin-assemblage, and delivering this package (vesicle) to the receptor site.

If one lists the reported effects of endorphins, such as relieving pain and producing a feeling of well being, and the effects of solutions of crystalline xeronine, the actions are similar. I am suggesting that they are similar because the endorphin receptor protein requires the simultaneous presence of both xeronine and endorphin.

Prostaglandins

Many of the beneficial actions of prostaglandins are identical to those produced by the xeronine-system. This similarity is so great that initially I believed that the active ingredient in commercial bromelain might be a new type of prostaglandin. However, more extensive research proved that the physiologically active ingredient in commercial bromelain could not possibly be a prostaglandin-type substance. I have covered this topic in Chapter 6.

Much interesting work remains to be done in this area. At present no experimental data exist in this area. To explain the observations I am suggesting that adsorption of prostaglandin alone to a prostaglandin-receptor produces a pain signal whereas adsorption of prostaglandin and xeronine to adjacent adsorption sites produces a signal that is definitely not a pain signal. The signal might initiate certain of the desirable responses that clinicians have attributed to prostaglandins.

Prostaglandins definitely can cause pain. To reduce this type of pain a physician now has two options; either he can reduce the synthesis of prostaglandins by prescribing aspirin or ibuprofen or he can modify the pain signal by adding a xeronine adjacent to the adsorbed prostaglandin—if my theory is correct. Although both approaches are effective, I would personally prefer the latter approach. To respond to signals from the environment, our body requires the synthesis of prostaglandins. If we really could inhibit the synthesis of prostaglandins, the side effects would be intolerable. Fortunately the inhibitors that we use, such as aspirin and ibuprofen, are only moderate inhibitors of prostaglandins in the cell. In test tube experiments these drugs truly do inhibit the synthesis of prostaglandins.

Non-Chemical Treatment of Health Problems

When pharmacologists test a new drug, they properly take great precautions to eliminate any possible placebo effect; if not properly controlled, the placebo effect introduces an uncontrolled variable in the testing. Although the placebo effect is something to be avoided in medical research on new drugs, it is something to use in treating a patient. A placebo effect is a biochemical action that is every bit as important in treating a patient as are drugs. Our only problem today is that we rarely have good control over the placebo effect and we cannot explain in biochemical terms precisely what biochemical systems take part in the placebo effect.

Similarly many physical manipulations, such as acupuncture, massage and chiropractic undoubtedly produce desirable health effects. Again we have only a meager amount of data that furnish us with clues about the biochemistry of the reactions. In this section I shall suggest certain biochemical mechanism that may serve as a starting point for research.

We need to explain these results in terms of quantifiable biochemical compounds. Behind every confirmed miracle—and anyone working with materials that are rich in the xeronine-system, such as Tahitian noni or the original bromelain preparations, has seen truly unbelievable results (miracles)—there are understandable, mechanically acceptable biochemical reactions to explain the results.

Acupuncture and Moxabustion

Today no scientist who examines the data can doubt that acupuncture produces a biochemical reaction in the body; this definitely is not a psychological effect. Several medical research workers who were dubious about the effectiveness of acupuncture visited certain hospitals in China that were using acupuncture. They saw Chinese doctors operating on patients who had received no pain killers other than that provided by acupuncture.

Even more impressive were experiments performed on rabbits. Rabbits, animals that may rank high on the cuddling scale but rank low on the intellectual scale, were excellent animals to use to obtain data on the acupuncture effect; psychological effects can be disregarded with confidence when working with rabbits. The scientist performed acupuncture on one rabbit and then used its blood to replace blood removed from an untreated rabbit. They discovered that something in the blood from the treated rabbit reduced the severity of induced inflammation in the untreated rabbit.

I have had some personal experiences with acupuncture but only indirect experiences with moxabustion. Being intrigued with the well-accepted practice of acupuncture, I brashly gave a lecture on acupuncture. (I am not a licensed acupuncturist.) I showed the audience the needles, explained the procedure and demonstrated how the acupuncturist inserted the needle in the arm. As I talked, I automatically continued to tap the needle. When I noticed that some of the people in the audience were becoming concerned, I looked at the needle. I had tapped it deeply into my arm. I had felt no pain during the procedure. Not having had any medical problems, I cannot say whether the treatment had any beneficial effects.

Moxabustion did not have the appeal for me that acupuncture had. In the moxabustion treatment, one buys from a druggist in Japan lightly compressed dried leaves of the Chinese wormwood plant. These are hand-pressed into small pyramids. When one feels the need for the treatment, one lights the tips of about three to four pyramids and places them on the arm and waits as the pyramids slowly burn themselves out.

One of my Japanese colleagues firmly believed in the efficacy of this treatment. At the company parties, where many toasts led to a certain amount of dizziness, he would excuse himself and go through the moxabustion treatment. When he would return about fifteen minutes later, his dizziness had disappeared and he was again ready to start toasting. Two or three moxabustion treatments generally got him safely through any party.

Acupuncture is easier to explain. Obviously the mechanical action of the needle on tissue membranes must produce a chemical that has a hormone-like action. The only body regulatory chemicals that a mechanical force can generate are prostaglandins.

The acupuncturist inserts his needles into the dermal layer of the skin. The skin is one of the body's warehouses for proxeronine. The act of inserting the needle and gently moving it displaces the cell membrane. This allows a prostaglandin-synthesizing enzyme to grab a released essential fatty acid and convert it into a prostaglandin molecule. However, since this area is rich in proxeronine, the Golgi complex probably packages the released prostaglandin into a prostaglandin-assemblage. This produces a feeling of well being similar to that of endorphin.

I had a dermatologist friend in Honolulu who told me that for all of his superficial dermatological work, he would inject a small amount of saline solution into the skin at several sites. He told me that this treatment was just as effective as injecting Novocaine®. Essentially what he was doing was practicing acupuncture.

Massage and Chiropractic

Both of these methods of treating ailments involve mechanical force. The people who are helped by these treatments are convinced that these treatments are effective. The doctors and scientists who are skeptical suggest that the results are strictly psychological. Whether the results are psychological or biochemical, that the treatments are effective is all that matters.

I am suggesting that any treatment, such as massage, chiropractic and exercise, which involves a certain amount of applied force to the body, will increase the synthesis of prostaglandins. Prostaglandins produced in this fashion are desirable; they are generally produced in areas of the body that are rich in proxeronine. This would lead to enhanced production of assemblages containing both the xeronine-assemblage and prostaglandin.

The Placebo Effect and Emotional Healing

The brain certainly initiates both the placebo effect and emotional healing. If we knew the biochemicals involved in this reaction and how the body controls the release and the use of these materials, we should be better able to enrich our lives. The common assumption is that the brain releases hormones that beneficially affect our systems. Just which hormones are released still remains to be determined. In addition to hormones, I am suggesting that proxeronine must also be released.

Under normal conditions, I am assuming that at approximately two-hour intervals the brain sends a signal to the liver to release a slug of proxeronine into the blood stream. This occurs without any conscious effort on our part. However, intense involvement in any activity, whether it is physical or mental, may cause the brain to send more signals to the liver to release proxeronine. If one believes that the "new drug" is going to help, this belief, this intense emotional activity, may induce the brain to send additional signals to the liver to release more proxeronine. The release of additional proxeronine makes one feel better even if the "new drug" is only a sugar pill placebo.

The hypothesis that the brain releases a signal every two hour to instruct the liver to release a slug of xeronine has some other interesting consequences. Why do we need to sleep and what can we do about it?

Sleep and Sweet Dreams

An enormous amount of research has been devoted to various phases of the sleeping phenomenon. E.Asernsky and N. Kleitman discovered that every two hours a sleeping infant moved its eyes around rapidly for no more than a few minutes. They called this period of activity REM (Rapid Eye Movement) and the long period between this activity NREM (Non-REM) sleep. Other research workers quickly showed that this same phenomenon also occurs in adults and that during the REM period we dream. Although this point is rarely mentioned, our entire body is in a state of increased activity during the REM periods. A progression of muscle contractions proceeds throughout the body.

An uninterrupted REM period is essential for normal activity. College students who volunteered for sleep experiments were allowed to sleep as long as they wanted. One group of students would be awakened as soon as they entered an REM period and were then allowed to go back to sleep. After three days of plenty of sleep but no REM sleep, this group of students were irritable and hallucinating. Obviously we need REM sleep.

Other animals have different sleep requirements. Cats spend most of the day catnapping. On the other hand, the cow spends its entire night chewing its cud and thinking about Mozart—or whatever subject tickles a cow's fancy. They do not need sleep. (Cows are one of the most intelligent animals on a farm. They actually do like Mozart and show their appreciation by producing more and higher-grade milk. I can see the potential here for an attractive milk advertising campaign.)

Since some animals seem to spend much of their day sleeping while others do not sleep at all, why do we need to sleep? One explanation that immediately caught the fancy of the Freudians was that we sleep to dream. During our dreaming periods they suggested that we get rid our brain of all of the accumulated frustrations so that we can start the next day with a cleansed brain. I checked out this hypothesis and found it most unlikely. The dream in the first REM period was a continuation of the mental activity just prior to drifting off to sleep. The next REM period dream continued from that point. At no time was there any suggestion of the dreams that so intrigued Freud.

I am suggesting that one of the prime reasons why we sleep is that we need to restock the local supply of proxeronine in our cells. Although there probably are still other reasons why we need to sleep, I believe that the restocking idea is the primary function of sleeping. If this theory is correct then we should find some evidence to support the theory.

Wide Awake Russians

During the 1960s I closely followed the work that certain Russian physiologists and biochemists were carrying out on the effect of certain plant extracts on animal behavior. The plant that they studied most intensively was a local species of Panex. The panex plant is related to ginseng. Their animal tests were very convincing even though the animal rights people would not allow such tests to be carried out in our laboratories today.

On the basis of these well-conducted experiments, the Russian Government built four large Panex processing plants in different parts of Russia to produce a plant extract for people who had stressful work or who needed to work long periods without adequate sleep. Some of the people who received the extract were blast furnace operators, miners, soldiers and air pilots. They reported that soldiers taking these extracts could go without sleep for several days and still be alert.

These studies came to the attention of the Western World during the 1980 Olympics. This was the Olympics that President Carter boycotted. At these Olympics the Russians took most of the medals. This prompted a complaint to the Olympic Committee that the Russians were "doping" their athletics. The Russians pointed out that what they were giving their athletes was a natural plant extract that they gave to all of their people who had stressful jobs. The Olympic Committee accepted their explanation.

From my own experience in drinking a teaspoonful of a very dilute solution of crystalline xeronine, I can attest to the effectiveness of xeronine in alleviating the feeling of sleepiness. We do not have to drink xeronine to ward off sleep. If we can become intensely involved in a project, such as happens when an artist paints a picture, or a musician composes a piece of music or one listens to an inspired orator, our brain probably releases proxeronine in greater amounts and at greater frequencies. Much of our emotional response at the molecular level is partially mediated by xeronine. Specific hormones are also involved in this reaction.

The Indian fakirs, through a period of intensive training that may take seven years, may have developed the ability to control the release of proxeronine. This may explain their ability to skewer themselves without feeling pain. (Certainly there should be more productive ways of using this increased supply of xeronine!)

Chapter Summary

• The physiologically effective ingredients in many natural products are components of the xeronine-system.

• The containers of the assemblages that the Golgi complex sends into the cytosol, namely the vesicles, are relatively stable structures.

• To open a vesicle containing assemblages and to initiate the biochemical work that the components of the assemblage are capable of requires special "keys" or ligands for each type of assemblage.

• A large number of different types of "keys" exist to open assemblages. Some are natural, some are plant pigments, some are inorganic and some are synthetic.

o Nitric oxide may be one of the natural "keys" that opens and/or activates the xeronine-assemblage. (There are many other keys.)

o Dilantin® (5,5-Diphenyl-2,4-imidazolidinedione), a drug that at low concentrations mimics the action of xeronine, probably works by opening the xeronine-assemblage and starting the synthesis of xeronine.

o Certain laboratory manipulations, such as the sequential treatment of a mixture of assemblages with anion and cation resins and then fractionating the assemblages by size, can open the xeronine-assemblage and release free xeronine.

• Acupuncture, massage and chiropractic probably work by the same biochemical sequence of events. They promote the synthesis of prostaglandins in areas that are particular rich in stored proxeronine.

ENDNOTE

1 For those people who might be interested the chemical formulae for DMSO and MSM, they are as follows:

O	O
CH3 S CH3	CH3 S CH3
	O
DMSO	MSM

CHAPTER 11

Treating Drug Addiction with Xeronine

I propose that we have the knowledge to cure the biochemical part of drug addiction. The treatment time is short, the cost is low and withdrawal symptoms do not occur. To understand this new approach, we need to understand what proteins do in the body, how the cell modifies the behavior of proteins by "pasting on" a variety of small molecules and how the body manufactures and folds the long polypeptide chain that becomes the working protein.

The globular proteins are biochemical devices for extracting energy from water. When the newly synthesized polypeptide chain folds in a specific way to form a protein, the new protein has the potential but not the ability to extract useful energy from water. Water stretches and compresses the newly formed protein in a completely random fashion. To convert this random stretching and compression of a protein into useful energy, the cell must add various structural modifiers onto the surface of the protein. Sometimes a single modifier is all that is required. At other times the protein may have an assortment of different modifiers and different numbers of any one of the modifiers.

Modifiers such as steroids, peptides and B-vitamins may have several different actions such as making proteins rigid or adding catalytic sites to the protein. Certain proteins involved in the transmission of signals to the brain are turned on when specific hormones adsorb onto the protein. These proteins are the hormone receptor proteins. Since this chapter is about the drug problem, I want to focus on one specific receptor protein, namely the endorphin receptor protein. When all of the proper attachments are applied to this protein, this is the complex that makes us feel good. This, according to excellent work done by the Chicago research group, is the same complex that is involved in drug addiction.

Endorphin and its Protein Receptor

In the mid 1980s several university research groups studied the interaction between foreign alkaloids and the protein receptor for endorphin. The research group at the University of Chicago found that if they exposed the endorphin receptor protein to a foreign alkaloid, the protein would not adsorb endorphin. Vice versa, they found that if they exposed the endorphin receptor protein to the endorphin molecule first, the receptor protein would not adsorb the alkaloid. Subsequent work with radioactive alkaloid and radioactive endorphin showed that the two molecules adsorbed onto the same general area of the protein. From this they drew the very logical and now accepted conclusion that the two molecules adsorbed onto the same adsorption site. The adsorption of one molecule on the adsorption site prevented the adsorption of the second molecule.

Later, another scientist showed that he could fold and twist the endorphin molecule, which is a chain of about seventeen amino acids, into a structure that had the same shape as the foreign alkaloid. This work supposedly supported the original theory. Nevertheless this model has several weaknesses.

Let us examine the proposition that the endorphin chain can be folded to simulate the shape of an alkaloid from a mechanical viewpoint. Physically an alkaloid and a polypeptide chain folded to occupy the same space as an alkaloid molecule have entirely different mechanical properties. Most alkaloids are generally rigid biochemical molecules. By contrast a folded polypeptide chain has no rigidity. If one of the receptor sites on the endorphin receptor protein (namely the xeronine adsorption site) requires a rigid molecule—which I believe that it does, then the folded polypeptide chain, which is not rigid, would not produce the hormone response even though the folded polypeptide chain might fit into the adsorption site.

Endorphin is a rope. From strictly mechanical considerations we can assume that the rope properties of endorphin modify the receptor protein so that it can perform its specific job. If we replace the rope with a rigid molecule, the endorphin receptor protein would not give the hormone response. From these strictly mechanical considerations I believe that we must modify the conclusions of the Chicago research group slightly to include two contiguous adsorption sites, one for xeronine and one for a specific polypeptide chain, namely endorphin.[1]

Types of Protein Modifiers

Protein modifiers affect the behavior of proteins in many different ways. Molecular boiler-plates, such as steroids, stiffen the portion of the protein that they occupy. Molecular ropes, such as the peptides, limit movement of two parts of a protein or produce closure of a cleft in a protein. Molecular girders are a completely new structural type of protein modifier. They provide crucial pivot points for increasing either the amount of movement or for increasing the force on a small amount of movement.

Only a few alkaloids have a girder structure. Of this small class of alkaloids only xeronine and tetrodotoxin have relatively "clean" structures. The other alkaloids of this class have a wide assortment of side chains that so clutter the structure that they cannot fit neatly into certain specific adsorption sites; they adsorb weakly to a site in contrast to the strong adsorption of either xeronine or tetrodotoxin.

The most intensively studied super toxic alkaloid is tetrodotoxin. I have covered this toxin in Chapter 8. That none of the conventional alkaloids prevent tetrodotoxin from killing a mouse injected with tetrodotoxin tells us something about the shape of the receptor site for xeronine. The tetrodotoxin molecule fits snugly into the xeronine adsorption site on the receptor protein whereas the other alkaloids, although adsorbing onto the site, fit poorly onto the site.

Proposed Model for the Endorphin-Xeronine-Protein Complex

I have drawn a highly simplified model of the endorphin receptor protein as a sphere with a prominent cleft in it. On one side of the cleft is an attachment for one end of the endorphin chain and on the other side of the cleft is an attachment for the other end of the chain. The chain is relatively taut with only a small amount of slack.

Xeronine, a basic molecule, fits into an adsorption cavity and keeps the width of the cleft at a precise distance. For a normal person this arrangement of the endorphin chain and the xeronine girder make a perfect fit on the surface of the protein. No one has the slightest idea of precisely what this combination does to make us feel happy. That is a problem to be worked on in the future.

Figure 1. Diagram of the xeronine-endorphin-receptor protein complex with the endorphin chain spanning the protein cleft and the xeronine

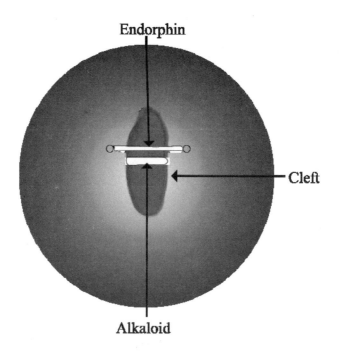

girder spacing the width of the cleft.

This model explains the observations that scientists made in the mid

1980s about the effect of "hard core" alkaloids blocking the adsorption of endorphin on the endorphin receptor protein. Since all foreign alkaloids are larger than xeronine, if the receptor protein is exposed to the foreign alkaloid before the endorphin, the foreign alkaloid will make the cleft wider than does xeronine. With a wider cleft the two ends of the endorphin molecule will not be able to attach to the two binding sites. Vice versa, if the receptor protein is exposed to the endorphin first, then the endorphin chain, which is attached to the two sides of the cleft, will keep the cleft opening narrow. This would prevent the foreign alkaloid from adsorbing onto the protein.

This model explains well all of the data and observations of the Chicago group. It does not explain the phenomenon of addiction. Addiction, which is becoming "hooked" on a drug, requires that the cell must produce a variant of the normal endorphin receptor protein, a variant protein that absolutely requires the foreign alkaloid in order to produce the endorphin response. Before I make any suggestions about how the cell might produce variants of the normal endorphin receptor protein, let us examine some of the observations that indicate that a cure for drug addiction is possible. (I am using the word cure intentionally and with confidence.)

Observations on Treatment of Drug Addiction

The cure for drug addiction can be unbelievably rapid, inexpensive and completely without withdrawal symptoms. Since our group was not licensed to work on hard-core drug addiction, we only treated nicotine addiction and a few cases of alcoholism. We used no double blind tests since in general the treatment worked spectacularly well with almost no recidivism.

Our group learned about the potential value of the xeronine-system in treating drug addiction from a Californian entrepreneur, Bill Hibbard. Bill knew nothing about the xeronine-system but he did know that the extract from leaves of the creosote bush successfully cured drug addiction. (The creosote leaves contain components of the xeronine-system.) Al Mosher, one of the members of our group and a two-pack-a-day smoker, enthusiastically agreed to try the creosote extract to treat his smoking habit. He warned us that he was doing this just for science and that as soon as we had finished the test that he planned to go back to smoking. He enjoyed smoking and had no intentions of giving it up. His wife asked us not to ask him to stop smoking because his withdrawal symptoms made him difficult to live with. After about two days into the test his wife suddenly realized that he was not smoking. She found this difficult to believe since he was behaving normally. Needless to say, Al never did go back to smoking; he became an enthusiastic campaigner to get his friends to stop smoking. His success rate with his friends was close to 99%.

In work that our group had done in Honolulu on nicotine addiction, we had one unanticipated, rather "serious" side effect from the treatment. One of the local doctors had asked me if we could cure his wife of smoking. I assured him that we could and supplied him with sufficient material for treating his wife for three days—our arbitrary length of time for the treatment. The evening of the first day the doctor called me and explained in a very agitated voice that we had to stop the treatment immediately. His wife was experiencing all sorts of weird reactions from the treatment. She had lost much of her muscular control. She could not dial a telephone (at that time in the history of our country all phones were dial phones), she could not walk across the room in a straight line, her speech was slurred and she could not carry on a coherent conversation.

Since this was the very first time that we had ever heard of such a reaction, I was deeply concerned. After thinking about the problem for several days, I called the doctor and asked him if his wife drank cocktails. He told me that his wife always had a martini or two before dinner. (This probably meant that she had two or more.) However, he assured me that she could "hold her liquor" and was never fazed by several cocktails. His reply immediately solved the problem. Curing her craving for nicotine had also made her naive to alcohol. Her problem was that before the treatment two martinis never fazed her whereas now two martinis made her uproariously drunk.

Whereas this was a completely serendipitous discovery, this experience supplied some valuable information about the rapidity of the switch between a foreign alkaloid endorphin receptor and the xeronine endorphin receptor. In less than eight hours our treatment had not only worked against nicotine addiction but it also worked against alcohol addiction; the treatment had made her naive to alcohol.

I had a clue to this action from my association with Bill Hibbard. Bill had a friend who drank a bottle of Scotch a day. Bill told his friend that he realized how much pleasure he was getting from drinking his bottle of Scotch and that he was not going to try to get him to stop drinking. He only wanted to save him some money. Instead of drinking a bottle of Scotch a day, Bill told him that he could get just as good a response by drinking just half a bottle of Scotch a day providing that he took some of the creosote bush extract.

His friend tried this regime and found that it worked. In fact it worked so well that he cut his consumption of Scotch to one quarter a bottle a day and continued to take the creosote bush extract. He felt so happy that he continued cutting down his Scotch consumption until finally he was drinking no Scotch at all. He felt better than he had ever felt before. Within a months time he had changed from being an alcoholic to becoming a strong advocate of continence.

What makes this case so exciting and unusual is that it goes against all the findings of scientists and against the warnings of Alcoholics Anonymous. (Their warnings are very legitimate and important to anyone in their program. I would most strongly advise anyone on their program to follow their instructions.) Bill's friend had no intention of stopping his drinking. His actions were voluntary and were made under no stress. He was the one who decided that he would keep cutting down his consumption of Scotch as long as he was feeling good.

With this as a background, Al got one of his friends, who had a serious drinking problem, to try the treatment. The treatment worked well with absolutely no withdrawal symptoms. After he had been cured, we asked him if he would be willing to take part in an experiment with alcohol. He agreed since he was now confident that if he should get rehooked on alcohol, that we could get him off alcohol with no problem. After work one Friday he joined his friends at the local cocktail bar. After ordering a martini, he toyed with it a while, took a sip, put it down and took another sip. In the meantime his companions were already on their second martini. Finally he looked at his watch, said that he had work to do and left his half drunk martini still on the table.

Anyone who has worked with alcoholics knows that this man's action is unbelievable. He was truly cured of addiction, something that few research workers believe can ever happen. Although this is all of the information that we really need to begin seriously attacking the problem of addiction, research workers would like to have a better picture of the biochemistry involved. Data in this area are sparse. What I have suggested in the following sections are possibilities that research workers should explore.

Chemically Breaking the Addiction

Getting hooked on a drug, whether the drug is alcohol, nicotine, heroin, a medicinal alkaloid drug or chocolate, probably involves the cell synthesizing an endorphin receptor that is a variant of the normal endorphin receptor; it is now an endorphin receptor that absolutely must have the foreign alkaloid in order to function properly. Without that specific alkaloid, the endorphin hormone will not produce the "good feeling" response.

Determining how a cell synthesizes new proteins is a research subject that many biochemists are working on. My work indicates that components of the xeronine-system—if properly administered—will cure the biochemical part of drug addiction. Since my theory suggests that this cure involves switching from the addictive variant of the endorphin receptor back to the body's normal xeronine-requiring endorphin receptor, exploring this concept might lead to a better understanding of one way that the cell produces variants of normal proteins. Thus the research could lead to both theoretical advances as well as lead to a better solution to our still unsolved problem of drug addiction.

The cell has two different methods of synthesizing new proteins, unlocking previously blocked genes to produce a new polypeptide chain or folding a given polypeptide chain in a different manner. To form a new type of endorphin receptor the cell might "open up" a previously locked gene that contains the code for forming a protein that requires the presence of the foreign alkaloid and endorphin to become active. There is a precedent for this suggestion. Certain bacteria that normally cannot use lactose as a source of energy can be trained to "eat" lactose by gradually substituting lactose for glucose in their food. Although these bacteria have a gene for the enzyme that works on lactose, normally the transcription of this gene is blocked. The "training" removes the block.

Today scientists would say that the cell produces a specific ligand (key) that opens a particular gene for transcription. Of course a problem still to be worked out in most cases is determining the structure of the ligand.

Another possibility that might explain how the cell forms different types of endorphin receptor proteins is for the cell to fold the same polypeptide chain for the endorphin receptor protein in different ways. It could do this by having the Golgi complex prepare new templates for folding the polypeptide chain. If a person starts taking drugs, very quickly the Golgi complex would make a template that would fold the polypeptide chain to produce a different type of endorphin receptor protein. For activity this protein would require the foreign alkaloid to adsorb adjacent to the adsorbed endorphin. At this point the person would be "hooked."

The Golgi Complex

Since the Golgi complex plays such critical roles in the formation of vesicles, assemblages and possibly templates for the folding of peptide chains, we should take a brief look at this cell structure. Many, many years ago when I took cytology in college the Golgi complex was a dubious structure with no known function. Today the Golgi complex is an important cell organelle. However biochemists are still attempting to discover new tasks for this structure. Its complex structure indicates that it probably has more important functions than we presently assign to it.

History of the Golgi Complex

In 1898 Camillo Golgi (1843-1926) discovered that staining a section of a cell with a solution of osmium tetroxide caused a structure close to the nucleus to stain black. Unfortunately the staining procedure that Golgi used was so erratic, that many cytologists believed that the spots were casual artifacts and did not correspond to any cellular structure. Not until the electron microscope became a routine tool in the 1950s for studying cell structure was everyone convinced that the Golgi black particles were part of an important organelle. Since Golgi, a truly brilliant Italian physician who made many discoveries about the structure of the cells and especially the nerve cells, was the first person to detect a part of this structure, scientists have honored him by calling this structure the Golgi complex.

Actually osmium tetroxide stains only a small portion of the Golgi complex, namely the plate facing the nucleus. Even on this plate the staining is erratic. The electron microscopic pictures show a structure that is much larger and much more complex than the structure that Golgi envisioned; it is a structure that is about one half to one third the size of the nucleus! Cells contain from one to several Golgi complexes.[2]

Structure of the Golgi complex

The structure of the Golgi complex consists of a number of curved plates attached to a post on one side. The number of plates varies with the type of cell and the organism. Bacteria have no discrete Golgi complexes. Plants can have very complex Golgi complexes. The number of plates varies from three to fourteen. Each plate is curved with a thickened rim and is separated from the adjoining plate by enough space to allow free circulation of the cytosol. Every component of the Golgi complex, including the pole, is interconnected. This allows free internal circulation of components.

From the surface of any plate, but especially from the top plate, bulges appear which grow and then are pinched off. Cytologists call the pinched-off structures vesicles. They contain molecules that the vesicles deliver to specific addresses that are written on the surfaces of the vesicles. Some of the vesicles contain digestive enzymes that cross the cell membrane and enter into ducts leading to the gastro-intestinal tract. (I suggest a more complex composition for the contents of these particular vesicles.) Plants have certain vesicles that contain complex carbohydrates that the cell uses to synthesize cell walls. Other vesicles contain contents whose function no one knows.

Just examining the structure of the Golgi complex gives us clues regarding what it does and how it performs. The Golgi complex has the structure of a complex automobile assembly plant; it can perform many tasks. It can receive ready-made molecules from the cytosol and assemble them with other molecules; it can receive molecules and modify them before it assembles them. The end products of the Golgi complex are integrated groups of molecules designed to perform a variety of specific tasks in the cell.

In addition to grouping molecules into assemblages, the Golgi complex also prepares templates that the cell uses for folding proteins. Other workers have called these proteins chaperon proteins. It prepares these from newly synthesized proteins that may have adsorbed certain materials from the cytosol. After the Golgi complex has completed its work on the template, it sends it back to the membrane that surrounds the nucleus (the smooth endoreticulum). This is where the newly synthesized polypeptides are folded into proteins.

A free polypeptide chain can be folded into a bewilderingly large number of different shapes; yet the cell unerringly folds this long polypeptide chain into a protein within a fraction of a second. The folding mechanism must be simple, unerring, inevitable and fast. From strictly mechanical considerations, we quickly realize that there is only one solution to this problem. If we attach different portions of the polypeptide chain to a template, thereby converting the long chain into a set of connected loops, we so greatly restrict the number of possible shapes for a protein, that the polypeptide chain almost immediately assumes its proper form.

Relationship between Assemblages and Vesicles

As so often happens in science, different groups studying a new problem approach the problem from different viewpoints. The cytologists studying the cell found a strange structure, the Golgi complex; they were interested in discovering functions for this structure. I had a completely different problem. I discovered that certain of the lines in the photographs of our disc—electrophoretic separation of commercial bromelain were not pure proteins or mixtures of closely related proteins as everyone thought; they were miniature shrink-wrapped manufacturing systems that synthesized xeronine and then used the xeronine in other reactions. My problem then was to discover how the cell produced this "shrink wrapped" assemblage of a number of different molecules. When I attempted to visualize how a cell could assemble, package and "shrink wrap" these diverse molecules, I realized that the structure that I was visualizing was the Golgi complex. The one point that the cytologists studying the Golgi complex and I have in common is their vesicle and my "shrink wrapped" package.

Since the terms vesicles and assemblages refer to different aspects of a structure, I believe that we can usefully use both terms. If we are interested in the container, vesicle would be the proper term. If we are interested in the contents, then assemblages would be more descriptive.

Chapter Summary

• Based on our work with nicotine addiction as well as observations that other people have made on hard core drug addiction, I am confident that the proper administration of components of the xeronine-system can cure the biochemical part of drug addiction rapidly, at relatively low cost and with no withdrawal symptoms.

• To stimulate specific research on this problem I have made specific suggestions regarding a model for drug addiction and cure. I am basing this model partly on the work done by research workers at the University of Chicago and partly on our own work. I am suggesting that for proper endorphin reaction the endorphin receptor protein must have both xeronine and endorphin adsorbed onto adjacent sites on the receptor protein.

• The normal and proper basic molecule for activating the endorphin receptor is xeronine, a basic protein that the body produces. (Chemists would call this basic protein an alkaloid.)

• Foreign alkaloids, being basic molecules, can also adsorb onto the xeronine adsorption site. Being more bulky than xeronine, they block the adsorption of endorphin.

• With continued exposure to a foreign alkaloid the cell forms a new variety of endorphin receptor protein that has an alkaloid adsorption site that conforms to the size and shape of the foreign alkaloid and endorphin. When this occurs the patient is "hooked"; he must have the foreign alkaloid to obtain the normal endorphin response.

• The mechanism that the cell uses to form the modified endorphin receptor protein still remains to be discovered. I have suggested two possibilities that could be explored quickly and easily.
  o The foreign alkaloid could uncover a previously blocked gene.
  o The foreign alkaloid could take part in forming a new template for folding a protein that is specific for the foreign alkaloid. Probably formation of the template for folding proteins occurs in the Golgi complex.

• The cure for the biochemical part of drug addiction is to provide the body with a potential supply of extra xeronine. This stimulates the body to synthesize endorphin receptor proteins that require xeronine for proper functioning.

• The cure requires little time—much less than three days, exhibits no withdrawal symptoms and is inexpensive.

ENDNOTES

[1]During the last four years scientists have made great advances in working out the three dimensional structures of proteins. Practically every issue of Science or Nature contains several articles describing the three-dimensional structure of some newly examined protein. Scientists now know where in the cell the recently synthesized polypeptide chain folds itself into a protein. However, the exact details of the folding process are still unclear. The folding process occurs in the smooth part of the folded structure that surrounds the nucleus of the cell (the smooth endoplasmic reticulum). They also know that certain proteins formed in the Golgi bodies move into the smooth endoplasmic reticulum. Here they "assist" the recently synthesized polypeptide chain to fold into the specific three-dimensional shape of the protein. Since these proteins assist the protein to

fold correctly, the specialists in this field call these proteins "chaperon proteins." I call these proteins "templates."

The chaperon proteins may play critical roles in several still unresolved health problems. I propose that the cure for the biochemical part of drug addiction is to reverse the addiction process. This can be done simply, rapidly and at relatively low costs by "flooding" the body with potential sources of xeronine. Very quickly the cells of the body switch from producing receptor proteins that require the foreign alkaloid back to the normal endorphin receptor proteins that require xeronine as the physiologically active basic molecule.

The chaperon or template proteins may be involved in another very serious health problem, namely the slowly developing brain diseases found in the brains of mammals suffering from mad cow disease. This is the only disease that is reputedly transmitted by a special protein, the prion protein. Even though the Noble prize committee in 1997 awarded Dr. S. B. Prusiner a solo prize for his "proof" that this disease was indeed transmitted by eating food contaminated by this protein, many in this field are still unconvinced that a disease can be transmitted by a protein because typically communicable diseases are transmitted by viruses or microorganisms. However, work done by Shigeki Nakagawa in 1968 proves that certain proteins can cross the intestinal tract. In a healthy person the liver strips out all traces of foreign proteins; however, if the liver is damaged, the intact foreign proteins can circulate throughout the body.

If we approach the problem of finding a method of folding a protein rapidly and precisely by using only mechanical techniques, we find that there is only one mechanical method that would work. We need a template to convert the long polypeptide chain into a series of loops. The chaperon or template protein must have on one face of its surface an image of the adsorption site of the desired receptor protein. Of course where the receptor protein has a positive charge, the template would have a negative charge and vice versa.

^{2} That only the "bottom" part—the side facing the nucleus—of the Golgi complex stains black, tells us something about the chemistry of the bottom surface of the complex. Osmium, the heaviest natural element, forms a strange oxide, osmium tetroxide. This compound has several unusual properties. In spite of its large molecular weight, 274, it is quite volatile and smells awful. This led to its name, smell or stink in Greek. When a section of a cell is treated with a solution of osmium tetroxide, any molecule that acts as a reducing agent converts the soluble tetroxide into an intensely dense, black precipitate. Silver solutions also stain the Golgi complex black for the same reason. This indicates that this surface of the complex facing the nucleus contains either an aldehyde or a sulfhydryl group or both. (Our data are compatible with both of these possibilities.)

SECTION IV: XERONINE IN THE FUTURE

CHAPTER 12

Future of the Xeronine-System in Research and Health

The xeronine-system is an entirely new subject in biochemistry, physiology and pharmacology. Only a few scientists have heard about this system. Therefore the scientific literature contains no mention of xeronine. Although a certain percentage of the population knows about this subject, the majority of people have never heard about it.

I believe that this situation will change dramatically within less than five years. We have health problems, including AIDS, we have social problems, such as drug addiction and we have industrial problems such as the safe disposal of sewage. We want answers to these problems now. A good reliable source of the xeronine-system, such as noni or properly prepared commercial bromelain, can do more to alleviate these problems than any other substance.

Once the public becomes aware that a solution to some of these problems exists today, they will demand that action be taken. This public demand will then drive the need for basic research on all aspects of these problems in terms of the xeronine-system.

The future looks promising for the solution of or at least the alleviation of some of the most intractable health problems. I feel very strongly about three critical health problems that a good source of the xeronine-system—for example Tahitian noni, or a properly prepared commercial bromelain preparation, or even an extract of the leaves of the creosote bush (Larrea dentata)—can treat today. These social-health problems are:

• Long term pain management

• The cure of the biochemical part of our country's drug problem
• The alleviation of the symptoms of AIDS.

These are all problems that we can treat today even though we still need much additional research on the various reactions involved in the action of components of the xeronine-system in treating these problems.

I am not talking about research projects that cost millions of dollars and take an unknown length of time to complete. Today we have available a reliable and dependable source of the xeronine-system in noni juice. We can use this material immediately to treat these very serious national health problems. In the meantime research scientists can study how xeronine functions in the various biochemical reactions involved in these problems. In this book I have attempted to furnish some guides for future research.

As a scientist, what I found most exciting about developing models for two of these health problems, namely the control of pain and the cure of the biochemical part of drug addiction, is that the same basic model applies to both of these two social-health problems. Even though pain management and drug addiction might initially appear to have few points in common, actually both phenomena have three common factors: 1) specific agonists (a biochemical compound that adsorbs onto a receptor protein to produce a response) 2) xeronine and 3) protein receptors. Of course the protein receptors and the agonists differ, yet the action is the same, namely to produce a signal that moves along the nerve to tell the other end of the nerve to do something. The other end of the nerve is frequently in the brain. The broad application of this hypothesis for two seemingly unrelated phenomena strengthens the appeal of this hypothesis. The model is simple, logical, biochemically feasible and of great scope.

Roles for Xeronine In Future Health Management

I believe noni juice can alleviate many health problems better than many of the medicines and treatments that health providers are currently prescribing. In addition, the costs of using noni are relatively low, beneficial results frequently appear quickly and undesirable side effects are absent.

Certainly providing the body with the components of the xeronine-system is not a specific cure for any single health problem. Generally a number of factors are involved in health problems. However, since xeronine is the key component of so many of the most basic reactions in a cell, before a clinician or a research worker studying a disease does anything else, he or she should first be certain that the body has an adequate supply of the components of the xeronine-system. Only when the health councilor is convinced that the components of the xeronine-system are available at an optimal level, should he or she begin looking for other possible limiting factors.

In a completely different field, growing pineapple, the disastrous consequences of failing to cure the most basic nutritional problem caused the industry to treat a bizarre group of hypothesized ailments that were never present. In the late 1930s the pineapple industry hired the most brilliant plant physiologist in the world. (At least he was the highest paid plant scientist in the world.) He was the world's authority on the nutritional requirements of plants. As would be expected, he immediately carried out a meticulous study on the micronutrient requirements of the pineapple plant.

He carried out this study at a time when plant scientists believed with considerable confidence that they knew what micronutrients a plant required; they had "proven" that plants do not require cobalt, selenium, chromium or vanadium. Also the sensitivity of chemical analyses at that time was too poor to alert them to the embarrassing fact that the pots in which they grew their plants contained sufficient trace elements to supply the plant with the very micronutrients that they were studying. His strange and literally unbelievable conclusion was that "for some strange reason, the pineapple plant appeared to be the only plant that does not require micronutrients!"

About twenty years later I discovered that the pineapple plant is one of a few plants that absolutely must have selenium for growth. The relationship is very simple: no selenium, no pineapple. The pineapple crises that threatened the existence of the Hawaiian pineapple industry in 1922, 1928 and 1943 were all caused by selenium deficiencies. The research workers at these times did not realize that each of the specific "cures" for the postulated problems supplied the plant with additional selenium. Today the former pineapple soils in Hawaii are now so deficient in a wide range of other micronutrients that growing high quality pineapple on Hawaiian soil is difficult.

Today we have a similar problem in the health industry. Xeronine is one of the cell's most critical protein regulators; it is critical for many basic cellular reactions. A deficiency of components of the xeronine-system can lead to a wide variety of different health problems. If research workers look for solutions for a specific health problem without first being certain that adequate amounts of components of the xeronine-system are present, their conclusions are apt to be highly ambiguous.

One example of such research work in the medical field is the past decade of research on Type II Diabetes. In a recent review (June 2000) of Type II Diabetes research, the author made two points. One was that Type II Diabetes is increasing rapidly and the other was that all of the seemingly well-postulated research conclusions may be invalid. Although he presented a number of excellent hypotheses, he more or less suggested that the research community must start the study from the beginning with no preset conclusions. Since numerous anecdotal reports indicate that Tahitian noni is providing varying degrees of relief from Type II Diabetes, xeronine may play a critical basic role in preventing this type of diabetes. I would suggest that in one study all of the patients be given Tahitian noni before any other research tests are performed.

Dr. Gary Tran, an innovative veterinarian, uses this method in his treatment of animals. Having found that many sick animals were probably deficient in components of the xeronine-system, he routinely gives all of the animals that he treats a dose of Tahitian noni. If this does not produce the desired results, then he combines the Tahitian noni treatment with certain specific drugs that he feels might aid in the cure.

Now let us examine certain specific health problems.

Pain Management

Abundant anecdotal reports plus the laboratory data from Gus Martin's research group indicate that the proper use of a good source of the xeronine-system, such as certain preparations of commercial bromelain, TAHITIAN NONI® Juice or a few other plant or animal tissue extracts, helps alleviate severe pain and at the same time improve one's spirits. This pain treatment is far superior to morphine, which has undesirable side effects.

Long-term pain management, such as caring for terminally ill cancer patients, is at present an unsatisfactory compromise between relieving pain and deadening one's responses to the environment. I would like to suggest to doctors that for the management of severe, chronic pain, that they consider recommending that the patient take frequent small doses (a half a teaspoonful or less) of noni juice from Tahiti (at least every hour) throughout the day—and at night if the patient should awaken. For an explanation on how this noni juice treatment might work to alleviate pain, please refer to Chapter 6 in the section "Prostaglandin, Pain and the Xeronine-System."

Prostaglandins, Xeronine and Hearing

Prostaglandin and xeronine may be involved in hearing. The movement of specific cilia in the ear by sound waves probably generates prostaglandins. The adsorption of these prostaglandins on specific receptors sends signals to the brain that the brain interprets as sounds.

I believe that xeronine must also be involved in this phenomenon. Several people who have had serious hearing problems have discovered—generally serendipitously—that taking noni juice dramatically improved their hearing.

The same hypothesis and model that I used for pain and kinesthetic perception could apply to hearing. The newly synthesized prostaglandin could either enter into the Golgi body and there be packaged with a xeronine-assemblage or the prostaglandin and the xeronine molecules could each be adsorbed onto the auditory-receptor protein independently.

How the Brain Perceives Pain

The brain has the ability to respond or not to respond to the pain signals that the pain receptors send to the brain. If we had the ability to cause our brain to modify the interpretation of the signals from the receptors as pain signals, then we would have another method for managing pain. The Indian fakirs, through intensive and extensive training, may have developed the ability to prevent the interpretation of the pain signals as pain. Alternately, they may have developed the ability to cause the brain to release extra amounts of proxeronine from the body's proxeronine warehouses. I know of no experimental work in this area.

We do have an anecdotal report that might have affected the brain's interpretation of the pain signal. The family of a very sick, comatose man, who was being kept alive by stomach tube feeding, finally consented to allow the attending doctor to perform an exploratory operation. As soon as the doctor had made an incision to examine the gastrointestinal tract, the doctor immediately saw that the man had such advanced gastrointestinal cancer that there was no hope of saving the man's life. He closed the incision and informed the family that there was nothing that could be done for him.

His granddaughter, who was the secretary of the army Colonel who had validated the action of some our products that contained the xeronine-system, knew about the biological action of a creosote leaf extract that we were investigating. She asked the doctor whether he would object to introducing the creosote leaf extract into the man's stomach. (This creosote extract contained components of the xeronine-system.) Since her grandfather was going to die shortly, the attending doctor felt that agreeing to this request might make the family feel better and certainly would not aggravate the sick man's health problems. The doctor pumped the solution into the man's stomach through the stomach tube. That evening the patient had recovered sufficiently to sit up in bed and to demand that the stomach tube be taken out and that he be given a plate of food and chop sticks so that he could eat like the other hospital patients. (He was Korean.) A week later he was out of the hospital and tending to his garden. A month later he started going to Korean bars and bantering with the hostesses.

The treatment did not cure his cancer. At his funeral a year later, the family told us that his last year was the happiest year of his life. He had no pain, he was in excellent spirits and he was determined to enjoy every moment left to him. Not only did the creosote leaf extract free him from all pain, but it also lifted his spirits.

This is the type of treatment that health providers should give to every terminally ill patient. One should demand the right to die with dignity, with no pain and in full possession of ones faculties. Of course, today the doctor would recommend Tahitian noni, which is easier to obtain and is just as effective if not more effective than creosote leaf extract.

From this one dramatic experience, we know that managing pain can be done. Certainly we were fortunate in testing the treatment on a patient who was unusually responsive to the treatment. Yet since the treatment worked once, we know that the treatment has the potential to work again. We may need to discover any unusual parameters that are necessary for success.

I should emphasize that this man, who literally came back from the portals of death, had an extremely positive attitude. He was determined to live his remaining days vigorously. Many people strongly believe—and I am one of them—that positive emotions produce good hormones. Good hormones and a good source of proxeronine can truly work miracles.

Providing complete pain relief for terminally ill people should be one of the highest priorities of research.

Cure of Drug Addiction

Our government's attempts to control drug addiction have been enormously expensive and futile. About two years ago when I contacted the division of NIH that dispensed funds for research on drug addiction, I discovered that every single project that NIH had funded the previous year dealt with methadone research! There was not a single innovative research project among the list of supported research proposals. When I mentioned this lack of new ideas to the government official, he told me that a review board of "experts in the field" had examined the submitted proposals and recommended which ones they believed that the government should support. He was merely following the opinion of the experts!

Methadone treatment is not a cure for drug addiction; it merely substitutes the dependency on one alkaloid with dependency on another alkaloid that is under better price control by the government. Recommending methadone treatment is not fair to the patient!

The only acceptable treatment for any type of drug addiction is a complete cure of the addiction problem. We should not even consider any other proposal. This can be done today without any further studies.

I feel quite frustrated that a cure for one part of our drug problem, namely the addiction aspect, has existed for years. Yet the problem persists. With the publication of this book, which contains proposed models illustrating a possible cause of addiction and how xeronine can affect a permanent cure, I am hoping the government agencies will take strong action in this area. The cost will be minimal and the benefits enormous.

Further Research On Noni and the Xeronine-System

The physiological research that I was able to carry out with solutions of crystalline xeronine were exciting and convincing. Yet they barely scratched the surface of the research that still needs to be done.

One of the areas in which we need additional research is in the separation and purification of assemblages. This would include simple assemblages, such as the xeronine-assemblage and more complex assemblages that contain the xeronine-assemblage plus a variety of other products, such as serotonin, the good feeling hormone, sex hormones and others. These purified assemblages might have many useful pharmacological applications.

Purified Assemblages

In an ideal world the body would obtain all of the proxeronine that it requires from food grown on nutrient-rich soil. It would use the proxeronine to make xeronine-assemblages and assemblages containing the xeronine-assemblage plus a variety of necessary hormones and agonists. Unfortunately few of us live in an ideal world. We live in a world with a variety of contaminants that may seriously compromise certain of our body's critical biochemical systems; we live in a world in which intense ultraviolet radiation may damage our chromosomes; we live in a world in which many of our crops grow on soils that suffer from severe micronutrient imbalances.

If we do not have access to an adequate source of components of the xeronine-system, the shortage may prevent the Golgi complexes from assembling the desired mixture of molecules. This shortage of appropriate assemblages could lead to a variety of health problems. The simplest and the most certain method for remedying this problem is to supplement our diet with noni juice from Tahiti.

Possibly at sometime in the future doctors might have available a supply of purified assemblages that they could inject directly into certain severely ill patients. This is a research project for the future. This is an exciting area for research since the xeronine-assemblage concept approaches health problems from an entirely different viewpoint from than that used by most drug companies. The xeronine-assemblage approach attempts to raise the effectiveness of normal body constituents and processes to operate at their optimal levels rather than to achieve a balance between various reactions by using drugs to block certain biochemical reactions. The present drug philosophy achieves metabolic balance at a lower level of metabolic activity or at a cost of many serious side effects.

Purified Prostaglandin

As one of the critical components of assemblages, we need to have purified, crystalline proxeronine available to carry out fundamental research.

Viruses and the Xeronine-System

During the last several years a number of research groups have discovered an entirely new method that cells can use to control the action of certain genes, especially of viral genes. This control occurs not at the DNA transcription level but at the messenger RNA level. Certain ribonucleases target for destruction the messenger RNA produced by a foreign gene or a mutated cellular gene. The ribonuclease splits the targeted messenger RNA into 22-24 nucleotide fragments.

Most of the research workers in this research field work with plants; they are still studying this phenomenon and consolidating their findings. They have suggested that similar reactions may occur in mammalian cells. This is a new and exciting field for research; this is a field of research that has enormous potential health applications.

The Xeronine-System on Peach Mosaic Virus

In the 1970s Bill Hibbard sprayed part of a virus infected peach orchard with a commercial product that contained the xeronine-system plus a chemical to move the ingredients across the cell membrane. The sprayed trees showed no visible signs of the mosaic virus and produced an excellent crop of peaches whereas the unsprayed trees produced no commercial peaches. No one knows whether the treatment eliminated the virus by the method discussed in the previous section or enabled the trees to tolerate the damaging action of the virus. Unfortunately for an answer to this question, the following year the State of California destroyed all of the trees in this orchard to minimize the possible spread of this virus.

These results were definitive but inexplicable at that time. On the basis of these results Jintan-Dolph of Osaka, Japan, had Dr. Ono of the Agricultural College of the University of Osaka test the action of this product on a plant virus. His studies were laboratory studies. He ran these tests many years before scientists had developed the exquisite tests that they now have for studying DNA and RNA. His results suggested an action of the product on the virus. However, the data were not sufficiently definitive to justify our continuing this research since at that time we were interested primarily in the pharmaceutical actions of some still to be identified physiologically active ingredient in commercial bromelain.

Reports of Noni Juice and AIDS

AIDS is also a disease produced by a virus. There are many anecdotal reports on the effect of Tahitian noni in alleviating most or all of the symptoms of AIDS. Several of the patients who were in the terminal stages of an AIDS infection are still living active lives many years later. Since an HIV virus causes AIDS, some research worker should investigate whether this alleviation of the symptoms of AIDS occurs at the messenger RNA stage or whether it occurs at the nuclear stage or whether it keeps the cell healthy in spite of the potential damage to the immune system.

Today experimental techniques are available to answer these questions. These were not available when Dr. Ono ran his studies on plant viruses with a commercial solution of the xeronine-system. The possible action of the xeronine-system on certain foreign RNA chains could represents an entirely new approach to the AIDS problem. Either xeronine is involved at certain stages in the transcription of the gene or it may be involved in the activation of the specific ribonucleases that destroys the foreign RNA. Since xeronine activates a number of enzymes, this latter possibility is an intriguing one.

This is an important problem that should be studied intensively. Its health implications could be far reaching, as well as the many other health-enhancing facets of the xeronine-system.

Chapter Summary

• A critical area for development should be the integration of our knowledge of the xeronine-system into our current concepts connected with cellular, physiological and medical research.

• The three public health issues that should be intensively studied immediately are
      o Long term management of pain
      o Cure of the biochemical part of drug addiction
      o Alleviation of the debilitating effects of aid

• The possible involvement of the xeronine-system in the newly discovered action of certain ribonucleases to destroy foreign RNA should be investigated. This could be a factor in several health problems such as AIDS and possibly other diseases.

APPENDIX

Derivation of the Structure for Xeronine

In this Appendix I have included some of the technical reasonings that I used in deriving my proposed structure for xeronine.

From the ability of solutions of crystalline xeronine to completely prevent the toxicity of tetrodotoxin, I knew that xeronine and tetrodotoxin had to be able to fit into a very unique adsorption site. Therefore they both had to have a similar size, shape and positioning of the positive charge. No previously known alkaloid has been able to prevent tetrodotoxin toxicity.

Let us look at Woodward's structure for tetrodotoxin and see in what respects this structure has properties that do not match the experimentally determined properties of crystalline xeronine.

Figure 1.

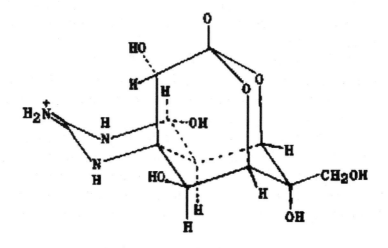

Tetrodotoxin

To really appreciate the structure of tetrodotoxin, we need a three-dimensional model of the diagram shown above. From such a model we immediately appreciate one unique feature of tetrodotoxin; this structure has an absolutely rigid three-dimensional core. It cannot be compressed, twisted or stretched. A Dreiding stereo molecular model of tetrodotoxin shows that this molecule can exist in two forms. The left end of the molecule in the diagram pictured above has three nitrogen atoms. This end can flip up and down. This movement does not affect the rigidity of the molecule but it does affect the energy absorption spectrum of the molecule.

To devise a structure for xeronine let us start with the molecular structure of tetrodotoxin and make appropriate changes so that our modified molecule will match the known properties of xeronine. The most likely atom to modify the chemical reactivity of the structure without greatly affecting the central part of the three dimensional structure is the far left nitrogen atom. This particular nitrogen atom differs from the two adjacent nitrogen atoms in having four valence bonds. The chemical name for this particular type of nitrogen atom is quaternary nitrogen. This nitrogen is so basic that it retains its positive charge even at high pH values. As a result, tetrodotoxin cannot be distilled even at extreme vacuum pressures and high temperatures. To make our structure for xeronine volatile, we must change the quaternary nitrogen atom of tetrodotoxin.

Although Woodward's diagram shows the puckered ring that contains the quaternary nitrogen as pointing upwards, the three dimensional model shows that the pucker can change readily from the up to the down position. I mention this point since the change that I shall make in this nitrogen is going to lock the pucker in the upward position—the "boat position"—with no chance of its changing position.

If we replace the quaternary nitrogen with a regular nitrogen atom, that is a three-valent nitrogen atom, this change does not affect the rigid core structure of tetrodotoxin; in other words, the essential shape of the molecule has remained the same. However, this substitution has made five significant changes to the original molecule in its physical and chemical properties.

• It makes the structure more rigid. It does this by preventing the shift of the puckered ring between the "boat" position (both ends up) and the "chair" position (one end up and the other down).

• It adds another puckered ring to the molecule, making it a more effective fulcrum.

• It converts the carbon atom to which the side chain nitrogen is attached into an optically active carbon. (This is a technical point that affects some of the physical properties of this molecule.)

• It makes the molecule volatile.

• It makes the hydroxyl group attached to the carbon atom at the top of the molecule (in the illustration) highly reactive.

This single change has produced a molecule that has all of the properties of xeronine!

Volatility of Xeronine

That xeronine readily distills at pH 9 under moderate conditions of temperatures and pressure and that it sublimes readily under alkaline conditions always amazes chemists who are familiar with alkaloids. The only volatile alkaloids are nicotine and coniine. Nicotine has a molecule weight of 162 and coniine a molecular weight of 127 whereas my proposed molecular weight for xeronine is 320 or 329. Few organic compounds with a molecular weight over 300 are volatile. I know of none that approaches xeronine in its degree of volatility.

Since the volatility of xeronine is a special property that only two much smaller alkaloids share, we should briefly examine some of the factors affecting volatility. One obvious factor affecting volatility is size. For example in the fatty acid series, the smaller acids are very volatile; some of them have a characteristic and identifiable smell (vinegar). Some smell awful! Even fatty acids having as many as twelve carbons can be identified by their odors—mostly highly unpleasant. Fatty acids of greater size are odorless. Palmitic acid, a common fatty acid used to make soaps, contains fourteen carbon atoms and is odorless.

Another important factor affecting the volatility of a molecule is the rigidity of the molecules. If a molecule is flexible, it absorbs most of the heat energy in flipping or twisting instead of using this energy to volatilize. By contrast a molecule that has rigid structure tends to be volatile. The best examples of such molecules are those containing planar rings. The smaller members of this class are so volatile that they give the name aromatic to any molecule containing such rings.

Nicotine, a relatively simple molecule has one aromatic ring and one rigid five-member ring. Also, since its molecular weight is relatively low, 162, its volatility is what we should expect.

Another very common type of ring is the six member puckered ring. Sugars have this type of structure. These rings are never volatile. Yet the structure that I am proposing for xeronine, has a structure made of linked, puckered rings. Its molecular weight, according to my proposal of about 320 (or 329), is high. Yet it is very volatile.

My proposed structure for xeronine immediately explains the unusual volatility of xeronine. The structure is so rigid, so compact and has so few side chains, which might absorb heat energy, that most of the heat energy contributes to the motion of the molecule. In other words, it makes xeronine volatilize readily.

As an example of the extreme volatility of xeronine I should mention the experience that I had in the laboratory. The isolation of xeronine includes several steps in which solutions are concentrated under a high vacuum. In one of my early runs I suddenly realized that the entire laboratory began smelling of nicotine. (Xeronine smells like nicotine.) Realizing that this was my product, I immediately installed a trap before the vacuum pump to collect the xeronine and to prevent the laboratory from smelling so bad.

This also illustrated another property of xeronine. Xeronine is insoluble in vacuum pump oil.

I am showing one of my proposed structure for xeronine.

Figure 2.

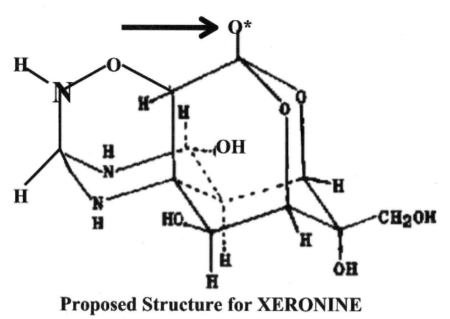

Proposed Structure for XERONINE

This proposed structure is a theoretical drawing based on the structure of tetrodotoxin. Changing the quaternary nitrogen to a three-valent nitrogen made the carbon between the two lower nitrogen atoms in the illustration above optically active.

The Lability of Xeronine

One of the major experimental problems that I had in isolating xeronine and in running experiments with xeronine is the great lability or instability of xeronine. Very early in my work, I noticed that frequently reddish solutions showed excellent initial biological activity. But then when I attempted to isolate the active component from the solution, I would lose biological activity and end up with a black colored mess.

When I finally developed an empirical method for isolating crystalline xeronine, I was able to follow the decomposition process of xeronine more closely. The initial solution of xeronine crystals in distilled water, which had been boiled to remove any absorbed oxygen, was water clear. In about a half an hour the solution had a touch of pink color. Five hours later the solution was red. After twenty-four hours the solution was black. My preliminary estimate of the half-life of a solution of xeronine is about one day or less.

Crystalline xeronine has a slightly longer half-life. In one experiment I was able to obtain large crystals. These showed no color. After two days the crystals had a metallic, mirror like surface. Five days later the mirror had turned black.

Obviously—at least so I thought—oxidation was the problem. I tried adding all of the conventional antioxidants at various points in the recovery process. I carried out the critical isolation steps under an atmosphere of argon. These measures helped somewhat but they failed to prevent the ultimate decomposition of xeronine. This indicated that some other process was involved. Free radicals were another possibility.

For the proposed model for xeronine to be a valid model, the model should indicate which atom is responsible for the great lability of the xeronine molecule. On the model illustrated above, the arrow points to the atom that is the source of the trouble.

In the model for tetrodotoxin, Woodward portrays this oxygen atom with a negative charge and the quaternary nitrogen with a positive charge. He did this because the carbon with this attached oxygen atom is unique in this molecule in being the only carbon with three attached oxygen atoms. Two of these oxygen atoms are part of the ring structure. These two ring-oxygen atoms affect the bond strength of the other oxygen atom. This oxygen atom readily loses its hydrogen atom and become negatively charged. Since tetrodotoxin has an internal salt structure, it is a stable molecule.

In my model for xeronine, I placed the hydrogen atom back onto the oxygen atom. I did this to avoid having a negative charge on this oxygen; a molecule having a negative charge would not distill from an alkaline solution. Yet the hydrogen is so weakly held, that it must be able to move off the oxygen atom occasionally. I am suggesting that the oxygen then becomes a free radical rather than a negatively charged ion. This would account for the spontaneous decomposition of xeronine.

This model also suggests some approaches that could be devised for stabilizing the xeronine molecule; it also suggests that the high reactivity of this oxygen atom may play a role in the reaction of the xeronine molecule with its protein receptor.

The Spectrum of Xeronine

During my studies on the recovery of xeronine, I used the recording UV spectrophotometer to follow the course of the recovery steps. This instrument was useful during the early stages of the recovery process. Certain of the intermediate materials had UV spectra that showed unique changes in acid and basic solutions. These materials were part of the xeronine-system. However, solutions of crystalline xeronine showed only "end absorption," a region of the UV absorption spectrum that is of little value in identifying materials.

Again, if my structural model for xeronine is a valid model, then the model should explain the lack of interesting UV peaks. The model contains no groups that would give strong UV peaks. Thus the lack of a definitive UV spectrum is exactly what we would expect from the proposed model.

Comparison of the Models of Xeronine and Tetrodotoxin

The structural model for xeronine depicted in this chapter is just one of two possible structures that I am proposing for xeronine. In Table 8-1 I describe another possible formulation for xeronine.

Table 8-1

Properties of Sturctures	Tetrodotoxin	Xeronine #1	Xeronine #2
Molecular Weight	319.28	319.28	329.29
Formula	$C_{11}H_{17}O_8N_3$	$C_{11}H_{17}O_8N_3$	$C_{13}H_{19}O_7N_3$
Total # Puckered Rings	5	6	7
# Puckered Rings on 1 side	2	0	0
# Puckered Rings on 2 sides	3	2	3
# Puckered Rings on 3 sides	0	2	2
# Puckered Rings on 4 sides	0	1	1
# Puckered Rings on 5 sides	0	0	1
# Quaternary Nitrogen Atoms	1	0	0
# Secondary Nitrogen Atoms	2	3	3

The figures for the two xeronine structures come from models of the hypothetical structures; these are not experimentally determined values. In the model for xeronine #2, I substituted a tetravalent carbon atom for one of the ring oxygen atoms. This substitution modifies the strength of the oxygen bonds of the attached OH group. I prefer the model that has a molecular weight of 329.

By attaching another carbon atom to the substituted ring carbon atom, the model shows that another puckered ring can readily form from the dangling side chain. This action would increase the volatility of the compound.

Molecular Weight of Xeronine

Determining the molecular weight of xeronine on a mass spectrometer will conclusively prove whether either of my two proposed structures for xeronine is correct. Since the mass spectrometer at the Chemistry Department was being used intensively during the time that I was isolating crystalline xeronine, I decided to run the physiological tests before I ran a mass spec on my crystals. Although I was rapidly using up my last batch of raw material that I had obtained from the Dole Bromelain Plant, I was not worried since I had worked out a method for crystallizing xeronine and I could always obtain more raw material—so I thought.

About this time the Dole management decided to modernize the bromelain operation. This took about six months. When they started operating again, the composition of the raw material that I had been using had changed. I could no longer obtain xeronine. By examining each step in their new plant, I located the source of the problem. They were now allowing the assemblages in the pineapple stems to open and produce functioning enzymes. This was good for their temporary profits but this operation eliminated the only factor that had made commercial bromelain such a valuable product for the consumer. It also meant that I would get no further crystals from that source.

I was able to make one mass spec run on crystals that I obtained from noni. Unfortunately by the time that I got on the mass spec machine, the crystals were black. The resulting spectrum was such a mixture of fragments and polymerizations that I originally considered the spectrum useless for determining the molecular weight. Nevertheless among the large number of peaks there were peaks at 319 and at 329. These are my two proposed molecular weights.

A high priority project should be getting a good mass spec on freshly prepared crystalline xeronine.

INDEX